Web Applications, Security & Maintenance: The Personal Trainer

IIS 7.0 & IIS 7.5

William Stanek

Cover Design: Creative Designs Ltd.
Editorial Development: Andover Publishing Solutions
Technical Review: L & L Technical Content Services

You can provide feedback related to this book by emailing the author at
williamstanek@aol.com. Please use the name of the book as the subject line.

Contents at a Glance

Table of Contents

Introduction

Welcome to *Web Applications, Security & Maintenance: The Personal Trainer for IIS 7.0 and IIS 7.5*. As the author of over 100 books, I've been writing professionally about Web publishing and Web servers for many years. Over the years, I've written about many different Web server technologies and products, but my favorite has always been Internet Information Services (IIS). From top to bottom, IIS 7.0 and IIS 7.5 are substantially different from earlier versions of IIS. For starters, the underlying configuration architecture for IIS is based entirely on Extensible Markup Language (XML) and XML schema.

Having also written many top-selling Web publishing and XML books, I was able to bring a unique perspective to this book—the kind of perspective you can gain only after working with server and application development technologies for many years. You see, long before IIS architecture was built on XML and related technologies, I was working with, researching, and writing about these technologies. The advantage for you, the reader, is that my solid understanding of these technologies allowed me to dig deeply into the IIS configuration architecture and to provide a comprehensive roadmap to this architecture.

Inside this book's pages, you'll find comprehensive overviews, step-by-step procedures, frequently used tasks, documented examples, and much more. One of the goals is to keep the content so concise that the book remains compact and easy to navigate while at the same time ensuring that the book is packed with as much information as possible—making it a valuable resource.

What's This Book About?

IIS provides the core services for hosting Web servers, Web applications, and Microsoft Windows SharePoint services. In this book, I teach you how features work, why they work the way they do, and how to customize them to meet your needs. I also offer specific examples of how certain features can meet your needs, and how you can use other features to troubleshoot and resolve issues you might have. In addition, this book provides tips, best practices, and examples of how to fine-tune key aspects of IIS.

What Do I Need to Know?

To get practical and useful information into your hands without the clutter of a ton of background material, I had to assume several things. If you are reading this book, I hope that you have basic networking skills and a basic understanding of Web servers. With this in mind, I don't devote entire chapters to understanding the World Wide Web, Web services, or Web servers. I do, however, provide complete details on the components of IIS and how you can use these components. I provide detailed guidance to help you quickly and easily perform common tasks, solve problems, and implement important features.

How Is This Book Organized?

Making this book easy to follow and understand was my number one goal! I really want anyone, skill level or work schedule aside, to be able to learn how to effectively manage IIS.

To make the book easy to use, this book is organized into multiple chapters. The chapters are arranged in a logical order, taking you from planning and deployment tasks to configuration tasks and beyond.

Web Applications, Security & Maintenance: The Personal Trainer is designed to be used with *Web Server Administration: The Personal Trainer*. While this book focuses on Web applications, application pools, worker processes, web server security, certificate management, optimization and maintenance, the latter book focused on core administration of IIS and key features.

What Conventions Are Used in This Book?

I've used a variety of elements to help keep the text clear and easy to follow. You'll find code terms and listings in monospace type, except when I tell you to actually enter a command. In that case, the command appears in **bold** type. When I introduce and define a new term, I put it in *italics*.

This book also has notes, tips and other sidebar elements that provide additional details on points that need emphasis.

Other Resources

Although some books are offered as all-in-one guides, there's simply no way one book can do it all. This book is intended to be used as a concise and easy-to-use resource. It covers everything you need to perform core tasks for IIS, but it is by no means exhaustive.

As you encounter new topics, take the time to practice what you've learned and read about. Seek additional information as necessary to get the practical experience and knowledge that you need.

I truly hope you find that *Web Applications, Security & Maintenance: The Personal Trainer* helps you manage IIS successfully and effectively.

Thank you,

William R. Stanek

(williamstanek@aol.com)

Chapter 1. Running IIS 7.0 and IIS 7.5 Applications

Not long ago, when Web sites were primarily static Hypertext Markup Language (HTML) pages, the most serious problems facing Web administrators were configuring multiple sites on the same server and keeping the server running without failure. With the growing importance of Web servers not just on the Internet but also everywhere within the organization, different issues have emerged. Web servers must do more—and not just with respect to handling and responding to requests. Web servers must provide services, host applications, and serve dynamic content, all of which IIS can do using Internet Server Application Programming Interface (ISAPI) applications, Common Gateway Interface (CGI) programs, Active Server Pages (ASP) applications, and Microsoft ASP.NET applications.

Managing ISAPI and CGI Application Settings

ISAPI and CGI are two basic types of IIS applications. ISAPI provides the core functionality for IIS when applications use classic pipeline mode. ISAPI acts as a layer over IIS that can be extended using ISAPI applications, Active Server Pages (ASP), ASP.NET, and third-party extensions. CGI programs pass information to servers through environment variables that capture user input in forms in addition to details about the user, the user's browser, and the user's operating system.

Understanding ISAPI Applications

Although ISAPI applications are being replaced by the new IIS modules API, IIS 7.0 and IIS 7.5 maintain support for ISAPI applications. ISAPI applications fall into two categories:

- ISAPI filters
- ISAPI extensions

You can use both filters and extensions to modify the behavior of IIS. ISAPI filters are dynamic-link libraries (DLLs) or executables that are loaded into memory when the World Wide Web Publishing Service is started and remain in memory until the IIS server is shut down. ISAPI filters are triggered when a Web server event occurs on the IIS server. For example, an ISAPI filter can control which files are mapped to a URL, modify the response sent by the server, and perform other actions to modify the behavior of the server.

You can apply ISAPI filters globally or locally. Global filters affect all IIS Web sites running on a server and are loaded into memory when the World Wide Web Publishing Service is started. Local filters are called site filters. Site filters affect a single IIS Web site and can be dynamically loaded into memory when a request that uses such a filter is made to the site.

ISAPI filters aren't ideal choices when you need to perform long-running operations, such as database queries, or when you want to process the entire body of requests. In these instances, ISAPI extensions work better.

Like ISAPI filters, ISAPI extensions are defined as DLLs or executables. Unlike global filters, which are loaded with the World Wide Web Publishing Service, extensions are loaded on demand and are executed in response to client requests. Normally, ISAPI extensions are used to process the data received in requests for specific types of files. For example, when a client makes a request for a file that has an .asp extension, IIS uses the Asp.dll ISAPI extension to process the contents of ASP and return the results to the client for display. IIS provides classic ASP.NET functionality through an ISAPI filter (aspnet_filter.dll), which in turn calls an ISAPI extension (aspnet_isapi.dll).

When you install ASP and ASP.NET, default ISAPI extensions are configured for use on the Web server. ISAPI extensions are configured to respond to specific types of Hypertext Transfer Protocol (HTTP) requests or all HTTP requests for files with a specific file extension. Table 1-1 summarizes the key types of HTTP requests.

TABLE 1-1 HTTP Request Types Use with ISAPI Extensions

DELETE	A request to delete a resource. This request normally isn't allowed unless the user has specific privileges on the Web site.
GET	A request to retrieve a resource. This is the standard request for retrieving files.

HEAD	A request for an HTTP header. The return request doesn't contain a message body.
OPTIONS	A request for information about communications options.
POST	A request to submit data as a new subordinate of a resource. It is typically used for posting data from filled-out forms.
PUT	A request to store the enclosed data with the resource identifier specified. It is typically used when uploading files through HTTP.
TRACE	A request to trace the client's submission for testing or debugging.

Configuring ISAPI and CGI Restrictions

ISAPI and CGI restrictions control the ISAPI and CGI extensions that are allowed to run on a Web server. You configure restrictions only at the server configuration level. In IIS Manager, to view currently configured restrictions as either a CGI (.exe) or an ISAPI (.dll) file extension, select the server node, and then double-click the ISAPI And CGI Restrictions feature. On the ISAPI And CGI Restrictions page, shown in Figure 1-1, extensions are listed by:

- **Description**   A brief description or friendly name for the related ISAPI or CGI application.
- **Restriction**   The restriction status. If an extension is permitted to run, its restriction status is listed as Allowed. Otherwise, its restriction status is listed as Not Allowed.
- **Path**   The execution path for the related ISAPI or CGI application.

Some of the commonly allowed extensions you'll see include:

- **ASP.DLL**   This ISAPI extension implements ASP functionality.
- **ASPNET_ISAPI.DLL**   This ISAPI extension provides the processing functions for ASP.NET in classic pipeline mode.
- **OCSPISAPI.DLL**   This ISAPI extension implements the certification status protocol for Certificate Services.
- **MSW3PRT.DLL**   This ISAPI extension provides the processing functions for Internet printing.

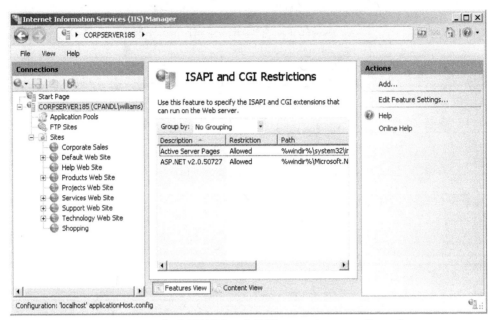

FIGURE 1-1 Determine which ISAPI and CGI extensions are allowed to run.

NOTE Because the ASPNET_ISAPI.DLL extension is version-specific, you may see multiple versions of the extension registered. Specifically, there'll be one extension for each version of the Microsoft .NET Framework configured. Remove older versions of this extension only when you are sure they are no longer in use.

By default, only extensions listed as Allowed can run on the server. You can modify this configuration to allow unspecified CGI modules, unspecified ISAPI modules, or both to run without restriction. To modify this behavior, as may be necessary during development or temporarily for troubleshooting, you can allow unspecified extensions to run by completing the following steps:

1. In IIS Manager, select the server node, and then double-click ISAPI And CGI Restrictions.

2. In the Actions pane, click Edit Feature Settings. The Edit ISAPI And CGI Restrictions Settings dialog box appears.

3. You can now allow unspecified CGI modules, unspecified ISAPI modules, or both to run by selecting the related check boxes. To prevent unspecified CGI modules, unspecified ISAPI modules, or both from running, clear the related check boxes. When you are finished, click OK to save your settings.

> **CAUTION** Allowing unspecified modules to run on a Web server is a serious security risk. To prevent possible malicious use of the extension functionality, you should rarely allow unspecified modules to run on a Web server.

You can configure an Allowed or Not Allowed restriction for an extension by completing the following steps:

1. In IIS Manager, select the server node, and then double-click ISAPI And CGI Restrictions.
2. In the Actions pane, click Add. The Add ISAPI Or CGI Restriction dialog box appears.
3. Click the selection button to the right of the ISAPI Or CGI Path text box, and then in the Open dialog box, select the executable to configure as either a CGI (.exe) or an ISAPI (.dll) file extension.
4. If you wish, type a description of the extension.
5. To allow the extension to run, select the Allow Extension Path To Execute check box. To prevent the extension from running, do not select this check box. Click OK to add the restriction.

You can work with restrictions in a variety of other ways, as follows:

- To change a currently set restriction from Allowed to Not Allowed, click the extension, and then in the Actions pane, click Deny.
- To change a currently set restriction from Not Allowed to Allowed, click the extension, and then in the Actions pane, click Allow.
- To modify an extension's execution path, description, and restriction status, click the extension, and then in the Actions pane, click Edit. In the Edit ISAPI Or CGI Restriction dialog box, make the necessary changes to the restriction configuration, and then click OK.
- To remove an extension from the restriction list, click the extension, and then in the Actions pane, click Remove. When prompted to confirm the action, click Yes.

By using the IIS command-line administration tool, you can configure ISAPI and CGI restrictions by using the Set Config command and the IsapiCgiRestriction section of the configuration file. Sample 1-1 provides the syntax and usage.

SAMPLE 1-1 Configuring ISAPI and CGI Restrictions Syntax and Usage

Syntax

```
appcmd set config ["ConfigPath"] /section:IsapiCgiRestriction
[/notListedIsapisAllowed:true|false]
[/notListedCgisAllowed:true|false]
```

Usage

```
appcmd set config "Default Web Site" /section:IsapiCgiRestriction
/notListedIsapisAllowed:true /notListedCgisAllowed:true
```

Configuring ISAPI Filters

ISAPI filters are DLLs that enhance the functionality provided by IIS. In IIS Manager, you can view currently configured filters by selecting a server or site node and then double-clicking the ISAPI Filters feature. On the ISAPI Filters page, you'll see a list of defined filters listed by name, executable, and entry type. Local entries are configured at the level you are working with. Inherited entries are configured at a higher level of the configuration hierarchy.

When you've configured a server to use ASP.NET, the standard filter you'll see is aspnet_filter.dll, which enables classic pipeline mode. Because this filter is version-specific, you may see multiple versions of the extension registered. Specifically, there'll be one extension for each version of the .NET Framework configured. Remove older versions of this extension only when you are sure they are no longer in use. Typically, no other standard filters are configured.

You can configure an ISAPI filter for use by completing the following steps:

1. In IIS Manager, select the server node, and then double-click ISAPI Filters.
2. In the Actions pane, click Add. This displays the Add ISAPI Filter dialog box.
3. In the Filter Name text box, type a descriptive name for the filter.
4. Click the selection button to the right of the Executable text box, in the Open dialog box, select the filter's DLL, and then click OK to add the filter.

You can edit, rename, or remove ISAPI filters by using the following techniques:

- To modify an ISAPI filter's executable path, click the filter entry you want to modify, and then click Edit. In the Edit ISAPI Filter dialog box, click the selection button to the right of the Executable text box, in the Open dialog box, select the filter's DLL, and then click OK to save your changes.
- To rename a filter, click the filter entry to select it, and then click Rename. Type the new name for the filter, and then press Enter.
- To remove a filter that is no longer needed, click the filter entry you want to remove, and then click Remove. When prompted to confirm the action, click Yes.

Configuring CGI Settings

You can control the way CGI applications are executed by using the settings on the CGI configuration page. You can set a time-out value for CGI applications, isolate CGI applications in their own console window, or configure CGI applications to run at the system or user level.

To view the currently configured CGI settings, in IIS Manager, navigate to the level of the configuration hierarchy you want to manage, and then access the CGI page by double-clicking the CGI feature. On the CGI page, you can configure the way CGI applications are used by using the following techniques:

- You can modify the time-out for CGI applications by typing the desired time-out in the Time-Out text box. Use the hh:mm:ss format where hh is for hours, mm is for minutes, and ss is for seconds. The default value is 00:15:00 (15 minutes). In most cases, you'll want a relatively short time-out value. The reason for this is that when CGI applications time out, IIS removes the related process and frees up the resources it used. Increase the time-out period only when users are experiencing problems with long-running requests that are processed through CGI applications.
- You can specify whether each CGI application runs in a separate console window by setting the Use New Console For Each Invocation option. The default value is False. If the value is set to True, each CGI application creates a new console window when started, which isolates each application and prevents problems with one CGI application from affecting another CGI application (in most cases). However, because creating a new console

window for each CGI application uses additional resources on the server, there is a trade-off to be made between application isolation and resource usage.

- You can specify whether a CGI application process is created in the system context or in the context of the requesting user by using the Impersonate User feature. The default value is True. When True, IIS creates CGI application processes in the context of the requesting user. When False, IIS creates CGI application processes in the system context. Run CGI applications in a system context only when there is a specific need to do so, such as when an application requires the additional permissions available to the system user. Otherwise, run CGI applications in the user context to enhance security and reduce the possibility of malicious use of elevated privileges.

By using the IIS command-line administration tool, you can configure CGI settings by using the Set Config command and the Cgi section of the configuration file. Sample 1-2 provides the syntax and usage.

SAMPLE 1-2 Configuring CGI Settings Syntax and Usage

Syntax
```
appcmd set config ["ConfigPath"] /section:Cgi
[/createCGIWithNewConsole:true|false]
[/createProcessAsUser:true|false]
[/timeout: "hh:mm:ss"
```

Usage
```
appcmd set config "Default Web Site" /section:Cgi
/createCGIWithNewConsole:true /createProcessAsUser:true
/timeout: "00:10:00"
```

Managing ASP Settings

ASP is a server-side scripting environment used to create dynamic Web applications. An ASP application is a collection of resource files and components that are grouped logically. Logically grouping files and components as an application allows IIS to share data within the application and to run the application as a shared, pooled, or isolated process. You can have multiple applications per Web site, and you can configure each application differently.

IIS resource files include ASP pages, HTML pages, GIF images, JPEG images, and other types of Web documents. An ASP page is a file that ends with the .asp extension that includes HTML, a combination of HTML and scripting, or only scripting. Scripts within ASP pages can be intended for processing by a client browser or the server itself. Scripts designed to be processed on the server are called server-side scripts and can be written using Microsoft Visual Basic Scripting Edition (VBScript), Microsoft JScript, or any other scripting language available on the server.

ASP provides an object-based scripting environment. Server-side scripts use the built-in objects to perform common tasks, such as tracking session state, managing errors, and reading HTTP requests sent by clients. ASP scripts can also use Component Object Model (COM) components. Prebuilt components are available in the standard IIS installation and are included in the %SystemRoot%\System32\Inetsrv directory on the IIS server.

Controlling ASP Behavior

To view the currently configured ASP behavior settings, in IIS Manager, navigate to the level of the confiuration hierarchy you want to manage, and then access the ASP page, by double-clicking the ASP feature. On the ASP page, shown in Figure 1-2, you'll find a variety of settings under the Behavior node.

For ASP, buffering is a key option that affects server performance and resource usage. When buffering is enabled, as per the default setting, IIS completely processes ASP pages before sending content to the client browser. When buffering is disabled, IIS returns output to the client browser as the page is processed. The advantage to buffering is that it allows IIS to respond dynamically to events that occur while processing the page. IIS can take one of the following actions:

- Abort sending a page or transfer the user to a different page
- Clear the buffer and send different content to the user

- Change HTTP header information from anywhere in your ASP script

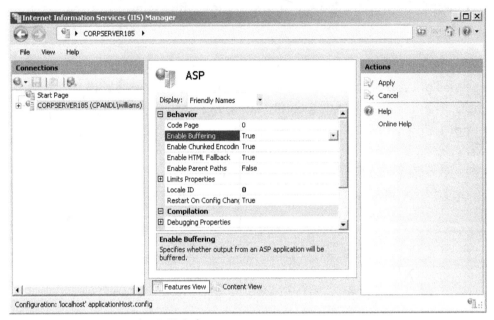

FIGURE 1-2 Review the ASP behavior settings.

A disadvantage of buffering is that users have to wait for the entire script to be processed before content is delivered to their browser. If a script is long or complex, the user might have to wait for a long time before seeing the page. To counter potential delays associated with buffering, developers often insert Flush commands at key positions within the script. If your development team does this, they should be aware that this causes additional connection requests between the client and server, which might also cause performance problems.

Other options that control the behavior of ASP include Code Page, Enable Chunked Encoding, Enable HTML Fallback, Enable Parent Paths, Locale ID, Restart On Config Change, and Script Language. Code Page sets the default code page that IIS should use when working with non-Unicode character data. The default setting is zero (0), which indicates that IIS should use the code page used by the server for storing and displaying non-Unicode character data.

Enable Chunked Encoding determines whether HTTP 1.1 chunked transfer encoding is enabled. The default is True. All HTTP 1.1–compliant applications, such as Web browsers, support chunked encoding. With chunked encoding, IIS transfers the body of responses as a series of message chunks, each with its own size indicator, following by an optional trailer containing entity-header fields. This allows dynamically generated content to be transferred along with the information necessary for the recipient to verify that it has received the full message. If chunked encoding is disabled, IIS transfers responses to requests using standard encoding, and client browsers have no way to verify that the full response has been received. If chunked encoding is enabled, IIS transfers responses to requests by using chunked encoding, and client browsers can verify that the full response has been received.

Enable HTML Fallback determines whether HTML is used as a fallback when the ASP request queue is full. The default is True. When set to True and the request queue is full, ASP will substitute an HTML file that has _asp added to the file name and return the file if found. For example, if the name of the requested .asp file is inventory.asp, the name of the .htm file that is returned will be inventory_asp.htm. If the file does not exist or you've disabled fallback and the request queue is full, IIS returns a 500.13 (Web Server is too busy) HTTP error to the client.

Enable Parent Paths determines whether ASP pages allows paths relative to parent directories in addition to the current directory. The default is False. When enabled, ASP pages can use relative paths to access parent directories of the current directory. For example, a script could reference ../Build.htm, where ".." is a reference to the current directory's parent directory. When disabled, ASP pages cannot use parent paths.

Locale ID sets the default locale identifier (LCID) for an application. Locale identifiers control the formatting of numbers, currencies, dates, and times. The default setting is zero (0), which indicates that IIS should use the locale identifier used by the server.

Restart On Config Change determines whether IIS automatically restarts ASP applications when you change critical configuration properties that affect how applications are used. The default is True. To restart an application, IIS stops and then starts the application. This means that all resources used by the application are freed. This also means, however, that any requests currently being processed will fail and that new requests for the application aren't processed until the application is started.

Script Language sets the default scripting language for ASP pages. Two scripting engines are installed with a standard IIS installation. These scripting engines are for VBScript and JScript. You can reference these scripting engines by using the values VBScript and JScript, respectively. The default scripting language in a standard IIS installation is VBScript. In ASP pages, you can override the default language by using the <%@LANGUAGE%> directive.

You manage ASP behavior settings by completing the following steps:

1. In IIS Manager, navigate to the level of the configuration hierarchy you want to manage, and then access the ASP page by double-clicking the ASP feature.

2. On the ASP page, under Behavior, set the following options to configure ASP behavior: Code Page, Enable Buffering, Enable Chunked Encoding, Enable HTML Fallback, and Enable Parent Paths.

3. On the ASP page, under Compilation, use the Script Language option to set the default scripting language.

In the Actions pane, click Apply.

By using the IIS command-line administration tool, you can configure ASP behavior settings by using the Set Config command and the ASP section of the configuration file. Sample 1-3 provides the syntax and usage.

SAMPLE 1-3 Configuring ASP Behavior Settings Syntax and Usage

Syntax

```
appcmd set config ["ConfigPath"] /section:Asp
[/codepage: "CodePage"]
[/bufferingOn: true|false]
[/enableChunkedEncoding: true|false]
[/enableAspHtmlFallback: true|false]
[/enableParentPaths: true|false]
[/lcid: "LocaleID"]
[/enableApplicationRestart: true|false]
```

```
[/scriptLanguage: "ScriptLanguage"]
```

Usage

```
appcmd set config "Default Web Site" /section:Asp
/bufferingOn: true /enableChunkedEncoding: true
```

Customizing Request Handling for ASP

Many different options control the way ASP handles and responds to requests. To view the related ASP settings, in IIS Manager, navigate to the level of the configuration hierarchy you want to manage, and then access the ASP page by double-clicking the ASP feature. On the ASP page, under Behavior, expand the Limits Properties node to see the related properties.

Client Connection Test Interval sets the period of time a request should be queued. If the request is queued longer than the specified time, ASP checks to determine whether the client is still connected before running a request. If the client is no longer connected, the request is not processed and is deleted from the queue. The default is 00:00:03 (3 seconds).

Maximum Requesting Entity Body Limit determines the maximum number of bytes allowed in the entity-body of an ASP request. The default is 200,000 bytes (195 KB). If the maximum value is exceeded, IIS truncates the request or generates an error.

Queue Length determines the maximum number of concurrent ASP requests that are permitted in the ASP request queue. The default is 3000. IIS does not allow any new requests when the queue has reached the maximum value. If you've disabled HTML fallback and the request queue is full, IIS returns a 500.13 (Web Server is too busy) HTTP error to the client.

Request Queue Timeout sets the period of time that an ASP request is allowed to wait in the queue. The default is 00:00:00 (infinite), allowing a request to be queued indefinitely. If you set a specific time-out, IIS removes requests older than the time-out period automatically and does not attempt to process them. All requests that wait in the queue are also subject to the Client Connection Test Interval.

Response Buffering Limit sets the maximum size of the ASP response buffer. If response buffering is enabled, this property controls the maximum number of bytes that an ASP page can write to the response buffer before a flush occurs. The default is 4,194,304 bytes (4096 KB).

Script Timeout determines the default length of time that IIS allows an ASP script to run before attempting to stop the script and writing an event to the Windows event log. The default is 00:01:30 (90 seconds).

Threads Per Processor Limit determines the maximum number of worker threads per processor that IIS can create to handle ASP requests. The default is 25. Once the per-processor thread limit is reached, IIS will not generate new threads to handle ASP requests. This doesn't necessarily mean that request processing will fail. Worker processes associated with application pools are responsible ultimately for handling requests. Worker processes can use additional threads to improve responsiveness and handling of requests. If no new threads are available, worker processes must handle requests by using currently allocated threads.

You can customize request handling for ASP by completing the following steps:

1. In IIS Manager, navigate to the level of the configuration hierarchy you want to manage and then access the ASP page by double-clicking the ASP feature.
2. On the ASP page, under Behavior, expand the Limits Properties node by double-clicking it.
3. Use the Limit Properties to configure request handling for ASP.
4. In the Actions pane, click Apply.

By using the IIS command-line administration tool, you can configure request-handling settings by using the Set Config command and the Asp\limits section of the configuration file. Sample 1-4 provides the syntax and usage.

SAMPLE 1-4 Configuring Request Handling Settings Syntax and Usage

Syntax

```
appcmd set config ["ConfigPath"] /section:Asp
[/limits.queueConnectionTestTime: "hh:mm:ss"]
```

```
[/limits.maxRequestEntityAllowed: "RequestLimit"]
[/limits.requestQueueMax: "QueueLength"]
[/limits.queueTimeout: "hh:mm:ss"]
[/limits.bufferingLimit: "BufferingLimit"]
[/limits.scriptTimeout: "hh:mm:ss"]
[/limits.processorThreadMax: "ThreadLimit"]
```

Usage

```
appcmd set config "Default Web Site" /section:Asp
/limits.queueConnectionTestTime: "00:00:05"
/limits.requestQueueMax: "5000"
```

Optimizing Caching for ASP

IIS compiles ASP pages at run time when they're first requested, and then the compiled code is stored in the file cache where it can be reused without recompiling. The way IIS caches ASP pages depends on these caching properties:

- **Cache Directory Path**   Sets the name of the directory that ASP uses to store compiled ASP templates to disk after overflow of the in-memory cache. The default is *%SystemDrive%* \Inetpub\Temp\ASP Compiled Templates.
- **Enable Type Library Caching**   Determines whether Type Library caching is enabled. The default value, True, enables Type Library caching.
- **Maximum Disk Cached Files**   Sets the maximum number of compiled ASP templates that can be stored on disk. The default value is 2000. The valid range is from 0 to 2147483647 files.
- **Maximum Memory Cached Files**   Sets the maximum number of precompiled script files to cache in memory. The default value is 500 files. The valid range is from 0 to 2147483647 files.
- **Maximum Script Engines Cached**   Sets the maximum number of scripting engines that IIS will keep cached in memory. The default value is 250 cached scripting engines. The valid range is from 0 to 2147483647 script engines.

You can optimize caching for ASP by completing the following steps:

1. In IIS Manager, navigate to the level of the configuration hierarchy you want to manage and then access the ASP page by double-clicking the ASP feature.

2. On the ASP page, expand the Caching Properties node by double-clicking it.

3. In Caching Properties, configure caching settings for ASP.

4. In the Actions pane, click Apply.

By using the IIS command-line administration tool, you can configure caching settings by using the Set Config command and the Asp\session section of the configuration file. Sample 1-5 provides the syntax and usage.

SAMPLE 1-5 Configuring Caching Settings Syntax and Usage

Syntax

```
appcmd set config ["ConfigPath"] /section:Asp
[/session.diskTemplateCacheDirectory: "DirectoryPath"]
[/session.enableTypelibCache: true|false]
[/session.maxDiskTemplateCacheFiles: "NumFiles"]
[/session.scriptFileCacheSize: "CacheSize"]
[/session.scriptEngineCacheMax: "NumEngines"]
```

Usage

```
appcmd set config "Default Web Site" /section:Asp
/session.enableTypelibCache: true
/session.maxDiskTemplateCacheFiles: "2500"
```

Customizing COM+ Execution for ASP

ASP can use different types of Component Object Model components. The way those components are used depends on these Com Plus Properties for ASP:

- **Enable Side By Side Component** Determines whether COM+ side-by-side assemblies are enabled. When True, ASP applications can use COM+ side-by-side assemblies to specify which version of a system DLL or COM component to use. The default is False.

- **Enable Tracker** Determines whether the COM+ tracker is enabled. When True, you can debug applications by using the COM+ tracker. The default is False.
- **Execute In MTA** Determines whether ASP can run scripts in a multithreaded execution mode. The default is False. When True, ASP can use multiple threads to execute scripts (but scripts must be designed for and compliant with multithreading).
- **Honor Component Threading Model** Determines whether IIS examines the threading model of any components that your application creates. The default is False. If True, IIS checks the threading model of any components that your application creates to ensure that it is appropriate. Otherwise, IIS does not check the threading model.
- **Partition ID** When COM+ partitioning is used, Partition ID sets the GUID of the COM+ partition. This value is not used when COM+ partitioning is disabled.
- **Side By Side Component** When side-by-side execution is enabled, sets the name of the COM+ application. This value is not used when side-by-side execution is disabled.
- **Use Partition** Determines whether COM+ partitioning is used to isolate applications into their own COM+ partitions. When this property is set to True, you must specify a value for the Partition ID element.

You can customize the way ASP uses COM+ components by completing the following steps:

1. In IIS Manager, navigate to the level of the configuration hierarchy you want to manage, and then access the ASP page by double-clicking the ASP feature.
2. On the ASP page, under Services, expand the Com Plus Properties node by double-clicking it.
3. Use Com Plus Properties to configure COM+ component handling for ASP.
4. In the Actions pane, click Apply.

By using the IIS command-line administration tool, you can configure COM+ settings by using the Set Config command and the Asp\comPlus section of the configuration file. Sample 1-6 provides the syntax and usage.

SAMPLE 1-6 Configuring COM+ Handling Settings Syntax and Usage

Syntax

```
appcmd set config ["ConfigPath"] /section:Asp
[/comPlus.appServiceFlags: true|false]
[/comPlus.appServiceFlags: true|false]
[/comPlus.executeInMta: true|false]
[/comPlus.trackThreadingModel: true|false]
[/comPlus.partitionID: "PartitionGUID"]
[/comPlus.sxsName: "AppName"]
[/comPlus.usePartition: true|false]
```

Usage

```
appcmd set config "Default Web Site" /section:Asp
 /comPlus.appServiceFlags: true
/comPlus.executeInMta: true
```

Configuring Session State for ASP

Session state plays a significant role in IIS performance and resource usage. When session state is enabled, IIS creates a session for each user who accesses an ASP or ASP.NET application. Session information is used to track the user within the application and to pass user information from one page to another. For example, your company might want to track individual user preferences within an application, and you can use sessions to do this.

By default, IIS uses in-process session state management. The way sessions work in this mode is fairly straightforward. The first time a user requests an ASP or ASP.NET page with a specified application, IIS generates one of the following:

- A *Session* object containing all values set for the user session, including an identifier for the code page used to display the dynamic content, a location identifier, a session ID, and a time-out value

- A *Session.Contents* collection, which contains all the items that the application has set in the session
- A *Session.StaticObjects* collection, which contains the static objects defined for the application

The *Session* object and its associated properties are stored in memory on the server. The user's session ID is passed to the user's browser as a cookie. As long as the browser accepts cookies, the session ID is passed back to the server on subsequent requests. This is true even if the user requests a page in a different application. The same ID is used in order to reduce the number of cookies sent to the browser. If the browser doesn't accept cookies, the session ID can't be maintained, and IIS can't track the user session by using this technique. In this case, you could track the session state on the server.

Session state is enabled by default for all IIS applications. By default, sessions time out in 20 minutes. This means that if a user doesn't request or refresh a page within 20 minutes, the session ends and IIS removes the related *Session* object from memory. Worker process recycling can affect session management. If a worker process is recycled or otherwise cleared out of memory, the session state could be lost. If this happens, you won't be able to recover the session data.

As you might imagine, tracking sessions can use valuable system resources. You can reduce resource usage by reducing the time-out interval or disabling session tracking altogether. Reducing the time-out interval allows sessions to expire more quickly than usual. Disabling session tracking tells IIS that sessions shouldn't be automatically created. You can still start sessions manually within the application. Simply place the <%@ENABLESESSIONSTATE = True%> directive in individual ASP pages.

For ASP pages, you control session state management by using the ASP feature. In IIS Manager, navigate to the level of the configuration hierarchy you want to manage, and then display the ASP page by double-clicking the ASP feature. On the ASP page, expand the Session Properties node by double-clicking it. You can then use the following Session properties to manage caching for ASP:

- **Enable Session State**   Determines whether session state persistence is enabled for applications. The default is True.
- **Maximum Sessions**   Sets the maximum number of concurrent sessions that IIS will allow. The default is 4294967295.
- **New ID On Secure Connection**   Determines whether IIS generates a new cookie when a transition from a non-secure to a secure connection is made. The default is True, and in most cases, you'll want to keep this value.
- **Timeout**   Sets the period of time that IIS maintains a session object after the last request associated with the object is made. The default is 00:20:00. For a high-usage application in which you expect users to move quickly from page to page, you might want to set a fairly low time-out value, such as 5 or 10 minutes. On the other hand, if it's critical that the user's session is maintained to complete a transaction, you might want to set a long time-out value, such as 60 minutes.

By using the IIS command-line administration tool, you can configure session state settings by using the Set Config command and the Asp\session section of the configuration file. Sample 1-7 provides the syntax and usage.

SAMPLE 1-7 Configuring Session State Settings for ASP Syntax and Usage

Syntax

```
appcmd set config ["ConfigPath"] /section:Asp
[/session.allowSessionState: true|false]
[/session.max: "MaxSessions"
 [/session.keepSessionIdSecure: true|false]
[/session.timeout: "hh:mm:ss"
```

Usage

```
appcmd set config "Default Web Site" /section:Asp
 /session.allowSessionState: true
/session.timeout: "00:15:00"
```

Configuring Debugging and Error Handling for ASP

One of the best ways to troubleshoot an IIS application is to enable debugging. Debugging is handled through server-side and client-side configuration settings. Server-side debugging allows IIS to throw errors while processing ASP pages and to display a prompt that allows you to start the Microsoft Script Debugger. You can then use the debugger to examine your ASP pages. Client-side debugging involves sending debugging information to the client browser. You can then use this information to help determine what's wrong with IIS and the related ASP page.

You can use the following debugging options to help you detect and diagnose problems. Calculate Line Numbers determines whether ASP should calculate and store the line number of each executed line of code. The default is True. If set to True, ASP can report the line number on which an error occurred during execution. Otherwise, ASP does not report the line number in error reports.

Catch COM Component Exceptions determines whether ASP pages trap exceptions thrown by COM components. The default is True. If set to True, ASP attempts to catch exceptions, which prevents the exception from being handled elsewhere, such as the scripting engine or the IIS worker process. If set to False, ASP does not attempt to catch exceptions, which could lead to the exception being handled elsewhere and could also cause termination of the worker process.

Other debugging options are:

- **Enable Client-Side Debugging**   Determines whether debugging is enabled for ASP on the client. The default is False. If set to True, client-side debugging is enabled, which may be necessary for troubleshooting and diagnostics.
- **Enable Log Error Requests**   Determines whether IIS writes ASP errors to the IIS log files. The default is True. If set to True, IIS writes ASP errors to the IIS log files.
- **Enable Server-Side Debugging**   Determines whether debugging is enabled for ASP on the server. The default is False. If set to True, server-side debugging is enabled, which may be necessary for troubleshooting and diagnostics.
- **Log Errors To NT Log**   Determines whether IIS writes ASP errors to the Windows event logs. The default is False. If set to True, IIS writes ASP errors to the Windows event logs, which may be necessary for troubleshooting and diagnostics.

- **Run On End Functions Anonymously**   Determines whether the *SessionOnEnd* and *ApplicationOnEnd* global ASP functions should be run as the anonymous user. The default is True. If set to True, the functions are run as the anonymous user. If set to False, the functions are not run at all.
- **Script Error Message**   Sets the error message to send to the browser if specific debugging errors are not sent to the client. The default message sent is "An error occurred on the server when processing the URL. Please contact the system administrator."
- **Send Errors To Browser**   Determines whether IIS writes ASP errors to client browsers. The default is False. If set to True, IIS writes ASP errors to client browsers, such as may be necessary for troubleshooting and diagnostics.

You manage debugging and error handling settings by completing the following steps:

1. In IIS Manager, navigate to the level of the configuration hierarchy you want to manage, and then access the ASP page by double-clicking the ASP feature.

2. On the ASP page, under Compilation, expand the Debugging Properties node by double-clicking it.

3. On the ASP page, under Compilation, set the Debugging Properties options to configure the way ASP should debug and handle errors.

4. In the Actions pane, click Apply.

> **CAUTION**   Server-side debugging of ASP applications is designed for development and staging servers and not necessarily for production servers. If you enable server-side debugging on a production server, you might notice a severe decrease in performance for the affected application.

By using the IIS command-line administration tool, you can configure debugging settings by using the Set Config command and the ASP section of the configuration file. Sample 1-8 provides the syntax and usage.

SAMPLE 1-8 Configuring Debugging for ASP Syntax and Usage

Syntax

```
appcmd set config ["ConfigPath"] /section:Asp
[/calcLineNumber: true|false]
[/exceptionCatchEnable: true|false]
[/appAllowClientDebug: true|false]
[/logErrorRequests: true|false]
[/appAllowDebugging: true|false]
[/errorsToNTLog: true|false]
[/runOnEndAnonymously: true|false]
[/scriptErrorMessage: true|false]
[/scriptErrorSentToBrowser: true|false]
```

Usage

```
appcmd set config "Default Web Site" /section:Asp
/exceptionCatchEnable: true
/errorsToNTLog: true
```

Managing ASP.NET Settings

ASP.NET moves away from the reliance on ISAPI and ASP to provide a reliable framework for Web applications that takes advantage of the Microsoft .NET Framework. ASP.NET is, in fact, a set of .NET technologies for creating Web applications. With ASP.NET, developers can write the executable parts of their pages using any .NET-compliant language, including Microsoft Visual C#, Microsoft Visual Basic, and Microsoft JScript.

Unlike ASP, ASP.NET has components that are precompiled prior to run time. These precompiled components are called *assemblies*. Compiled assemblies not only load and run faster than ASP pages, but they also are more secure. Whereas ASP.NET can process requests in either classic pipeline mode or integrated pipeline mode, only the integrated mode allows IIS to process requests directly.

> **NOTE** Server-level configuration changes for ASP.NET features are made in the Web.config file in the %SystemRoot%\Microsoft.NET\Framework*Framework Version*

> \Config folder, where *FrameworkVersion* is the version of the .NET Framework you are using, such as V2.0.50727 or V4.0.30319. Site-level and application-level configuration changes for ASP.NET features are made in the Web.config file stored in the site or application folder.

Configuring Session State Settings for ASP.NET

In the default configuration, IIS manages session state for ASP.NET in much the same way as it manages session state for ASP. Beyond the basic settings, however, you have many more options. For ASP.NET pages, you use the Enable Session State setting of the Pages And Controls feature as the master control to turn on or off session state management or to configure IIS to use a read-only session state. You use the Session State feature to fine tune how session state management is used.

By default, IIS maintains session state in process as does ASP. Each ASP.NET application configured on your server can have its own session state settings. When you've activated the ASP.NET State Service and configured it to start automatically, you can use out-of-process session state management for ASP.NET. Out-of-process state management ensures that session state information is preserved when an application's worker process is recycled. You can configure out-of-process state management to use a State Server or a Microsoft SQL Server database. Before you configure a SQL Server for session state, you must run the InstallSqlState.sql script on the server. By default, this script is stored in *%SystemRoot%*\Microsoft.NET\Framework*FrameworkVersion*, where *FrameworkVersion* is the version of the .NET Framework you are using, such as V2.0.50727 or V4.0.30319.

You turn on or off session state management or use a read-only session state by following these steps:

1. In IIS Manager, navigate to the level of the configuration hierarchy you want to manage, and then display the Pages And Controls page by double-clicking the Pages And Controls feature.

2. On the Pages And Controls page, shown in Figure 1-3, the Enable Session State text box shows the current session state. As necessary, change this

setting to False to disable session state maintenance, True to enable session state maintenance, or ReadOnly to use a read-only session state.

3. In the Actions pane, click Apply to save your settings.

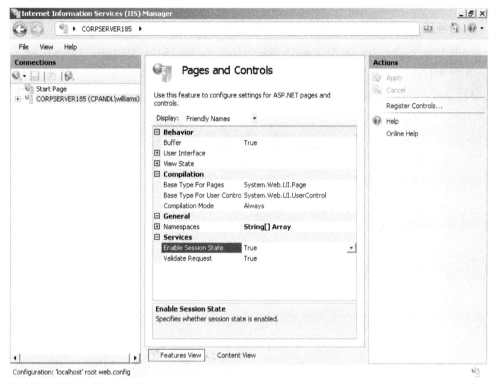

FIGURE 1-3   Review the Pages and Controls settings.

Once you've enabled a ReadWrite or ReadOnly session state, you can use the settings of the Session State feature to optimize the session state configuration. Follow these steps:

1. In IIS Manager, navigate to the level of the configuration hierarchy you want to manage, and then display the Session State page by double-clicking the Session State feature.

2. On the Session State Mode Settings frame in the main pane, shown in Figure 1-4, use the following options to set the session state mode:

- **Not Enabled**   Select this option to disable session state.
- **In Process**   Select this option to store session state data for a managed-code application in the worker process where the application runs. This is the default setting.

- **Custom**   Select this option to configure IIS to use a custom provider to handle session state for ASP.NET applications.
- **State Server**   Select this option to enable the ASP.NET State Service and store session state data outside the worker process where the application runs. The ASP.NET State Service stores the session state in an internal database by default or in a database of your choosing. You must start the service and configure it for automatic startup.
- **SQL Server**   Select this option to configure IIS to use a SQL Server database to store session state data instead of storing it in the worker process where the application runs. The ASP.NET State Service stores the session state in the SQL Server database you designate. You must start the service and configure it for automatic startup.

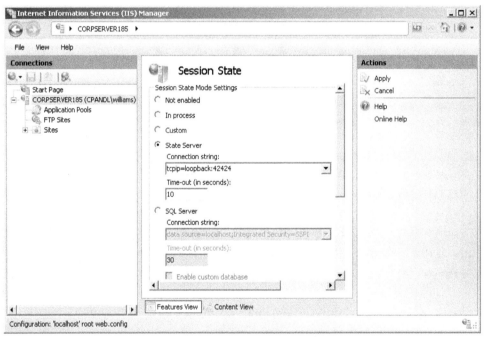

FIGURE 1-4 Configure the session state mode for ASP.NET.

3. With the State Server or SQL Server option, the Connection String text box sets the connection string that is used to connect to the state server or SQL Server. If you click the related selection drop-down list, you can choose a previously created connection string to use. If you click the related Create button, you create the required connection string by using the Create Connection String dialog box.

4. With the State Server or SQL Server option enabled, the related Time-Out text box sets the time, in seconds, that the connection will be maintained. The default for a state server is 10 seconds. The default for a server running SQL Server is 30 seconds.

5. With the SQL Server option enabled, you can select the Enable Custom Database check box to enable a custom SQL Server database for storing session state data.

6. On the Cookie Settings pane, in the Mode drop-down list, select the desired item to specify how cookies are used to store session state data. The items are:

- **Auto Detect**   IIS uses cookies if the browser supports cookies and cookie support is enabled. Otherwise, IIS doesn't use cookies.
- **Use Cookies**   Allows IIS to track the session state by using cookies. IIS passes the session state in cookies for all requests between a client browser and the Web server. Because cookies do not require redirection, cookies allow you to track session state more efficiently than any of the methods that do not use cookies. Using cookies also has several other advantages. Cookies allow users to bookmark Web pages, and they ensure that state is retained if a user leaves one site to visit another and then returns to the original site.
- **Use Device Profile**   IIS uses cookies if the device profile supports cookies regardless of whether cookie support is enabled or disabled. The only time that IIS doesn't use cookies is when the device profile indicates that the browser doesn't support cookies.
- **Use URI**   IIS inserts the session ID as a query string in the Uniform Resource Identifier (URI) request, and then the URI is redirected to the originally requested URL. Because the changed URI request is used for the duration of the session, no cookie is necessary.

7. Keep the following in mind when you are specifying how cookies are used to store session state data:

- When you use the Auto-Detect cookie, Use Device Profile, or Use URI modes, the Regenerate Expired Session ID check box is selected automatically. This ensures that IIS rejects and reissues session IDs that do not have active sessions. You should require that expired session IDs be regenerated because this ensures that IIS expires and regenerates tokens, which gives a potential attacker less time to capture a cookie and gain access to server content. If you want to disable session ID regeneration, as may be necessary when initially testing a new deployment in a development environment, clear this check box. Be sure to re-enable this feature later to enhance server security.

- When you use the Auto-Detect cookie, Use Cookies, or Use Device Profile modes, the entry in the Time-Out (In Minutes) text box sets the period of time that IIS maintains a session object after the last request associated with the object is made. The default time-out is 20 minutes. For a high-usage application in which you expect users to move quickly from page to page, you might want to set a fairly low time-out value, such as 5 or 10 minutes. On the other hand, if it's critical that the user's session is maintained to complete a transaction, you might want to set a long time-out value, such as 60 minutes.

- When you use the Auto-Detect cookie, Use Cookies, or Use Device Profile modes, the Name text box sets a name for the cookie. The default is ASP.NET_SessionId. To enhance security, you may want to change this value to a name that isn't as readily identifiable as the session ID.

- The Use Hosting Identity For Impersonation option enables Windows authentication for remote connections using the host process identity. Typically, this is the setting you want to use to ensure that IIS can read and write session state data.

8. In the Actions pane, click Apply to save your settings.

Configuring SMTP E-Mail Settings

E-mail services are an important part of most Internet, intranet, and extranet server operations. Often, you'll find that applications installed on a server generate e-mail messages that need to be delivered. For this purpose, IIS includes the Simple Mail Transfer Protocol (SMTP) feature so that IIS can deliver e-mail messages for Web applications that use the System.Net.Mail API. The configuration restricts the sending of messages that are generated by remote users, which include the Internet Guest account and any other named user on the Web server. The configuration also restricts relaying of e-mail through SMTP.

SMTP is just one of several components that make up a typical e-mail system. Windows Server 2008 and Windows Server 2008 R2 includes the optional SMTP Server feature to provide a more robust solution. However, if you want to receive e-mail and store it on the server so that users and applications can retrieve it, you need to install a full-featured messaging server in the enterprise, such as Microsoft Exchange Server.

You can use the SMTP E-mail feature in two key ways. You can use this feature to deliver e-mail messages generated by applications to a specific SMTP server running on the local system or a remote server. Or you can use this feature to drop e-mail directly into the pickup directory for later processing by an application or for direct processing by an SMTP server running on the local system. Because SMTP servers monitor their pickup directories continuously for new messages, any message placed in this directory is picked up and transferred to a queue directory for further processing and delivery.

E-mail messages have To, Cc, Bcc, and From fields to determine how the message should be handled. To, Cc, and Bcc fields are used to determine where the message should be delivered. The From field indicates the origin of the message. E-mail addresses, such as *williams@tech.microsoft.com*, have three components:

- An e-mail account, such as *williams*
- An at symbol (@), which separates the account name from the domain name
- An e-mail domain, such as *tech.microsoft.com*

The key component that determines how the server handles messages is the e-mail or service domain. Service domains can be either local or remote. A *local service domain* is a Domain Name System (DNS) domain that's serviced locally by the server. A *remote service domain* is a DNS domain that's serviced by another server or mail gateway.

You can deliver e-mail to a locally hosted or remote SMTP server by completing the following steps:

1. In IIS Manager, navigate to the level of the configuration hierarchy you want to manage, and then display the SMTP E-Mail page by double-clicking the SMTP E-Mail feature.

2. On the SMTP E-Mail page, shown in Figure 1-5, in the E-Mail Address text box, type the address you want to use as the default address from which e-mail messages are sent.

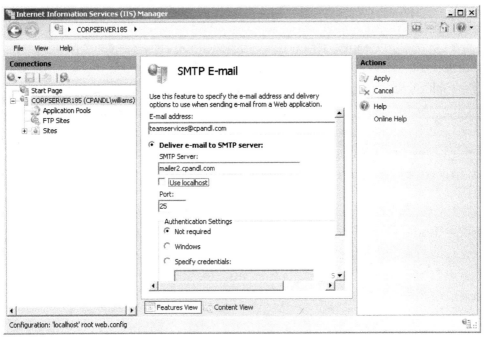

FIGURE 1-5 Configure SMTP E-mail settings.

3. Select the Deliver E-Mail To SMTP Server option.

4. In the SMTP Server text box, type the fully qualified domain name of the SMTP server, such as mailer5.imaginedlands.com. Or select the Use Localhost check box to set the name of the SMTP server to localhost, allowing System.Net.Mail to send e-mail directly to the SMTP server on the local computer.

5. In the Port text box, type the TCP port number to use to connect to the SMTP server. The standard TCP port for SMTP is 25, so this is the default and recommended setting.

6. The Authentication Settings options allow you to specify the authentication mode and credentials. If your SMTP server does not

require authentication, choose Not Required. Otherwise, choose one of the following options:

- **Windows**   Choose this to use the application identity for connecting to the SMTP server.
- **Specify Credentials**   Choose this to specify a user name and password for connecting to the SMTP server. Credentials are sent as clear text across the network. To specify credentials, click Set. Type the user name, type and then confirm the user password, and then click OK.

7. In the Actions pane, click Apply to save your settings.

You can deliver e-mail to a pickup directory by completing the following steps:

1. In IIS Manager, navigate to the level of the configuration hierarchy you want to manage, and then display the SMTP E-Mail page by double-clicking the SMTP E-Mail feature.

2. On the SMTP E-Mail page, in the E-Mail Address text box, type the address you want to use as the default address from which e-mail messages are sent.

3. Select the Store E-Mail In Pickup Directory option, and then click Browse.

4. Use the Browse For Folder dialog box to specify the location of the pickup directory, and then click OK.

5. In the Actions pane, click Apply to save your settings.

Configuring Key/Value Pairs for ASP.NET Applications

When you are working with managed code applications, you may need to store information used by an application as key/value pairs in the application's Web.config file. Storing application settings in this way ensures that the stored values can be accessed from anywhere within the application. If you store application settings at the server or site level, multiple applications could access and use the same settings. With this in mind, you can view and work with key/value pairs for applications by completing the following steps:

1. In IIS Manager, navigate to the level of the configuration hierarchy you want to manage.

2. Access the Application Settings page by double-clicking the Application Settings feature.

3. In the main pane, you'll see a list of the currently defined key/value pairs. Be sure to note whether the entry type is listed as local or inherited. Local entries are configured at the level you are working with. Inherited entries are configured at a higher level of the configuration hierarchy.

4. Use the following techniques to work with application settings:

- **Add a setting** Click Add. In the Add Application Setting dialog box, type the name and value for the application setting, and then click OK.
- **Edit a setting** Click the setting you want to modify, and then click Edit. In the Edit Application Setting dialog box, type the desired name and value for the application setting, and then click OK.
- **Remove a setting** Click the setting you want to remove, and then click Remove. When prompted to confirm the action, click Yes.

Configuring Settings for ASP.NET Pages and Controls

Web applications that use ASP.NET include Web pages to provide the user interface and controls to provide drop-in functionality. As with ASP, you can optimize the way ASP.NET is used through a variety of configuration settings. You can also make additional functionality available by registering custom controls that applications can use.

Registering Custom Controls

Managed code applications can use any custom controls that are registered for use with IIS. As an administrator, you probably won't need to install controls, but you may need to validate control configurations. To view currently registered controls, in IIS Manager, navigate to the level of the configuration hierarchy you want to manage, double-click the Pages And Controls feature, and then in the Actions pane, click Register Controls. In the main pane, you should then see a list of the currently registered controls. Controls are listed by tag prefix, associated source or assembly, and entry type. Local entries are configured at the level you are working with. Inherited entries are configured at a higher level of the configuration hierarchy.

You can add a custom control by following these steps:

1. In IIS Manager, navigate to the level of the configuration hierarchy you want to manage, double-click the Pages And Controls feature, and then, in the Actions pane, click Register Controls.

2. In IIS Manager, on the Controls Page, click Add Custom Control. The Add Custom Control dialog box appears as shown in Figure 1-6.

3. In the Tag Prefix text box, type the tag prefix assigned to the control, such as **aspx**.

4. In the Namespace text box, type the ASP.NET namespace in which the custom control type is defined, such as **System.Web.UI.WebControls.WebParts**.

5. In the Assembly text box, type the assembly details associated with the custom control. This includes the control's top-level namespace, version, culture, and any additional information required to register the assembly properly, such as its public key token. Then click OK.

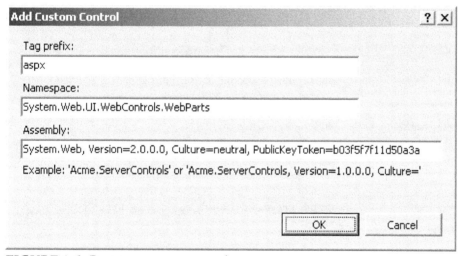

FIGURE 1-6 Register a custom control.

You can edit registered control entries by clicking the control entry you want to modify and then clicking Edit. In the Edit Custom Control dialog box, modify the settings as necessary, and then click OK to save your changes. To remove a registration entry for a custom control that is no longer needed, click the control entry you want to remove, and then click Remove. When prompted to confirm the action, click Yes.

Configuring ASP.NET Settings for Pages and Controls

You can modify the way ASP.NET is used by Web applications by using the configuration settings on the Pages And Controls page in IIS Manager. To access this page, navigate to the level of the configuration hierarchy you want to manage, and then double-click the Pages And Controls feature.

Table 1-2 summarizes the available ASP.NET settings for pages and controls. In the related server, site, or application Web.config file, you manage these settings by using the sessionState configuration section.

TABLE 1-2 Settings for Pages and Controls

Base Type for Pages (pageBaseType)	Sets the base type that .aspx pages inherit by default. The default value in most cases is System.Web.UI.Page. This value can be overridden by the *Inherits* attribute.
Base Type for User Controls (userControlBaseType)	Sets the base type that user controls inherit by default. The default value in most cases is System.Web.UI.UserControl.
Buffer (buffer)	Determines whether .aspx pages and .ascx controls use response buffering. The default setting is True. When True, IIS uses response buffering in much the same way as it uses response buffering for ASP.
Compilation Mode (compilationMode)	Determines whether an ASP.NET page or control should be compiled at run time. The default is Always, which ensures that pages and controls are always compiled at run time. A value of Never specifies that pages and controls are not compiled and should be interpreted instead. A value of Auto allows IIS to compile pages and controls as necessary and otherwise set them to be interpreted.
Enable Authenticated View State (enableViewStateMAC)	Determines whether ASP.NET should run a message authentication code (MAC) on the page's view state when the page is posted back from the client. The default setting is True.
Enable Session State (enableSessionState)	Specifies whether and how IIS maintains session state information for ASP.NET applications. The default setting is True. When True, IIS maintains session state information for ASP.NET. Alternately, you can use a value of ReadOnly to have IIS maintain non-editable, read-only session state data. If you don't want IIS to maintain session state information for ASP.NET, configure this setting to False.

Enable View State (enableViewState)	Determines whether the page maintains the view state and the view state of any server controls it contains when the current page request ends. The default setting is True.
Master Page File (masterPageFile)	Sets an optional master page path relative to the local configuration file. This allows applications to reference locations in the master page path by name rather than full file path.
Maximum Page State Field Length (maxPageStateFieldLength)	Sets the maximum number of characters for individual view state fields. When the value is greater than zero (0), IIS breaks the view state field into chunks that are less than the specified length. Clients receive this chunked view state as a series of view state fields rather than a single, possibly very long view state field. When the value is set to -1, IIS does not chunk the view state field and instead sends the entire value to the client in a single view state field.
Namespaces (namespaces)	Specifies the namespaces included for all pages. IIS imports these namespaces during assembly pre-compilation. If you expand the Namespaces node, you'll see a list of namespaces that will be imported.
Style Sheet Theme (styleSheetTheme)	Sets the optional name of the theme folder that IIS will use to apply a theme before control declarations. You can specify a theme to apply after control declaration by using the theme attribute.
Theme (theme)	Sets the optional name for the theme that is used for pages that are in the scope of the configuration file. The specified theme must exist as either an application or a global theme. If the theme does not exist, IIS generates an HttpException exception.
Validate Request (validateRequest)	Determines whether ASP.NET validates requests to screen for potentially dangerous or malicious input. The default setting is True, which causes ASP.NET to validate input from client browsers. Although you should rarely disable validation, you can do so by using a value of False.

You can configure the list of namespaces that IIS imports during assembly pre-compilation by completing the following steps:

1. To view currently configured Pages And Controls settings, in IIS Manager, navigate to the level of the configuration hierarchy you want to manage, and then double-click the Pages And Controls feature.

2. On the Pages And Controls page, expand the Namespaces node to display a list of namespaces that will be included during assembly pre-compilation.

3. If you click the Namespaces entry, IIS Manager displays a selection button on the far right side of the second column. Clicking this button displays the String Collection Editor dialog box, which you can use to edit the imported namespace values. Edit the namespace entries as necessary. Add additional namespaces by typing each additional namespace on a separate line.

4. When you are finished editing namespace values, click OK. In the Actions pane, apply the changes to the configuration by clicking Apply.

Connecting to Data Sources

IIS can store connection strings used by managed code applications to connect to local and remote data sources, which can include SQL Server databases and other types of databases. To view currently configured connection strings, in IIS Manager, navigate to the level of the configuration hierarchy you want to manage, and then access the Connection Strings page by double-clicking the Connection Strings feature. In the main pane, you'll see a list of the currently defined connection strings. Local entries are configured at the level you are working with. Inherited entries are configured at a higher level of the configuration hierarchy.

You can create a connection string for SQL Server by completing the following steps:

1. In IIS Manager, navigate to the level of the configuration hierarchy you want to manage, and then access the Connection Strings page by double-clicking the Connection Strings feature.

2. On the Connection Strings page, in the Actions pane, click Add. This displays the Add Connection String dialog box, shown in Figure 1-7.

3. In the Name text box, type the name of the connection string, such as **SqlServerCustDb.** This name must be the same name that you reference in your application code to retrieve data that uses this connection string. You cannot change the name later without re-creating the connection string.

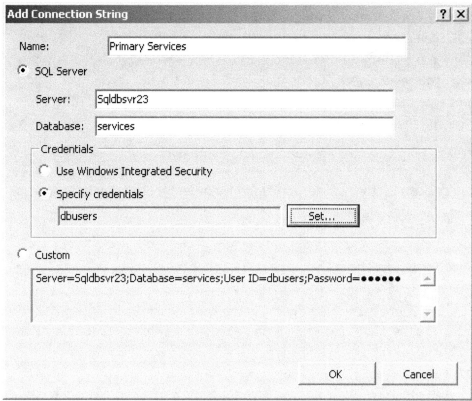

FIGURE 1-7 Add a connection to a SQL Server database.

4. In the Server text box, type the name of the SQL server that hosts the database.

5. In the Database text box, type the name of the SQL server database.

6. Select one of the following Credentials options to specify the security credentials that are used to connect to the database:

- **Use Windows Integrated Security** Configures the connection string so that the application uses the current Windows identity established on the operating system thread to access the SQL Server database. Use this option to pass through authenticated Windows domain credentials to the database.

NOTE You can use integrated security only when SQL Server runs on the same computer as IIS or when you've configured delegation between computers. Additionally, all application users must be in the same domain so that their credentials are available to IIS.

- **Specify Credentials** Configures the connection string to use a specific SQL Server user name and password. Use this option when you do not want to pass through user credentials to the database for authentication. After you select Specify Credentials, click Set in the Set Credentials dialog box, type the SQL Server user name to use for the connection. After you type and then confirm the password for this user, click OK.

7. Click OK to close the Add Connection String dialog box.

You can create a custom connection string for other types of database servers by completing the following steps:

1. In IIS Manager, navigate to the level of the configuration hierarchy you want to manage, and then access the Connection Strings page by double-clicking the Connection Strings feature.

2. On the Connection Strings page, in the Actions pane, click Add. This displays the Add Connection String dialog box, with the Custom option enabled, as shown in Figure 1-8.

3. In the Name text box, type the name of the connection string, such as **LocalSqlServer**. This name must be the same name that you reference in your application code to retrieve data that uses this connection string. You cannot change the name later without re-creating the connection string.

4. Select the Custom option, and then type the connection string. The connection string should by formatted as appropriate for the type of database to which you are connecting. Your organization's application developer or database administrator should be able to provide the required connection string. The following example connects to a local SQL Express database, which is stored in the aspnetdb.mdf file:

```
Data source=.\SQLEXPRESS;Integrated Security=SSPI;
AttachDBFilename=|DataDirectory|aspnetdb.mdf;User Instance=true
```

5. Click OK to close the Add Connection String dialog box.

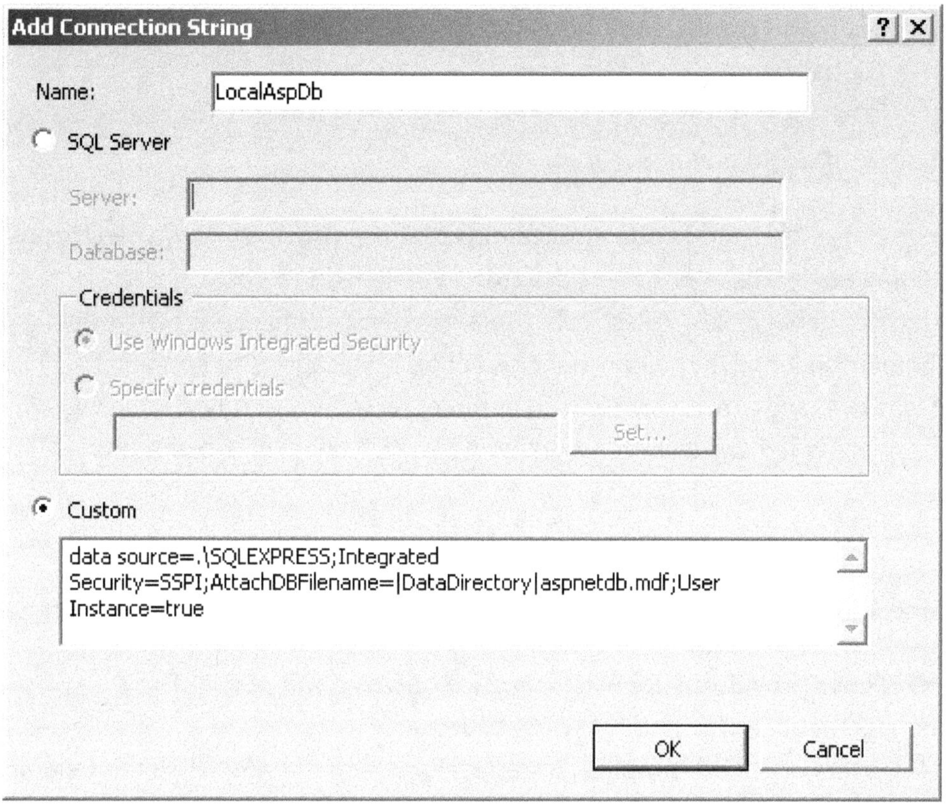

Add Connection String   ? X

Name: `LocalAspDb`

○ SQL Server

     Server: [ ]

     Database: [ ]

     ┌─ Credentials ──────────────────┐
     │ ● Use Windows Integrated Security │
     │ ○ Specify credentials │
     │ [ ]   Set... │
     └───────────────────────────┘

● Custom

```
data source=.\SQLEXPRESS;Integrated
Security=SSPI;AttachDBFilename=|DataDirectory|aspnetdb.mdf;User
Instance=true
```

                    [OK]   [Cancel]

FIGURE 1-8 Add a connection to a data source.

To edit an existing connection string, select the string that you want to modify, and then click Edit. In the Edit Connection String dialog box, modify the settings as necessary, and then click OK to save your changes. To remove a connection string that is no longer needed, select the connection string you want to remove, and then click Remove. When prompted to confirm the action, click Yes.

Managing .NET Framework Settings

In ASP.NET applications, you can use the functions and features provided by the .NET Framework to establish connections to databases, control access to applications, and much more. Key configuration areas for connecting to databases include Connection Strings and .NET Providers. Key configuration areas for controlling applications include: .NET Profiles, .NET Users, and .NET

Roles. You can also configure settings for .NET Trust Levels, .NET Compilation, and .NET Globalization.

Configuring .NET Providers

When you have managed code applications that use provider-based services to store data in a database or other data store, you'll need to configure .NET providers to manage .NET roles, .NET users, and .NET profiles. .NET providers have helper functions that allow managed code applications to connect to databases by using previously defined connection strings and perform the necessary management tasks for working with .NET roles, .NET users, and .NET profiles.

Because .NET roles, .NET users, and .NET profiles all have different purposes, different .NET providers are required for working with each of these features:

- .NET Roles providers supply an interface between the ASP.NET role management service and role data sources.
- .NET Users providers supply an interface between the ASP.NET membership service and membership data sources.
- .NET Profile providers supply an interface between the ASP.NET profile service and profile data sources.

To view the default .NET providers and any additional providers that you've created, in IIS Manager, navigate to the level of the configuration hierarchy you want to manage, and then double-click the Providers feature. On the Providers page, in the Feature drop-down list, choose the type of .NET provider you want to view and manage. Associated providers are listed by:

- **Name** Show the descriptive name that is assigned to the provider for easy identification.
- **Type** Shows the .NET type for the provider. All providers are implemented in managed code.
- **Entry Type** Shows the scope of the provider as either Local or Inherited.

Table 1-3 provides an overview of the default .NET providers that are available when you've enabled ASP.NET for application development.

TABLE 1-3 Default .NET Providers

AspNetSqlRoleProvider	For working with .NET roles stored in the Windows Internal Database associated with the IIS installation. .NET type: System.Web.Security. SqlRoleProvider.
AspNetWindowsTokenRoleProvider	For working with Windows security tokens associated with .NET roles. .NET type: System.Web.Security. WindowsTokenRoleProvider.
AspNetMembershipProvider	For managing .NET user memberships stored in the Windows Internal Database associated with the IIS installation. .NET type: System.Web.Security. SqlMembershipProvider.
AspNetSqlProfileProvider	For managing .NET profiles stored in the Windows Internal Database associated with the IIS installation. .NET type: System.Web.Profile. SqlProfileProvider.

You can configure additional .NET providers for managing .NET roles, .NET users, and .NET profiles stored in a database or other data store by following these steps:

1. Each .NET provider requires a connection string to the data source you want to use. If you haven't already created the required connection string as discussed in the "Connecting To Data Sources" section earlier in this chapter, do so now.

2. On the Providers page in IIS Manager, in the Feature drop-down list, select the feature you want to manage with the provider. Choose .NET Roles if you want to use the provider to create or manage .NET Roles in the related data source. Choose .NET Users if you want to use the provider to create or manage .NET Users in the related data source. Choose .NET Profile if you want to use the provider to create or manage .NET Profiles in the related data source.

3. In the Actions pane, click Add. As shown in Figure 1-9, this displays the Add Provider dialog box.

4. In the Type selection drop-down list, choose the .NET type to associate with the .NET provider, such as AuthorizationStoreRoleProvider.

5. In the Name text box, type a unique name for the .NET provider, such as **AspNet AuthorizationStoreRoleProvider**.

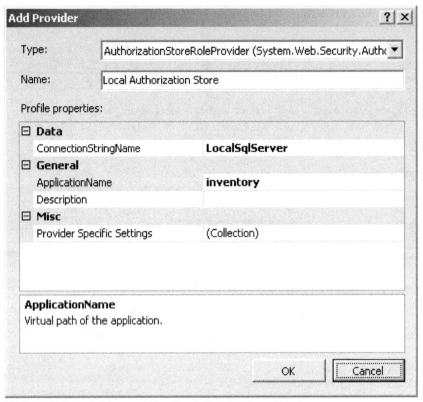

FIGURE 1-9 Add a provider for ASP.NET applications.

6. If you are creating a .NET provider for .NET users, use the Behavior options to specify these profile properties:

- EnablePasswordReset for enabling the password reset functionality
- EnablePasswordRetrieval for enabling password retrieval from a data store
- RequiresQuestionAndAnswer for requiring a security question and correct answer to reset a user password
- RequiresUniqueEmail for requiring a unique e-mail address for each user
- StorePasswordInSecureFormat for storing the user password in a secure (encrypted) format

7. Click in the ConnectionStringName text box to activate the related selection list. In the drop-down list, choose the previously created connection string that the .NET provider should use.

8. The entry in the ApplicationName text box sets the virtual path of a specific application that uses the provider. If you do not specify a value,

the value is set at run time to that of the current application making the connection request, per HttpContext.Current.Request.ApplicationPath.

9. In the Description text box, type an optional description of the provider, and then click OK.

Although you cannot edit or remove default .NET providers, you can edit, rename, or remove any .NET providers you've created:

- To edit user-created .NET providers, click the provider entry you want to modify, and then click Edit. In the Edit Provider dialog box, modify the settings as necessary, and then click OK to save your changes.
- To rename a user-created provider, click the provider entry to select it, and then click Rename. Type the new name for the provider, and then press Enter.
- To remove an entry for a user-created provider that is no longer needed, click the provider entry you want to remove, and then click Remove. When prompted to confirm the action, click Yes.

Configuring .NET Trust Levels

The active .NET Trust Level sets the level of trust that is applied to managed modules, handlers, and applications. The trust levels you can use for servers, sites, and applications follow:

- **Full (internal)**   Indicates that ASP.NET applications are fully trusted. This grants application permissions to access any resource that is subject to operating system security and allows all privileged operations.
- **High (web_hightrust.config)**   Indicates that ASP.NET applications are highly trusted. This restricts application permissions so that an application cannot perform any of the following actions: call unmanaged code, call serviced components, write to the event log, access Microsoft Message Queuing (MSMQ) service queues, or access data sources.
- **Medium (web_mediumtrust.config)**   Indicates that ASP.NET applications are moderately trusted. This restricts application permissions so that in addition to not being able to perform any of the actions restricted by the High trust level, an application cannot perform any of the following tasks

by default: access files outside the application directory, access the registry, or make network or Web service calls.

- **Low (web_lowtrust.config)**   Indicates that ASP.NET applications are somewhat trusted. This restricts application permissions so that in addition to not being able to perform any of the actions restricted by the High and Medium trust levels, an application cannot perform either of the following tasks by default: write to the file system or call the *Assert* method.
- **Minimal (web_minimaltrust.config)**   Indicates that ASP.NET applications are minimally trusted. This restricts application permissions so that it has only execute permissions. No other permissions are granted by default.

You can configure the .NET trust level for a server, site, or application by completing the following steps:

1. In IIS Manager, navigate to the level of the configuration hierarchy you want to manage, and then display the .NET Trust Levels page by double-clicking the .NET Trust Levels feature.
2. On the .NET Trust Levels page, in the Trust Level drop-down list, set the desired trust level. Click Apply to save your settings.

In the related server, site, or application Web.config file, you can configure the trust level by using the level attribute of the trust configuration section. The valid values are: Full, High, Medium, Low, and Minimal.

Configuring .NET Profiles

.NET profiles allow you to store any custom information that applications require. Generally speaking, you'll have two types of properties: global properties that you want to use for all applications, and application-specific properties that apply only to a specific application. You can make it easier to work with properties by grouping similar properties. You can do this according to the application they are used with or according to how the property is used.

In IIS Manager, you can view currently configured properties for .NET profiles by double-clicking the .NET Profile feature. This feature is available only at or below a site level. On the .NET Profile page, you'll see a list of the currently defined properties. Local entries are configured at the level you are working with. Inherited entries are configured at a higher level of the configuration hierarchy.

You can work with .NET profiles in a variety of ways:

- To disable or enable the .NET Profile feature, in the Actions pane, click Disable or Enable.
- To set the default provider for .NET profiles, in the Actions pane, click Set Default Provider, select a default provider, and then click OK. By default, ASP.NET uses a SqlProfileProvider instance named AspNetSqlProfileProvider to connect to a SQL Server database on the local computer. A Windows Internal Database is provided for this purpose.
- To create a group container for properties, in the Actions pane, click Add Group, type a group name, and then click OK.
- When you select a group, you can add a new property to the group by clicking Add Property To Group, providing the property details, and then clicking OK.
- To add a property without placing it in a group, click Add Property, provide the property details, and then click OK.
- When you select a property, you can edit, rename, or remove it by configuring the related settings in the Actions pane.

You can set the following details for profile properties:

- **Name**   Sets the name of the profile property.
- **Data Type**   Sets the data type of the property. This can be either a common data type such as String, or a custom data type.
- **Default Value**   Sets the default value of the property.
- **Serialization Option**   Sets the serialization formatting for the property as string, binary, XML, or provider-specific.

Properties can also be read-only and accessible to anonymous users.

Configuring .NET Roles

.NET Roles allow you to group a set of users and perform security-related operations, such as authorization, on a whole set of users. In IIS Manager, to view currently configured .NET Roles, double-click the .NET Roles feature. This feature is available at or below a site level only. On the .NET Roles page, enable roles that are currently disabled by clicking Enable in the Actions pane. You'll see a list of the currently defined roles. Roles are listed by name and by the number of users assigned to a role.

You can work with .NET Roles in a variety of ways:

- To set the default provider for .NET profiles, in the Actions pane, click Set Default Provider, select a default provider, and then click OK. By default, the ASP.NET Role Manager uses a SqlRoleProvider instance named AspNetSqlRoleProvider, which stores role information in a SQL Server database. A Windows Internal Database is provided for this purpose.
- To define a role, in the Actions pane, click Add, provide the necessary role details, and then click OK. The role uses the default provider automatically.
- To change the default provider for a role, click the role you want to edit, and then click Edit. In the Edit .NET Role dialog box, select the default provider to use, and then click OK.

> **NOTE** The ASP.NET Role Manager is designed to support custom role and user assignment and cannot be used to manage Windows users and groups. This is why the default provider is set as SqlRoleProvider and not as WindowsTokenRoleProvider. SqlRoleProvider supports custom user and role assignment through SQL Server and is ideally suited to medium and large deployments. The WindowsTokenRoleProvider uses role information based on Windows domain accounts and is useful only if your application runs on a network in which all users have domain accounts. The WindowsTokenRoleProvider relies on Windows authentication to determine the groups in which a user is allowed to be a member.

Configuring .NET Users

You can use .NET Users to help you manage user identities that are defined for applications. .NET Users can be used to perform authentication, authorization, and other security-related operations.

To view currently configured .NET Users, in IIS Manager, double-click the .NET Users feature. This feature is available at or below a site level only. On the .NET

Users page, you'll see a list of the currently defined users. Users are listed by name, e-mail address, date created, and last login.

You can work with .NET Users in a variety of ways:

- To set the default provider for .NET users, in the Actions pane , click Set Default Provider, select a default provider, and then click OK. By default, the ASP.NET Users Manager uses a SqlMembershipProvider instance named AspNetSqlMembershipProvider, which stores user information in a SQL Server database. A Windows Internal Database is provided for this purpose.
- To create a user, in the Actions pane, click Add., and then follow the wizard prompts. You'll need to supply the user name and default e-mail address. Type and then confirm the password for the user. You can also select or type a security question and provide an answer for this question. If the RequiresQuestionAndAnswer property is set for the .NET Users provider, this question and answer can be used to reset the user password.
- To specify the roles to associate with a .NET user, select a user, and then in the Actions pane, click Add . Then use the options provided to specify the roles associated with the user.
- To change the default provider for a user, click the user you want to edit, and then click Edit. In the Edit .NET Users Settings dialog box, select the default provider to use, and then click OK.

Configuring .NET Compilation

.NET Compilation properties allow you to manage the way IIS performs batch compilations of ASP.NET application code. In IIS Manager, to view currently configured .NET compilation settings, navigate to the level of the configuration hierarchy you want to manage, and then double-click the .NET Compilation feature. On the .NET Compilation page, you'll see a list of the currently defined settings. These settings are used as described in Table 1-4. In the related server, site, or application Web.config file, you can use the compilation configuration section to configure these settings.

TABLE 1-4 .NET Compilation Settings

Assemblies (assemblies)	Specifies the assemblies to include during compilation. If you expand the Assemblies node, you'll see a list of assemblies that will be included. Click Select to edit the assemblies list.
Batch Compilations (batch)	Determines whether batch processing is supported. The default is True, enabling batch compilation. To disable batch compilation, use a value of False.
Code Sub Directories	Specifies the subdirectories that contain code. If you expand the Code Sub Directories node, you'll see a list of subdirectories that will be included. Click Select to edit the subdirectories list.
Debug (debug)	Determines whether the debugger is enabled or disabled. The default is False, disabling debugging. To enable debugging, use a value of True.
Default Language (defaultLanguage)	Sets the default programming language to use in dynamic compilation files. The default is Visual Basic ("vb"). You can also select C#.
Explicit Compile Option (explicit)	Determines whether to set the Visual Basic explicit compile option. The default is True. If True, all variables must be declared explicitly by using a Dim, Private, Public, or ReDim statement. To remove the requirement for explicit declarations, use a value of False.
Maximum File Size (maxBatchGeneratedFileSize)	Sets the maximum size, in kilobytes, of the generated source files per batched compilation. The default is 1000 KB. If a source file exceeds the maximum size, the compiler reverts to single compilation mode for the source file.
Maximum Size of Batch (maxBatchSize)	Sets the maximum number of pages per batched compilation. The default is 1000. When ASP.NET reaches the maximum number of files, it closes the current batch session and starts a new one as necessary.
Number of Recompiles (numRecompilesBeforeAppRestart)	Specifies the number of dynamic recompiles of resources that can occur before IIS restarts the application. The default is 15. If this value is reached, IIS restarts the application.

Strict Compile Option (strict)	Determines whether to set the Visual Basic strict compile option. The default is False, meaning that the strict compile option is not set.
Timeout (batchTimeout)	Sets the time-out period for batch compilation. If compilation cannot be completed in the time-out period, the compiler reverts to single compilation mode for the current page. The default is 00:15:00 (15 minutes).
Temporary Directory (tempDirectory)	Sets the directory to use for temporary file storage during compilation. The default value is an empty string, which allows ASP.NET to use its default working directory.
Url Line Pragmas (urlLinePragmas)	Determines whether the line pragmas (used to introduce machine-dependent code in a controlled fashion) generated by ASP.NET should use URLs instead of physical paths. The default is False, meaning that ASP.NET will use physical paths. To use URLs instead, use a value of True.

You can configure the list of assemblies to use during .NET Compilation by completing the following steps:

1. To view currently configured .NET compilation settings, in IIS Manager, navigate to the level of the configuration hierarchy you want to manage, and then double-click the .NET Compilation feature.

2. On the .NET Compilation page, expand the Assemblies node to display a list of assemblies that will be included for compilation.

3. If you click the Assemblies entry, IIS Manager displays a selection button on the far right side of the second column. Clicking this button displays the String Collection Editor dialog box, which you can use to edit the included assemblies. Edit the assembly entries as necessary. Add additional assemblies by entering each additional assembly on a separate line. Enter * as the last entry to include all other assemblies.

4. When you are finished editing assembly values, click OK. In the Actions pane, click Apply to apply the changes to the configuration.

Configuring .NET Globalization

IIS is capable of supporting multiple language environments. *Globalization* is the process of internationalizing application code, then localizing the application to other languages and cultures. With applications that have been globalized, IIS can present application content in the appropriate encoding and format for the client locale.

You can configure globalization options to support globalized applications on the .NET Globalization page. To access this page, in IIS Manager, navigate to the level of the configuration hierarchy you want to manage, and then double-click the .NET Globalization feature. On the .NET Globalization page, you'll see a list of the currently defined settings. These settings are used as described in Table 1-5. In the related server, site, or application Web.config file, you can configure these settings by using the globalization configuration section.

TABLE 1-5 .NET Globalization Settings

Culture (culture)	Sets the default culture for processing incoming Web requests.
Enable Client Based Culture (enableClientBasedCulture)	Determines whether the client culture settings are evaluated. The default is False, meaning that the client culture settings are not evaluated. If True, ASP.NET sets the Culture and UICulture properties based on the AcceptLanguage header field value that is sent by the client browser.
File (fileEncoding)	Sets default the file encoding for .aspx, .asmx, and .asax file parsing. Unicode and UTF-8 files that are saved with the byte-order mark prefix are automatically recognized, regardless of the value for this attribute. The default file encoding in the U.S. is Windows-1252.
Requests (requestEncoding)	Sets the assumed encoding for incoming requests, including posted data and query strings. If a request includes a request header that contains an *Accept-Charset* attribute, the value of this attribute overrides this setting. The default encoding is UTF-8. In most case, requests, response headers, and responses encoding should be set in the same way.
Response Headers (responseHeaderEncoding)	Sets the content encoding of response headers. The default encoding is UTF-8.

Responses (responseEncoding)	Sets the content encoding of responses. The default encoding is UTF-8.
UI Culture (uiCulture)	Sets the default UI culture for use in processing incoming Web requests.

Chapter 2. Managing Applications and Application Pools

The previous chapter discussed the essentials for customizing the application environment. That chapter's focus was broad and discussed issues related to all types of applications that you can host on IIS. In this chapter, I focus on advanced application configuration issues that are specific to running dynamic applications, such as:

- Managing .NET configurations
- Creating applications and application pools
- Configuring multiple worker processes for applications
- Recycling worker processes manually and automatically
- Optimizing application performance

As you might expect, the discussion in this chapter applies primarily when you are working with Active Server Pages (ASP) and Microsoft ASP.NET, and you must be logged on as an administrator or run commands as an administrator to perform the tasks this chapter discusses.

Defining Custom Applications

You use IIS Manager to configure custom applications. As part of the standard installation, Web sites have a prespecified application that allows you to run custom programs without making changes to the environment. You could, for example, copy your ASP files to a site's base directory and run them without creating a separate application. Here, the ASP application runs as a default application within the context of the site's application pool.

Each application has a starting point. The starting point sets the logical namespace for the application. That is, the starting point determines the files and folders that are included in the application. Every file and folder in the starting point is considered part of the application.

You can set application starting points for the following:

- An entire site
- A directory
- A virtual directory

When you specify a site-wide application, all files in all the Web site's subdirectories are considered to be a part of the application. When you specify an application for a standard or virtual directory within a site, all files in all subdirectories in this directory are considered part of the application and are no longer considered to be a part of the site application.

To get better control over sites and related applications, you should configure separate contexts for key applications. Application contexts are specified using basic and advanced application settings. Basic application settings include the following:

- **Alias**   Sets the relative URL path for the application.
- **Physical Path**   Sets the base directory for the application. All files in all subdirectories of the base directory are considered to be part of the application.
- **Application Pool**   Determines which application pool is used with the application. You can configure multiple application pools, and each can have a different worker process configuration.

Advanced application settings include Physical Path Credentials and Physical Path Credentials Logon Type. Physical Path Credentials sets the credentials for the user identity that should be impersonated when IIS accesses application files on a remote share. If you need to use alternate credentials to connect to the remote server specified in a Universal Naming Convention (UNC) path, you can specify user credentials or use the default pass-through authentication mode. With pass-through authentication, IIS uses the credentials of the requesting user. For authenticated requests, IIS uses the logged on credentials of the authenticated user. For non-authenticated requests, IIS uses the Internet Guest account (IUSR_*hostname*).

Physical Path Credentials Logon Type specifies the type of logon operation to perform when acquiring the user token necessary to access the physical path. The logon types you can use are as follows:

- **ClearText** IIS uses a clear-text logon to acquire the user token. As IIS passes the logon user call over the back end on an internal network, using a clear-text call typically is sufficient. This is the default logon type.
- **Interactive** IIS uses an interactive logon to acquire the user token. This gives the related account the Interactive identity for the logon session and makes it appear that the user is logged on locally.
- **Batch** IIS uses a batch logon to acquire the user token. This gives the related account the Batch identity for the logon session and makes it appear that the user is accessing the remote server as a batch job.
- **Network** IIS uses a network logon to acquire the user token. This gives the related account the Network identity for the logon session and makes it appear that the user is accessing the remote server over the network.

These basic and advanced settings create an application context within which an application runs. Application contexts are specified at the directory level. All files in all subdirectories of an application's base directory are considered to be part of the application. Because of this, one way to create applications is to follow these steps:

1. In Microsoft Windows Explorer, create a directory that will act as the application's starting point, and then set appropriate Windows access permissions on the directory.
2. Use IIS Manager to create an application that maps to the physical directory.
3. Configure application settings for the directory as described in the "Creating Applications" section later in this chapter.

Because IIS Manager now allows you to create a required physical directory and set Windows permissions, you can also create applications by using the following technique:

1. Use IIS Manager to create an application that maps to a new directory.

2. Configure application settings for the directory as described in the "Creating Applications" section later in this chapter.

3. In IIS Manager, use the application's Edit Permissions setting to set appropriate Windows access permissions on the directory.

Managing Custom IIS Applications

As part of the standard installation, all Web sites created in IIS have a default application that's set as a site-wide application, meaning that its starting point is the base directory for the Web site. The default application allows you to run custom applications that use the preconfigured application settings. You don't need to make any changes to the environment. You can, however, achieve better control by specifying applications with smaller scope, and the sections that follow tell you how to do this.

Viewing Applications

To view all applications associated with a site, in IIS Manager, select the site node, and then in the Actions pane, click View Applications. As Figure 2-1 shows, you'll then see the applications created within the site.

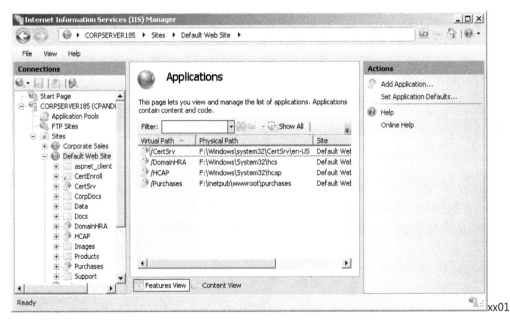

FIGURE 2-1 Review the applications associated with a site.

These applications are listed by:

- **Virtual Path** Lists the virtual path to the application within the site context
- **Physical Path** Lists the physical path to the base directory for the application
- **Site** Lists the site to which the application belongs
- **Application Pool** Lists the application pool in which the application runs

With the IIS command-line administration tool, you can list applications by using the List App command. Sample 2-1 provides the syntax and usage.

SAMPLE 2-1 List App Syntax and Usage

Syntax

```
appcmd list app [[/app.name:]AppNameOrURL] [/site.name:"SiteName"]
[/apppool.name:"AppPoolName"][/path: "VirtualPath"]
[/parameter1:value1 ...]
```

Usage

```
appcmd list app "Default Web Site/Sales"


appcmd list apps /site.name:"Default Web Site"


appcmd list apps /apppool.name:"DefaultAppPool"


appcmd list apps /path:/Sales
```

Configuring Default Settings for New Applications

In a standard configuration, new applications are configured to use the default application pool, pass-through authentication, and clear text for the logon type. If you use the same settings for most applications, you may want to modify the default settings. To do this, follow these steps:

1. In IIS Manager, select the site node you want to work with, and then in the Actions pane, click View Applications.

2. On the Applications page, in the Actions pane, click Set Application Defaults.

3. The Application Pool text box lists the current default application pool. To change the default value, click the selection button. In the Select Application Pool dialog box, select the application pool to use in the Application Pool drop-down list, and then click OK.

4. The Physical Path Credentials text box is blank by default to indicate that IIS uses pass-through authentication. If you need to use alternate credentials to connect to the remote server specified in a UNC path, click the selection button. In the Connect As dialog box, choose Specific User, and then click Set. In the Set Credentials dialog box, type the name of the user account to use for authentication, type and confirm the account password, and then click OK.

5. The Physical Path Credentials Logon Type text box lists the default type of logon operation to perform when acquiring the user token necessary to access the physical path. The logon types you can use are ClearText, Interactive, Batch, and Network. Click OK to save your settings.

With the IIS command-line administration tool, you can configure the default application pool by using the *applicationPool* attribute of the applicationDefaults configuration section. You can configure the Physical Path Credentials and Physical Path Credentials Logon Type by using the *username*, *password*, and *logonMethod* attributes of the virtualDirectoryDefaults configuration section. Samples 9-2 and 9-3 provide the syntax and usage.

SAMPLE 2-2 Setting the Default Application Pool Syntax and Usage

Syntax
```
appcmd set config ["ConfigPath"] /section:applicationDefaults
[/applicationPool:"AppPoolName"]
```

Usage
```
appcmd set config "Default Web Site" /section:applicationDefaults
/applicationPool:"Standard App Pool"
```

SAMPLE 2-3 Configuring Default Path Settings Syntax and Usage

Syntax
```
appcmd set config ["ConfigPath"] /section:virtualDirecdtoryDefaults
```

```
[/userName:"UserName"] [/password:"Password"]
[/logonMethod:"LogonType"]
```

Usage

```
appcmd set config "Default Web Site"
/section:virtualDirecdtoryDefaults /logonMethod:"ClearText"
```

Creating Applications

IIS applications are collections of resource files and components that are grouped together to take advantage of key IIS features. You can create an application by completing the following steps:

1. In IIS Manager, right-click the site, directory, or virtual directory under which you want to create the application, and then select Add Application. This displays the dialog box shown in Figure 2-2.

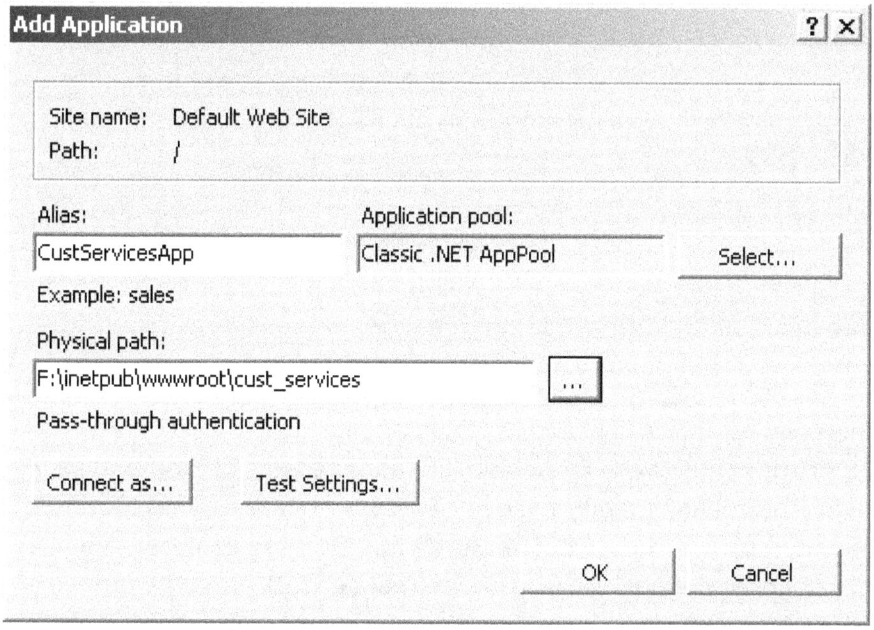

FIGURE 2-2 Use the Add Application dialog box to configure custom applications.

2. In the Alias text box, type the relative URL of the application. For example, if you are creating the application under the default Web site at *http://www.reagentpress.com* and set the alias as Inventory, the application can be accessed using the URL *http://www.reagentpress.com/Inventory*.

> **CAUTION**   Make sure you use an appropriate alias. You cannot change an application's alias.

3. The default application pool is listed in the Application Pool text box. Although you can use the default application pool, it's better to create pools for specific types of applications. To do so, click the Select button. In the Select Application Pool dialog box, select the application pool to use in the Application Pool drop-down list, and then click OK.

> **NOTE**   When you select an application pool in the Select Application Pool dialog box, the Microsoft .NET Framework version and pipeline mode are listed as properties. Be sure to select an application pool using the appropriate .NET Framework version and pipeline mode.

4. In the Physical Path text box, type the path to the physical directory where the application content is stored, or click the selection button to the right of the Physical Path text box to search for a directory. The directory must be created before you can select it. If necessary, in the Browse For Folder dialog box, click Make New Folder to create the directory before you select it. However, don't forget about checking and setting permissions at the operating system level as discussed in Chapter 4, "Enhancing Web Server Security."

5. If you need to use alternate credentials to connect to the remote server specified in a UNC path, click Connect As. In the Connect As dialog box, choose Specific User, and then click Set. In the Set Credentials dialog box, type the name of the user account to use for authentication, type and confirm the account password, and then click OK twice.

> **TIP**   When you set logon credentials for an application, the account name you provide must exist. By default, IIS Manager sets the logon type to ClearText. This means that IIS will use clear text when acquiring the user token necessary to access the physical path. Because IIS passes the logon user call over the back end on an internal network, using a clear-text call typically is sufficient. By editing an application's properties, you also have the option to set the logon type to Interactive, Batch, or Network. See the "Changing Application Settings" section later in this chapter for more information.

With the IIS command-line administration tool, you can create applications by using the Add App command. Sample 2-4 provides the syntax and usage.

SAMPLE 2-4 Add App Syntax and Usage

Syntax

```
appcmd add app /site.name: "ParentSiteName" /path: "VirtualPath"
/physicalPath: "Path"
```

Usage

```
appcmd add app /site.name:"Default Web Site" /path: "/Sales"
/physicalPath: "c:\inetpub\wwwroot\Sales"
```

When you create an application, a related virtual directory is created automatically. You can use this virtual directory to set the logon type and credentials for an application. The related command is Add Vdir. Sample 2-5 provides the syntax and usage.

SAMPLE 2-5 Setting the Logon Type and Credentials Syntax and Usage

Syntax

```
appcmd add vdir /app.name:"ParentAppName" /path: "VirtualPath"
[/physicalPath: "Path"] [/logonMethod:Method] [/userName:User]
[/password:Password]
```

Usage

```
appcmd add vdir /app.name:"Default Web Site/Sales" /path:"/Support"
/physicalPath:"c:\support"
```

```
appcmd add vdir /app.name:"Sales Site/" /path:"/Invoices"
/physicalPath:"c:\salesroot\invoices" /logonMethod:ClearText
/userName:SupportUser /password:RainyDayz
```

Converting Existing Directories to Applications

Existing physical and virtual directories can be easily converted to applications, giving them separate contexts. To convert a directory to an application, follow these steps:

1. In IIS Manager, right-click the directory or virtual directory that you want to convert to an application, and then select Convert To Application. This displays the Add Application dialog box shown previously in Figure 2-2.

The application alias and physical path are set automatically based on the directory you selected and cannot be changed.

2. The default application pool is listed in the Application Pool text box. To use a different application pool, click the Select button. In the Select Application Pool dialog box, select the application pool to use in the Application Pool drop-down list, and then click OK.

3. If you need to use alternate credentials to connect to the remote server specified in a UNC path, click Connect As. In the Connect As dialog box, choose Specific User, and then click Set. In the Set Credentials dialog box, type the name of the user account to use for authentication, type and confirm the account password, and then click OK twice.

With the IIS command-line administration tool, you can convert a directory to an application in the same way as you create an application. See Samples 9-4 and 9-5 for examples.

Changing Application Settings

An application's alias (virtual path) cannot be changed. You can change any other application's settings by following these steps:

1. In IIS Manager, select the site node you want to work with, and then in the Actions pane, click View Applications.

2. On the Applications page, click the application you want to work with, and then do one or both of the following:

- To edit the application's basic settings (which includes all settings except the logon type), select the application, and then, in the Actions pane, click Basic Settings. This displays the Edit Application dialog box, which you can use to change the application settings in much the same way as you set them in the first place by using the Add Application dialog box.
- To edit the application's advanced settings, in the Actions pane, click Advanced Settings. This displays the Advanced Settings dialog box, which you can use to change the application settings.

3. Applications can have associated virtual directories. To view and manage the virtual directories associated with an application, select the application you want to work with, and then click View Virtual Directories. You can

now work with the virtual directories associated with the previously
selected application.

With the IIS command-line administration tool, you can change application
settings via the virtual directory associated with the application. See Sample 2-6
for the related syntax and usage. Several application settings are configurable
only from a command prompt. These settings control the bindings and
protocols that are enabled for an application. With IIS 7.5, you also can specify
whether the application should start automatically and the related autostart
provider that the Windows Process Activation Service will use.

SAMPLE 2-6 Set Application Attributes Syntax and Usage

Syntax

```
appcmd set app [/app.name:]AppNameOrURL
[/bindings:value1 ...]
[/enabledProtocols:value1 ...]
```

IIS 7.5 only:

```
[/serviceAutoStartEnabled: true|false]
[/serviceAutoStartProvider: "ProviderName"]
```

Usage

```
appcmd set app "Default Web Site/Sales" /bindings:
http://www.imaginedlands.com:8080


appcmd set app "Default Web Site/Sales" /enabledProtocols:http
```

Configuring Output Caching for Applications

Output caching improves performance by returning a processed copy of a
served content from cache, resulting in reduced overhead on the server and
faster response times. IIS supports output caching in both user mode and kernel
mode. Kernel-mode caching is enabled by default to ensure that cached
responses are served from the kernel rather than from IIS user mode, giving IIS
an extra boost in performance and increasing the number of requests IIS can
process. Whether an individual application uses user-mode caching or kernel-

mode caching depends on the application configuration as well as the caching rules that you define.

With the attributes of the Caching configuration section, you can control the way caching is used. Sample 2-7 provides the syntax and usage. The *enabled* attribute turns user-mode output caching on or off. If set to True, user mode is enabled for output caching. Otherwise, user-mode output caching is disabled. The *enableKernelModeCache* attribute controls whether kernel-mode output caching is enabled. If set to True, kernel mode is enabled for output caching. Otherwise, kernel-mode caching is disabled. The *maxCacheSize* attribute sets the maximum size, in megabytes, of the in-memory cache used for both the user-mode and kernel-mode caches. If this attribute is set to zero (0), IIS uses half the available physical or virtual memory (whichever is less) for caching. *maxResponseSize* sets the maximum size, in bytes, of responses that can be stored in the output cache for both the user-mode and kernel-mode caches. The default value is 262144 bytes (256 KB). If the response size is large than this value, the response is not stored in the output cache.

> **NOTE** At the server level, you set the master caching configuration and all the configuration options are available. At other configuration levels, you can control only whether output caching, kernel caching, or both are enabled.

SAMPLE 2-7 Configuring Output Caching Syntax and Usage

Syntax

```
appcmd set config ["ConfigPath"] /section:caching
[/enabled:true|false] [/enableKernelModeCache:true|false]
[/maxCacheSize:"MaxStoredCacheInMB"]
[/maxResponseSize:"MaxSizeInBytes"]
```

Usage

```
appcmd set config "Default Web Site" /section:caching
/enableKernelModeCache:true
```

In IIS Manager, you can configure the maximum cached response size and cache size limit for output caching by completing the following steps:

1. Navigate to the level of the configuration hierarchy you want to manage, and then double-click the Output Caching feature.

2. On the Output Caching page, click Edit Feature Settings. This displays the Edit Output Cache Settings dialog box, shown in Figure 2-3.

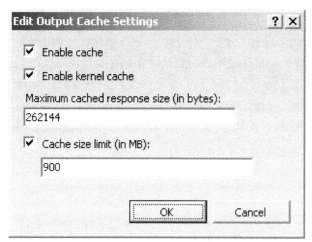

FIGURE 2-3 Configure output caching.

3. If you are working at the server configuration level, you can configure user-mode and kernel-mode caching:

   ▪ To enable user-mode caching, select Enable Cache. Clear this option to disable user-mode caching.
   ▪ To enable kernel-mode caching, select Enable Kernel Cache. Clear this option to disable kernel-mode caching.

4. In the Maximum Cached Response Size text box, type the maximum cached response size in bytes. The default value, 262144 bytes (256 KB), is appropriate in many instances. However, if your site has applications which can return large responses, such as database result sets, you'll want to increase this value accordingly.

5. To have IIS manage the cache size, clear the Cache Size Limit check box. To set a specific limit, select this check box, and then type a limit value in megabytes (MB). Click OK to save your settings.

> **TIP** On a dedicated Web server, you can set a specific cache limit to allow IIS to use more than half of the available physical or virtual memory. Before you do this, however, you should determine memory usage baselines for the server through monitoring. On a non-dedicated server,

you can set a specific cache limit of less than half of the available physical or virtual memory to ensure that memory is available for other applications running on the server. In this configuration, you sacrifice IIS performance and responsiveness to ensure other applications can run on the server.

You can also create output-caching rules that control how IIS performs output caching for specific types of files. You can cache files until they change or until a specified time interval has elapsed. You also can have multiple cached versions of files based on query string variables or HTTP headers. For example, you may want to allow multiple cached versions of files based on locale. This would allow IIS to store different language versions of a file in cache.

The best way to configure output-caching rules is as follows:

- At the server level, you set the caching rules that you want to apply to all sites and applications running on the server.
- At the site and application level, you set the remote caching rules that you do not want to apply at that level.
- At the site and application level, you add caching rules as necessary that use the default settings for cache monitoring.

In IIS Manager, you can create an output caching by completing the following steps:

1. Navigate to the level of the configuration hierarchy you want to manage, and then double-click the Output Caching feature. Keep in mind that you can customize the caching process only at the server level. At other levels, you can apply only the default settings.
2. On the Output Caching page, click Add. This displays the Add Cache Rule dialog box, shown in Figure 2-4.
3. In the File Extension text box, type the file extension for which the rule will be applied, such as .aspx or .axd.

NOTE   Be sure to use the correct file extension. You cannot change the file extension later. Because of this, you would need to delete and then re-create the rule using the correct file extension.

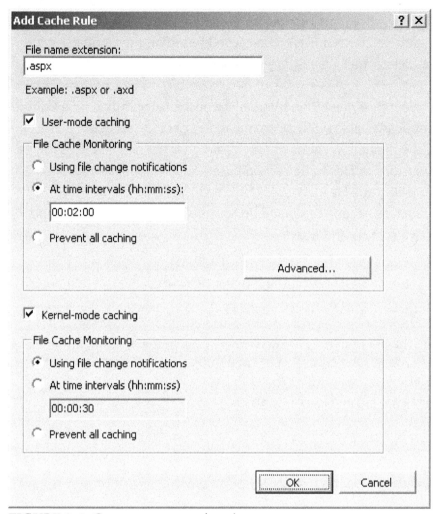

FIGURE 2-4 Create an output cache rule.

4. To prevent user-mode caching for this file extension, select the User-Mode Caching check box and then select Prevent All Caching. To enable and configure user-mode caching, select the User-Mode Caching check box and then perform one or more of the following actions as necessary:

- Once IIS caches a file, it monitors the file to determine whether the cache needs to be updated. To configure monitoring based on change notifications, select the Using File Change Notifications option. To configure monitoring for a specified time interval, select At Time Intervals, and then type an appropriate time interval, such as 00:01:00.

- IIS can cache multiple versions of files based on query string variables. To allow multiple versions of files to be cached based on the language, click Advanced. Select the Query String Variables check box, and then type Locale. To allow multiple versions of files to be cached based on regional settings, select the Query String Variables check box, and then type Culture. Separate multiple values with a comma and a space.
- IIS can cache multiple versions of files based on HTTP headers. To allow multiple versions of files to be cached based on a header value, click Advanced. Select the Headers check box, and then type the header keyword, such as Accept-Language or Accept-Charset. Separate multiple values with a comma and a space.

5. To prevent kernel-mode caching for this file extension, select the Kernel-Mode Caching check box and then select Prevent All Caching. To enable and configure user-mode caching, select the User-Mode Caching check box and then configure file cache monitoring. Once IIS caches a file, it monitors the file to determine whether the cache needs to be updated. To configure monitoring based on change notifications, select the Using File Change Notifications option. To configure monitoring for a specified time interval, select At Time Intervals, and then type an appropriate time interval, such as 00:01:00.

6. Click OK to create the cache rule.

You can work with cache rules in a variety of other ways:

- To modify the rule definition, click the rule, and then click Edit. In the Edit Cache Rule dialog box, make the necessary changes to the rule, and then click OK.
- To block an inherited rule so that IIS doesn't apply at the current configuration level, click the rule, and then click Remove.
- To remove a rule permanently, click the rule, and then in the Actions pane, click Remove. When prompted to confirm the action, click Yes.

Deleting IIS Applications

If you find that you no longer need an application, you should remove it to free up the resources that it's using. Deleting an application removes the application context only; it does not remove the underlying directories or content.

To delete an application, follow these steps:

1. In IIS Manager, select the site node you want to work with, and then in the Actions pane, click View Applications.
2. On the Applications page, click the application you want to remove, and then in the Actions pane, click Remove.
3. When prompted to confirm that you want to remove the application, click Yes.

With the IIS command-line administration tool, you can delete an application by using the Delete App command. Sample 2-8 provides the syntax and usage.

SAMPLE 2-8 Delete App Syntax and Usage

Syntax
```
appcmd delete app [/app.name:]AppNameOrURL
```

Usage
```
appcmd delete app "Default Web Site/Sales"
```

Managing ASP.NET and the .NET Framework

Every Web administrator should become intimately familiar with ASP.NET and the .NET Framework. You should know how to configure and manage the related components and applications. As you've seen in Chapter 1, ASP.NET and .NET Framework configurations are fairly complex. To ensure success, you'll need to work closely with your organization's engineers and developers during planning, staging, and deployment.

Installing ASP.NET and the .NET Framework

To use applications that incorporate the .NET Framework, you must install ASP.NET on your IIS servers. ASP.NET is the central Windows component that allows an IIS server to run ASP.NET applications. Like the .NET Framework, ASP.NET technology is advancing rapidly. Several implementations of ASP.NET are already available, and many more will be developed in the coming months and years.

Unlike many application implementations, in which you have to remove previous application or component versions before installing new applications or components, you don't have to remove previous versions of ASP.NET. The reason is that the .NET Framework supports side-by-side execution of applications and components running different versions of ASP.NET. Side-by-side execution is made possible because applications and the components they use run within isolated process boundaries. Each worker process runs its own instance of the ASP.NET components that it needs and is isolated from other processes.

You can install multiple versions of ASP.NET on an IIS server. You enable the default version of ASP.NET and .NET by installing and enabling the ASP.NET and .NET Extensibility role services. You can install additional versions of ASP.NET on an IIS server. Typically, you do this by running the .NET Framework setup program (Dotnetfx.exe) for the version you want to install. Installing a newer version of the .NET Framework could reconfigure ASP.NET applications installed on the IIS server to use the version you're installing. Specifically, this happens when the version you're installing is a new version that represents a minor revision (as determined by the version number). For example, if ASP.NET applications are currently configured to use ASP.NET version 2.0.50727 and you're installing a newer version, ASP.NET applications would be configured to use components in the new version automatically. Here, 50727 represents the build number, and 2.0 are the major and minor version numbers, respectively.

After you install a new version of the .NET Framework, you'll need to ensure that IIS is configured properly so that the new version of ASP.NET it contains can be used in both the Classic and Integrated pipeline modes. You do this by ensuring that the related aspnet_filter.dll is added as an ISAPI filter and that the related aspnet_isapi.dll is allowed as an ISAPI and CGI restriction. Each version of the .NET Framework installed on a server has different components and tools. The base directory for the .NET Framework is *%SystemRoot%*\Microsoft.NET\Framework. Below the base directory, you'll find separate subdirectories for each version of the .NET Framework you've installed.

One of the tools in the version subdirectory is the ASP.NET IIS Registration tool. This tool controls the mapping of ASP.NET applications to a specific ASP.NET version. If you want to install an additional ASP.NET version so that it can be used on the server, you can use this tool to do it. Complete the following steps:

1. On the Start menu, choose Run.
2. In the Open field, type **cmd,** and then click OK.
3. At the command prompt, type cd %SystemRoot%\Microsoft.NET\Framework, and then press Enter.
4. Run the **dir** command to obtain a directory listing. Note the available version subdirectories, and then change to the directory containing the ASP.NET version you want to use.
5. List the installed versions of ASP.NET and view how those versions are configured by running **aspnet_regiis -lv** and then **aspnet_regiis -lk**. Then do one of the following:

- If you want all application pools to use this ASP.NET version (as long as it's a newer version and represents a compatible build as determined by the version and build number), run **aspnet_regiis -i**.
- If you want to register this ASP.NET version on the server but don't want to reconfigure application pools to use it, run **aspnet_regiis -ir**.

> **TIP** It's important to note that each version of ASP.NET installed on a server has a separate set of performance counter objects. Because of this, if you want to monitor a particular ASP.NET application's performance, you'll need to configure monitoring of the performance counter objects specific to the version of ASP.NET used by the application.

Deploying ASP.NET Applications

Now that you've configured the application directory structure, you're ready to deploy your ASP.NET applications. To deploy applications, copy the necessary ASP.NET files, such as .asmx or .aspx files, to the application directory. Application binaries and assemblies (DLLs) are copied to the Bin subdirectory for the application.

Any time you need to update or change the files in the deployment directory, simply copy the new versions of the ASP.NET files and binaries to the appropriate directory. When you do this, ASP.NET automatically detects that files have been updated. In response, ASP.NET compiles a new version of the application and loads it into memory as necessary to handle new requests. Any current requests are handled without interruption by the previously created application instance. When that application instance is no longer needed, it's removed from memory.

ASP.NET handles changes to the Web.config file in the same way. If you modify the Web.config file or application pool properties while IIS is running, ASP.NET compiles a new version of the application and loads it into memory as necessary to handle new requests. Any current requests are handled without interruption by the previously created application instance. When that application instance is no longer needed, it's removed from memory.

Uninstalling .NET Versions

Sometimes you no longer want an older version of ASP.NET to run on a server. In this case you can uninstall the unneeded ASP.NET version. When you uninstall an older version of ASP.NET, ASP.NET applications that used the version are reconfigured so that they use the highest remaining version of ASP.NET that's compatible with the version you're uninstalling.

Remember, the version number determines compatibility. If no other compatible versions are installed, applications that used the version of ASP.NET you're uninstalling are left in an unconfigured state, which might cause the entire contents of ASP.NET pages to be served directly to clients, thereby exposing the code those pages contain.

If you want to uninstall an additional version of ASP.NET, follow these steps:

1. On the Start menu, choose Run.

2. In the Open field, type **cmd,** and then click OK.

3. At the command prompt, type **cd %SystemRoot%\Microsoft.NET \Framework**, and then press Enter.

4. Run the **dir** command to obtain a directory listing. Note the available version subdirectories and then change to the directory containing the ASP.NET version you want to remove.

5. List the installed versions of ASP.NET and view how those versions are configured by running **aspnet_regiis -lv** and then running **aspnet_regiis -lk**.

6. To uninstall the ASP.NET version whose components are in the current subdirectory, run **aspnet_regiis -u**. This uninstalls the ASP.NET version and the performance counter objects used by the ASP.NET version.

> **NOTE** If you want to uninstall all ASP.NET versions installed on a server, run **aspnet_regiis -ua**.

Working with Application Pools

Application pools set boundaries for applications and specify the configuration settings that applications they contain use. Every application pool has a set of one or more worker processes assigned to it. These worker processes specify the memory space that applications use. By assigning an application to a particular application pool, you're specifying that the application:

- **Can run in the same context as other applications in the application pool** All applications in a particular application pool use the same worker process or processes, and these worker processes define the isolation boundaries. These applications must use the same version of ASP.NET. If applications in the same application pool use different versions of ASP.NET, errors will occur and the worker processes might not run.

- **Should use the application pool configuration settings** Configuration settings are applied to all applications assigned to a particular application pool. These settings control recycling of worker processes, failure detection and recovery, CPU monitoring, and much more. Application pool settings should be optimized to work with all applications they contain.

The sections that follow provide techniques for creating, configuring, and optimizing application pools.

Viewing Application Pools

You manage application pools on a per-server basis. In IIS Manager, you can view all the application pools configured on a server by expanding the server node and then clicking the Application Pools node. As Figure 2-5 shows, you'll then see a list of applications created within the site.

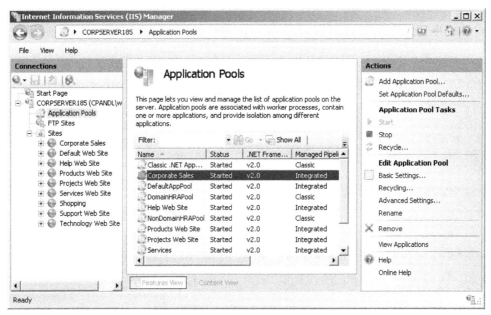

FIGURE 2-5 Review the application pools configured on the server.

These applications are listed by:

- **Name** Lists the name of the application pool
- **Status** Lists the status of an application pool as Started or Stopped
- **.NET Framework Version** Lists the .NET Framework version that the application pool uses
- **Managed Pipeline Mode** Lists the request processing mode used by the application as Integrated or Classic

- **Identity**   Lists the account under which the application pool runs, such as NetworkService
- **Applications**   Lists the number of applications that are configured to run in the application pool

With the IIS command-line administration tool, you can list a server's application pools by running the List AppPool command. Sample 2-9 provides the syntax and usage.

SAMPLE 2-9 List AppPool Syntax and Usage

Syntax

```
appcmd list apppool [[/apppool.name:]"AppPoolName"]
[/managedRuntimeVersion:"Version"]
[/managedPipelineMode: Integrated|Classic]
[/queueLength:"queueLength"]
[/autoStart:true|false]
```

IIS 7.5 only:

```
[/managedRuntimeLoader "ManagedLoader"]
[/CLRConfigFile "AppPoolConfigFile"]
[/startMode "AlwaysRunning" | "OnDemand"]
```

Usage

```
Appcmd list apppool

appcmd list apppool "DefaultAppPool"

appcmd list apppool /autoStart:false
```

Several utility commands are provided to help you work with application pools and track their worker processes. With the List Wp command, you can list the worker processes currently running on a server. Sample 2-10 provides the syntax and usage.

SAMPLE 2-10 List Wp Syntax and Usage

Syntax

```
appcmd list wp [[/process.name:]"ProcessID"] [/wp.name:"ProcessID"]
[/apppool.name:"AppPoolName"]
```

Usage

```
appcmd list wp

appcmd list wp "4291"

appcmd list wp /apppool.name:"DefaultAppPool"
```

With the List Request command, you can list the requests currently executing on a server and optionally find requests that have been executing for longer than a specified time in milliseconds. Sample 2-11 provides the syntax and usage.

SAMPLE 2-11 List Request Syntax and Usage

Syntax

```
appcmd list request [[/process.name:]"ProcessID"]
[/request.name: "ProcessID"] [/site.name:"SiteName"]
[/wp.name:"WpName"] [/apppool.name:"AppPoolName"]
[/elapsed:Milliseconds]
```

Usage

```
appcmd list request

appcmd list request /wp.name:4125

appcmd list request /apppool.name:DefaultAppPool

appcmd list request /site.name:"Default Web Site"
```

Configuring Default Settings for New Application Pools

In a standard configuration, new application pools are configured to use a number of settings that determine exactly how an application pool works. If you use the same settings for most application pools, you may want to modify the default settings. To do this, follow these steps:

- In IIS Manager, expand the node for the server you want to work with, and then click the Application Pools node.
- On the Application Pools page, in the Actions pane, click Set Application Pool Defaults.
- In the Application Pool Defaults dialog box, configure the default settings for application pools, and then click OK.

Table 2-1 provides a summary of the default settings for application pools. Each setting is listed alphabetically according to its related configuration area, such as CPU or Process Model. With the IIS command-line administration tool, you can configure these settings using the following syntax:

```
appcmd set config /section:applicationPools
/applicationPoolDefaults.SubAttribute:Value
```

where SubAttribute is a listed sub attribute and Value is the desired value, such as:

```
appcmd set config /section:applicationPools
/applicationPoolDefaults.enable32BitAppOnWin64:true
```

All time intervals are set hh:mm:ss format. These same sub attributes are used with application pools when you want to configure their settings from a command prompt. To configure settings for an individual application pool, use the following syntax:

```
appcmd set apppool "AppPoolName" /[Attribute.]SubAttribute:Value
```

where AppPoolName is the name of the application pool, Attribute is a listed attribute, SubAttribute is a listed sub attribute, and Value is the desired value, such as:

```
appcmd set apppool "CustServicesAppPool" /cpu.resetInterval:30
```

> **NOTE** Hyphens are added in this table for readability. Sub attribute names do not have hyphens in actual usage.

Table 2-1 Settings for Configuring Application Pools

GENERAL	
clrConfigFile	Sets the .NET configuration file for a pre-loaded application pool. (IIS 7.5 only)
enable32BitAppOnWin64	When True, enables 32-bit applications to run using 32-bits on a 64-bit system.
.NET Framework Version (managedRuntimeVersion)	Sets the .NET Framework version.
Managed Runtime Loader	Sets the managed loader to use for pre-loading the application. The default is webengine4.dll. (IIS 7.5 only)
Managed Pipeline Mode (managedPipelineMode)	Sets the managed pipeline mode
Name (name)	Sets the application pool name.
Queue Length (queueLength)	Sets the maximum number of queued requests.
Start Automatically (autoStart)	When True, the application pool starts when it is created or when IIS starts.
Start Mode (startMode)	Sets the startup type for a pre-loaded application pool as either "AlwaysRunning" or "OnDemand". (IIS 7.5 only)
CPU	
Limit (cpu.limit)	Sets the maximum CPU time in 1/1000th of a percent that the worker processes in an application pool can use over the limit interval.
Limit Action (cpu.action)	Sets the action IIS takes if the CPU limit is reached as either NoAction for logging only or KillW3WP to stop the application pool for the duration of the limit interval.
Limit Interval (cpu.resetInterval)	Sets the period of time in minutes for tracking the CPU limit or resetting an application pool if a limit is reached.
Processor Affinity Enabled (cpu.smpAffinitized)	When True, forces worker processes for an application to run on specific CPUs.

Processor Affinity Mask (cpu.smpProcessorAffinityMask)	Sets a hexadecimal mask that controls which CPUs worker processes are associated with when processor affinity is enabled.

PROCESS MODEL

passAnonymousToken	When True, allows passing an anonymous user token.
processModel.manualGroupMembership	When True, allows manual group membership assignment.
Identity (processModel.identityType)	Sets the user account under which the worker processes run. In IIS 7.5, the default identity is the ApplicationPoolIdentity.
Idle Time-Out (processModel.idleTimeout)	Sets the amount of time a worker process can remain idle before it shuts down.
Load User Profile (processModel.loadUserProfile)	When True, IIS loads the user profile for the application pool identity.
logonType	Set the logon type for the process identity. (IIS 7.5 only)
Maximum Worker Processes (processModel.maxProcesses)	Sets the maximum number of worker processes.
Password (processModel.password)	Sets the password for a "SpecificUser" identity. Available in UI when you are setting credentials.
Ping Enabled (processModel.pingingEnabled)	When True, IIS periodically checks worker processes to ensure that they are active.
Ping Maximum Response Time (processModel.pingResponseTime)	Sets the maximum time that a worker process is given to respond to a ping. If this time is exceeded, IIS terminates the process.
Ping Period (processModel.pingInterval)	Sets the interval between pings.
Shutdown Time Limit (processModel.shutdownTimeLimit)	Sets the maximum amount of time a worker process is given to finish processing requests and shutdown. If this time is exceeded, IIS terminates the process.
Startup Time Limit (processModel.startupTimeLimit)	Sets the maximum amount of time a worker process is given to start and initialize. If this time is exceeded, IIS terminates the process.

UserName (processModel.userName)	Sets user name for the "SpecificUser" identity. Available in UI when you are setting credentials.

PROCESS ORPHANING

Enabled (failure.orphan WorkerProcess)	When True, a nonresponsive worker process is abandoned instead of terminated. This allows debugging and should be used only during troubleshooting.
Executable (failure.orphan ActionExe)	Sets the executable to run when a worker process is abandoned, such as %SystemDrive%\Dbgtools\Ntsd.exe.
Executable Parameters (failure.orphan ActionParams)	Sets the parameters to pass to the executable that is run when a worker process is abandoned.

RECYCLING

Disable Overlapping Recycle (recycling.disallowOverlappingRotation)	If an application does not support multiple instances, set this value to True. When True, IIS waits for an existing process to exit before starting another process during recycling.
Disable Recycling for Configuration Changes (recycling.disallow RotationOnConfigChange)	When True, IIS doesn't recycle the application pool when the configuration is changed (and as a result some changes aren't applied until a later restart).
Generate Recycle Event Log Entry (recycling.logEventOnRecycle)	Determines the types of events that IIS logs when recycling application pools.
Private Memory Limit (recycling.periodicRestart.privateMemory)	Sets the maximum amount of private memory in kilobytes that a worker process can use before IIS recycles it. Use a value of zero to set no limit.
Regular Time Interval (recycling.periodicRestart.time)	Sets the period of time in minutes after which IIS routinely recycles an application pool. Use a value of zero to set a regular recycling interval.
Request Limit (recycling.periodicRestart.requests)	Sets the maximum requests an application pool can process before IIS recycles it. Use a value of zero to set no limit.
Specific Times (recycling.periodicRestart.schedule. [value='timespan'] .value	(Sets specific times when the application pool is recycled.)

Virtual Memory Limit (recycling.periodicRestart.memory)	Sets the maximum amount of virtual memory in kilobytes that a worker process can use before IIS recycles it. Use a value of zero to set no limit.

RAPID-FAIL PROTECTION

"Service Unavailable" Response Type (failure.loadBalancerCapabilities)	When rapid-fail protection is enabled, determines how "Service Unavailable" errors are handled. With HttpdLevel, an HTTP 503 error is returned. With TcpLevel, IIS resets the connection.
Enabled (failure.rapidFailProtection)	When True, rapid-fail protection is enabled.
Failure Interval (failure.rapidFailProtectionInterval)	When rapid-fail protection is enabled, sets the time interval during which the maximum number of failures must occur before the application pool is shut down.
Maximum Failures (failure.rapidFailProtectionMaxCrashes)	When rapid-fail protection is enabled, sets the maximum number of failures permitted in the failure interval before the application pool is shut down.
Shutdown Executable (failure.autoShutdownExe)	When rapid-fail protection is enabled, sets the executable to run when an application pool is shut down.
Shutdown Executable Parameters (failure.autoShutdownParams)	When rapid-fail protection is enabled, sets the parameters to pass to the executable to run when an application pool is shut down.

Creating Application Pools

Application pools specify the isolation boundaries for Web applications. You can use application pools to optimize the performance, recovery, and monitoring of Web applications. An application's scope can range from an entire Web site to a single virtual directory. This means that you can specify default applications for Web sites that your IIS server hosts, and you can specify Web applications with very specific scopes.

To create an application pool, follow these steps:

1. In IIS Manager, expand the node for the server you want to work with, and then click the Application Pools node.

2. On the Application Pools page, in the Actions pane, click Add Application Pool. This displays the Add Application Pool dialog box shown in Figure 2-6.

FIGURE 2-6 Use the Add Application Pool dialog box to set the name, .NET Framework version, and pipeline mode for the application pool.

3. In the Name text box, type the name of the application pool. The name should be short but descriptive.

TIP You might want to number the application pools to identify them uniquely. For example, you might create AppPool #1, AppPool #2, and so on. Or you might want to identify the purpose of the application pool in the name. For example, you might have CustRegPool, ProdCatPool, and TechNetPool.

4. You can now use the .NET Framework Version drop-down list to select the .NET Framework version that the application pool should use. If the application pool is not for ASP.NET applications and has no managed code components, you can select No Managed Code.

5. In the Managed Pipeline Mode drop-down list, you can choose either the Integrated or Classic pipeline mode. If an application pool uses Classic mode, IIS processes the requests in the application pool by using separate processing pipelines for IIS and ISAPI. If an application pool uses

Integrated mode, IIS processes the requests in an application pool by using an integrated processing pipeline for IIS and ASP.NET.

6. By default, the application pool is configured to start as soon as you click OK, and it is also configured to start automatically whenever you start IIS. If you'd rather start the application pool manually, clear the Start Application Pool Immediately check box.

7. Click OK to create the application pool.

With the IIS command-line administration tool, you can create an application pool by using the Add AppPool command. Sample 2-12 provides the syntax and usage. Attributes listed in Table 2-1 are valid also. The only mandatory attribute is the application pool name. If you don't set additional attributes, AppCmd uses the current default settings to determine the appropriate values.

SAMPLE 2-12 Add AppPool Syntax and Usage

Syntax
```
appcmd add apppool /name:"AppPoolName"
[/managedRuntimeVersion:"Version"]
[/managedPipelineMode: Integrated|Classic]
[/queueLength:"queueLength"]
[/autoStart:true|false]
```

Usage
```
Appcmd add apppool /name:CustServicesAppPool
/managedPipelineMode: Integrated

Appcmd add apppool /name:CustServicesAppPool
/autoStart:false
```

Changing Application Pool Settings

In IIS Manager, you can change application pool settings on the Application Pools page. To rename an application pool, click the entry to select it, and then click Rename. Type the new name for the application pool, and then press Enter.

You can change any other application pool settings by following these steps:

1. In IIS Manager, expand the node for the server you want to work with, and then click the Application Pools node.

2. On the Application Pools page, click the application pool you want to work with, and then do one of the following:

   - To edit the application pool's basic settings, in the Actions pane, click Basic Settings. This displays the Edit Application Pool dialog box, which you can use to change the application pool's .NET Framework, version, managed pipeline mode, and startup setting.
   - To edit the application pool's advanced settings, in the Actions pane, click Advanced Settings. This displays the Advanced Settings dialog box, which you can use to change all application pool settings.

3. Application pools can have associated applications. To view and manage the applications associated with an application pool, click the application pool you want to work with, and then click View Applications. You can now work with the applications associated with the previously selected application pool.

With the IIS command-line administration tool, you can change basic application pool settings by using the Set AppPool command. See Sample 2-13 for the related syntax and usage. Attributes listed in Table 2-1 are valid as well.

SAMPLE 2-13 Set AppPool Syntax and Usage

Syntax

```
appcmd set apppool [/apppool.name:]"AppPoolName"
[/managedRuntimeVersion:"Version"]
[/managedPipelineMode: Integrated|Classic]
[/queueLength:"queueLength"]
[/autoStart:true|false]
```

IIS 7.5 only:

```
[/managedRuntimeLoader "ManagedLoader"]
[/CLRConfigFile "AppPoolConfigFile"]
[/startMode "AlwaysRunning" | "OnDemand"]
```

Usage

```
Appcmd set apppool /name:CustServicesAppPool
```

```
/managedRuntimeVersion:"v2.0"
```

```
Appcmd set apppool /name:CustServicesAppPool
/queueLength:"1100"
```

Assigning Applications to Application Pools

Applications assigned to the same pool share the same configuration settings. These settings control recycling of worker processes used by applications in the pool, failure detection and recovery, the identity under which the worker processes run, and more. You should assign applications to the same pool only when they have similar requirements. If an application has unique requirements, you might want to assign it to a separate application pool that's used only by that application.

To assign an application to an application pool, follow these steps:

1. In IIS Manager, select the node for the site you want to work with, and then in the Actions pane, click View Applications.
2. On the Web Applications page, click the application you want to work with, and then click Basic Settings. This displays the Edit Application dialog box.
3. The Application Pool text box lists the application pool currently associated with the application. To change this value, click the Select button. In the Select Application Pool dialog box, select the application pool to use in the Application Pool list. Then click OK twice to save your settings.

Applications assigned to the same application pool can't use different versions of ASP.NET. If you assign applications that use different ASP.NET versions to the same pool, the worker process might not run at all.

Configuring Application Pool Identities

The application pool identity determines the account under which the application pool's worker processes run. Starting with IIS 7.5, application pools run under the ApplicationPoolIdentity account by default and access resources as the "IIS AppPool*AppPoolName*" identity. These individual, isolated identities allow you to specify permissions that pertain only to the identity under which the application pool is running.

In contrast, with IIS 7.0, the default identity typically is the Network Service account, which has limited permissions and privileges. With IIS 7.0, if a particular application needs additional permissions or privileges, it's a good idea to create a separate application pool for that application and then configure the application pool identity to use an account that has those permissions. In most cases you should use one of the other predefined accounts, such as Local Service or Local System, but you can also use the IWAM account or any other account that you configure.

To configure the application pool identity, follow these steps:

1. In IIS Manager, expand the node for the server you want to work with, and then click the Application Pools node.
2. On the Application Pools page, click the application pool you want to work with, and then click Advanced Settings.
3. Under Process Model, click the Identity entry, and then click the related selection button.
4. Do one of the following:

   - If you want to use the built-in Network Service, Local Service, or Local System accounts, select Built-in Account, and then in the drop-down list, select the appropriate account. Click OK and skip the remaining steps.
   - If you want to specify a user account, select Custom Account, and then click Set. In the Set Credentials dialog box, type the user name for the account. Type and then confirm the account password, and then click OK twice.

> **MORE INFO** For detailed information on working with the Network Service, Local Service, Local System, and accounts, see the section titled "IIS User and Group Essentials" in Chapter 4.

Chapter 3. Managing Worker Processes and Performance

Each application pool can have a different worker process configuration. Worker processes associated with application pools perform request handling. When additional threads are available, worker processes can use the additional threads to improve responsiveness and overall application performance. When additional processes aren't available, worker processes must handle requests by using currently allocated threads.

Starting, Stopping, and Recycling Worker Processes Manually

Sometimes you might want to restart or recycle the worker processes that an application pool is using. You might want to do this if you suspect that an application is leaking memory or is otherwise affecting server performance or if users are experiencing undetermined or intermittent problems.

Starting and Stopping Worker Processes Manually

When you stop worker processes for an application pool, the related IIS processes (W3wp.exe) are terminated, and as a result, all resources used by the worker processes are freed. This also means, however, that any requests currently being processed will fail and that new requests for the applications aren't processed until you start the application pool again, at which time Http.sys looks for requests in the application pool queue and then starts new worker processes as necessary to handle any pending requests.

The World Wide Web service can also stop an application pool. Typically, this occurs when rapid-fail protection is triggered, meaning that there were a certain number of worker process failures in a specified time period. In the standard configuration, five worker process failures within a five-minute interval trigger rapid-fail protection. Application pools can also be stopped when they're configured to use a nonexistent identity or if different applications use different versions of ASP.NET.

To stop and then start an application pool, follow these steps:

1. In IIS Manager, expand the node for the server you want to work with, and then click the Application Pools node.

2. On the Application Pools page, click the application pool you want to stop, and then click Stop.

3. Worker processes used by applications in the application pool are terminated. To start request processing for applications in the pool, click the application pool, and then click Start.

> **TIP** Clients trying to access an application in a stopped application pool might see an HTTP Error 503: Service Unavailable message. If users tell you they're seeing this message, and you haven't stopped the application pool, check to see if the application pool is started. If it isn't, start it, and then check the error logs to determine what happened while closely monitoring for additional failures.

With the IIS command-line administration tool, you can start and stop application pools by using the Start AppPool and Stop AppPool commands respectively. See Samples 3-1 and 3-2 for the related syntax and usage. The *Wait* attribute determines whether AppCmd waits for the application pool to start or stop before returning. When you wait for the application pool to start or stop, you can use the *timeout* attribute to specify the maximum amount of time in milliseconds to wait.

SAMPLE 3-1 Start AppPool Syntax and Usage

Syntax
```
appcmd start apppool [[/apppool.name:]"AppPoolName"] [/wait]
[/timeout:WaitTimeMilliseconds]
```

Usage
```
appcmd start apppool "MyAppPool"
```

SAMPLE 3-2 Stop AppPool Syntax and Usage

Syntax
```
appcmd start apppool [[/apppool.name:]"AppPoolName"] [/wait]
[/timeout:WaitTimeMilliseconds]
```

Usage
```
appcmd stop apppool "MyAppPool"
```

Recycling Worker Processes Manually

An alternative to abruptly terminating worker processes used by an application pool is to mark them for recycling. Worker processes that are actively processing requests continue to run while IIS starts new worker processes to replace them. Once the new worker processes are started, Http.sys directs incoming requests to the new worker processes, and the old worker processes are able to continue handling requests until they shut down. With this approach, you minimize any service interruptions while ensuring that any resources used by old worker processes are eventually freed.

With recycling, the startup and shutdown processes can be limited by the Startup Time Limit and Shutdown Time Limit values set for the application pool. If IIS can't start new worker processes within the set time limit, a service interruption would occur because IIS would be unable to direct requests to the new processes. If IIS stops old worker processes when the shutdown time limit is reached and those processes are still handling requests, a service interruption would occur because the requests wouldn't be processed further.

To recycle the worker processes used by an application pool, follow these steps:

1. In IIS Manager, expand the node for the server you want to work with, and then click the Application Pools node.
2. On the Application Pools page, click the application pool you want to recycle, and then click Recycle.

With the IIS command-line administration tool, you can recycle application pools by using the Recycle AppPool command. See Sample 3-3 for the related syntax and usage.

SAMPLE 3-3 Recycle AppPool Syntax and Usage

Syntax
```
appcmd recycle apppool [[/apppool.name:]"AppPoolName"]
[/parameter1:value1 ...]
```

Usage
```
appcmd recycle apppool "MyAppPool"
```

Configuring Worker Process Startup and Shutdown Time Limits

Whenever IIS starts or shuts down worker processes, it attempts to do so within prescribed time limits. The goal is to ensure timely startup of worker processes so that Http.sys can direct incoming requests to new worker processes and shut down old worker processes after they complete the processing of existing requests.

Graceful startup and shutdown of worker processes, however, is dependent on the amount of time allowed for startup and shutdown. If these values are set too low, service might be interrupted—a new worker process might not get started in time to accept incoming requests, or an old worker process might be terminated before it can finish processing requests. If these values are set too high, system resources might be tied up waiting for a transition that isn't possible. An existing worker process might be nonresponsive, or the server might be unable to allocate additional resources to start new worker processes while the old processes are still running.

> **REAL WORLD**   Listen carefully to user complaints about failed requests, time-outs, and other errors. Frequent complaints can be an indicator that you need to take a close look at the worker process recycling configuration as discussed in the "Configuring Worker Process Recycling" section later in this chapter. If you believe you've optimized worker process recycling but users are still experiencing problems, take a look at the startup and shutdown time limits.
>
> Ideally, you'll select a balanced startup and shutdown time that reflects the server's load and the importance of the applications in the application pool. By default, the startup and shutdown time limits are both set to 90 seconds. Here are some rules of thumb for setting startup and shutdown time limits:
>
> For application pools with applications that have long-running processes, such as those that require extensive computations or extended database lookups, you might want to reduce the startup time limit and extend the shutdown time limit, particularly if the server consistently experiences a moderate or heavy load.

For application pools in which it's more important to ensure that the service is responsive than to ensure that all requests go through, you might want to reduce both the startup and shutdown time limits, particularly if applications have known problems, such as memory leaks or frequent hangs.

To configure worker process startup and shutdown time limits, complete the following steps:

1. In IIS Manager, expand the node for the server you want to work with, and then click the Application Pools node.

2. On the Application Pools page, click the application pool you want to work with, and then click Advanced Settings.

3. Under Process Model, in the Startup Time Limit and Shutdown Time Limit fields, set the maximum time allowed for worker process startup and shutdown respectively (in seconds). Click OK.

Configuring Multiple Worker Processes for Application Pools

Multiple worker processes running in their own context can share responsibility for handling requests for an application pool. This configuration is also referred to as a *Web garden*. When you set up a Web garden, each new request is assigned to a worker process according to a round-robin scheme. Round-robin is a load balancing technique used to spread the workload among the worker processes that are available.

NOTE It's important to note that worker processes aren't started automatically and don't use resources until they're needed. Rather, they're started as necessary to meet the demand based on incoming requests. For example, if you configure a maximum of five worker processes for an application pool, there may be at any given time from zero to five worker processes running in support of applications placed in that application pool.

If a single application is placed in an application pool serviced by multiple worker processes, all available worker processes will handle requests queued for the application. This is a multiple worker process—single application configuration, and it's best used when you want to improve the application's request-handling performance and reduce any possible contention for resources with other applications. In this case the application might have heavy usage during peak periods and moderate-to-heavy usage during other times, or individuals using the application might have specific performance expectations that must be met if possible.

If multiple applications are placed in an application pool serviced by multiple worker processes, all available worker processes handle requests queued for any applicable application. This is a multiple worker process—multiple application configuration, and it's best used when you want to improve request-handling performance and reduce resource contention for multiple applications but don't want to dedicate resources to any single application. In this case the various applications in the application pool might have different peak usage periods or might have varying resource needs.

To configure multiple worker processes for an application pool, follow these steps:

1. In IIS Manager, expand the node for the server you want to work with, and then click the Application Pools node.

2. On the Application Pools page, click the application pool you want to work with, and then click Advanced Settings.

3. Under Process Model, in the Maximum Worker Processes text box, specify the number of worker processes that the application pool should use, and then click OK.

> **REAL WORLD** When you assign multiple worker processes to a busy application pool, keep in mind that each worker process uses server resources when it's started and might affect the performance of applications in other application pools. Adding worker processes won't resolve latency issues caused by network communications or bandwidth, and it can reduce the time it takes to process requests only if those requests were queued and waiting and not being actively processed. A poorly engineered application will still respond poorly, and at some point, you'd need to look at optimizing the application code for efficiency and speed.

Configuring Worker Process Recycling

Manual recycling of worker processes might work when you're troubleshooting, but on a day-to-day basis you probably don't have time to monitor resource usage and responsiveness for worker processes. For IIS to handle worker process recycling for you, you'll want to configure some type of automatic worker process recycling. Automatic worker process recycling can be configured to occur:

- **After a specific time period**   Recycles worker processes based on the amount of time they've been running. This is best used when applications have known problems running for extended periods of time.
- **When a certain number of requests are processed**   Recycles worker processes based on the number of requests processed. This is best used when applications fail based on usage.
- **At specific scheduled times during the day**   Recycles worker processes based on a defined schedule. This is best used when applications have known problems running for extended periods of time and you don't want processes to be recycled during a peak usage period. Here, you'd schedule recycling when you expect application usage to be at its lowest for the day.
- **When memory usage grows to a specific point**   Recycles worker processes when they use a certain amount of virtual (paged) or private (nonpaged) memory. This is best used when applications have known or suspected memory leaks.

The sections that follow discuss techniques for configuring automatic worker process recycling. When you configure recycling, keep in mind that unless you disable overlapped recycling, active worker processes continue to run while IIS starts new worker processes to replace them. Once the new worker processes are started, Http.sys directs incoming requests to the new worker processes, and the old worker processes are able to continue handling requests until they shut down. The startup and shutdown processes can be limited by the Startup Time Limit and Shutdown Time Limit values set for the application pool. If these values are set inappropriately, new worker processes might not start, and old worker processes might shut down before they've finished processing current requests.

Recycling Automatically by Time and Number of Requests

When applications have known problems running for extended periods of time and handling requests in peak loads, you probably want to configure automatic recycling by time, by number of requests, or both. To configure automatic recycling by time and number of requests, follow these steps:

1. In IIS Manager, expand the node for the server you want to work with, and then click the Application Pools node.

2. On the Application Pools page, click the application pool you want to work with, and then click Advanced Settings.

3. If any application running in the application pool does not support multiple instances, set Disable Overlapped Recycle to True. Otherwise, you'll want to allow overlapped recycling (in most cases) by setting this option to False.

4. To recycle worker processes after a specified period of time, select Regular Time Interval (In Minutes), and then type the number of minutes that you want to elapse before worker processes are recycled.

> **TIP** In most cases it's prudent to schedule worker process recycling to take place at specific off-peak usage times rather than to set hard limits based on run time or number of requests handled. If you schedule recycling, you control when recycling occurs and can be reasonably sure that it won't occur when the application usage is high.

5. To recycle a worker process after processing a specified number of requests, select Request Limit, and then type the number of requests that you want to be processed before the worker process is recycled.

6. To recycle worker processes according to a specific schedule, select Specific Times, and then click the related selection button. You can use the TimeSpan Collection Editor to:

  - **Add a scheduled recycle time**   Click Add. In the right pane under TimeSpan, click in the Value text box. Set a recycle time on a 24-hour clock.
  - **Edit a scheduled recycle time**   Click the recycle time you want to change, and then in the right pane, under TimeSpan, in the Value text box, type the desired recycle time.

- **Remove a scheduled recycle time**   Click the recycle time you want to delete, and then click Remove.
- **Save the scheduled recycle times**   Click OK to close the TimeSpan Collection Editor and save your recycle times.

7.   Click OK to apply the settings.

Recycling Automatically by Memory Usage

When applications have known or suspected memory leaks, you probably want to configure automatic recycling based on virtual or private memory usage. To configure automatic recycling of worker processes based on memory usage, follow these steps:

1.   In IIS Manager, expand the node for the server you want to work with, and then click the Application Pools node.

2.   On the Application Pools page, click the application pool you want to work with, and then click Advanced Settings.

3.   Virtual memory usage refers to the amount of paged memory written to disk that the worker process uses. To limit virtual memory usage and automatically recycle a worker process when this limit is reached, select Virtual Memory Limit (KB), and then type the virtual memory limit in the corresponding field.

> **TIP**   In most cases, you'll want to establish the baseline virtual and private memory usage for an application before configuring memory recycling. If you don't do this, you might find that worker processes are being recycled at the most inopportune times, such as when the server is experiencing peak usage loads. A good rule of thumb is to allow private memory usage of at least 1.5 times the baseline usage you see and to allow virtual memory usage of at least 2 times the private memory usage. For example, if your baseline memory usage monitoring shows that the application typically uses 128 MB of private memory and 96 MB of virtual memory, you might allow memory usage of up to at least 192 MB for private memory and 256 MB for virtual memory.

4.   Private memory usage refers to the amount of physical RAM that the worker process uses. To limit private memory usage and automatically recycle a worker process when this limit is reached, select Private Memory

Limit (KB), and then in the corresponding field, type the memory limit. Then click OK to apply the settings.

Maintaining Application Health and Performance

Maintaining the health and performance of Web applications is an important part of your job as a Web administrator. Fortunately, IIS has many built-in functions to make this task easier, including:

- CPU monitoring and automated shutdown of runaway worker processes
- Worker process failure detection and recovery
- Request queue limiting to prevent server flooding
- Idle worker process shutdown to recover resources

Each of these tasks is discussed in the sections that follow.

Configuring CPU Monitoring

Typically, when a process consistently uses a high percentage of CPU time, there's a problem with the process. The process might have failed or might be running rampant on the system. You can configure IIS to monitor CPU usage and perform either of the following CPU performance monitoring options:

- **Take No Action (NoAction)** IIS logs the CPU maximum usage event in the System event log but takes no corrective action.
- **Shut Down the Worker Process (KillW3wp)** IIS logs the event and requests that the application pool's worker processes be recycled, based on the Shutdown Time Limit, set in the Process Model section.

To enable and configure IIS to monitor the CPU usage of worker processes, follow these steps:

1. In IIS Manager, expand the node for the server you want to work with, and then click the Application Pools node.
2. On the Application Pools page, click the application pool you want to work with, and then click Advanced Settings.

3. Under CPU, in the Limit field, set the maximum percentage of CPU usage that triggers event logging, worker process recycling, or both, in 1/1000ths of a percent.

> **TIP** Typically, you'll want to set a value to at least 90000 (90 percent). However, to ensure that worker processes are recycled only when they're blocking other processes, you should set the value to 100000 (100 percent).

4. Use the Limit Interval (In Minutes) to specify how often IIS checks the CPU usage.

> **CAUTION** In most cases you won't want to check the CPU usage more frequently than every five minutes. If you monitor the CPU usage more frequently, you might waste resources that could be better used by other processes.

5. Next, choose one of the following:

- If you want to log the CPU usage event but not have IIS attempt to shut down worker processes, in the Limit Action list, select NoAction.
- If you want to log the CPU usage event and have IIS attempt to shut down the worker processes used by the application pool, in the Limit Action list, select KillW3wp.

6. Click OK.

If you want to disable CPU monitoring, follow these steps:

1. In IIS Manager, expand the node for the server you want to work with, and then click the Application Pools node.

2. On the Application Pools page, click the application pool you want to work with, and then click Advanced Settings.

3. Disable CPU monitoring by setting the Limit Interval to zero (0), and then click OK.

Configuring Failure Detection and Recovery

You can configure application pools to monitor the health of their worker processes. This monitoring includes processes that detect worker process failure and then take action to recover or prevent further problems on the server.

Process pinging is central to health monitoring. With *process pinging*, IIS periodically checks to see if worker processes are responsive. This means that IIS sends a ping request at a specified interval to each worker process. If a worker process fails to respond to the ping request, either because it doesn't have additional threads available for processing incoming requests or because it's hung up, IIS flags the worker process as unhealthy. If the worker process is in an idle but unresponsive state, IIS terminates it immediately, and a replacement worker process is created. Otherwise, the worker process is marked for recycling as discussed previously in this chapter.

To configure health monitoring, complete the following steps:

1. In IIS Manager, expand the node for the server you want to work with, and then click the Application Pools node.
2. On the Application Pools page, click the application pool you want to work with, and then click Advanced Settings.
3. To enable process pinging, set Ping Enable to True, and then use the Ping Period and Ping Maximum Response Time options to set the ping interval and the maximum time to wait for a ping response in seconds. Here are some guidelines:

- For low-priority applications or applications that are used infrequently, you might want to use intervals of several minutes. This ensures that the responsiveness of applications is checked only as often as necessary and that IIS waits an appropriate amount of time for a response.
- On a busy server or a server with many configured applications, you might want to set longer intervals than usual. This will reduce resource usage due to ping requests and give the application pool longer to respond.
- For high-priority applications in which it's critical that applications run and be responsive, you might want to set a ping interval of five minutes or less and a maximum response time of one minute (60 seconds) or less. This

ensures that the application pool is checked frequently and that the responsiveness of applications is checked frequently.

4. To improve responsiveness for important applications by preventing idle processes from being shut down after a specified period of time, set Idle Time-out to zero (0).

5. Click OK.

You can also configure application pools for rapid-fail protection. When rapid-fail protection is enabled, IIS stops an application pool if there are a certain number of worker process failures in a specified time period. In the standard configuration, five worker process failures within a five-minute interval trigger rapid-fail protection.

To configure rapid-fail protection, complete the following steps:

1. In IIS Manager, expand the node for the server you want to work with, and then click the Application Pools node.

2. On the Application Pools page, click the application pool you want to work with, and then click Advanced Settings.

3. To enable rapid-fail protection, under Rapid-Fail Protection, set Enabled to True.

4. To cause IIS to stop the application pool if there are a certain number of worker process failures in a specified time period, set the Failure Interval and Maximum Failures options respectively.

5. Set the Service Unavailable Response Type option to HttpLevel to have IIS return an HTTP 503 error when the application pool is stopped because of rapid-fail protection. Set this option to TcpLevel to have IIS reset the connection otherwise.

6. Click OK to save your settings.

> **NOTE** Keep in mind that these monitoring and recovery techniques aren't perfect, but they're helpful. They won't detect all types of failures. For instance, they won't detect problems with the application code, such as conditions that cause the application to return an internal error, and they won't detect a nonblocking error state, such as when the worker process can allocate new threads but is unable to process current threads.

Shutting Down Idle Worker Processes

Although worker processes start on demand based on incoming requests, and thus resources are allocated only when necessary, worker processes don't free up the resources they use until they're shut down. In a standard configuration, worker processes are shut down after they've been idle for 20 minutes. This ensures that any physical or virtual memory used by the worker process is made available to other processes running on the server, which is especially important if the server is busy.

> **TIP** Shutting down idle worker processes is a good idea in most instances, and if system resources are at a premium, you might even want idle processes shut down sooner than 20 minutes. For example, on a moderately busy server with many configured sites and applications and on which there are intermittent resource issues, reducing the idle time-out could resolve the problems with resource availability.
>
> **CAUTION** Shutting down idle worker processes can have unintended consequences. For example, on a dedicated server with ample memory and resources, shutting down idle worker processes clears cached components out of memory. These components must be reloaded into memory when the worker process starts and requires them, which might make the application seem unresponsive or sluggish.

To configure the idle process shutdown time, follow these steps:

1. In IIS Manager, expand the node for the server you want to work with, and then click the Application Pools node.

2. On the Application Pools page, click the application pool you want to work with, and then click Advanced Settings.

3. Choose one of the following:

   - To allow idle processes to be shut down after a specified period of time, set Idle Time-Out to the desired shutdown time in minutes.
   - To prevent idle processes from being shut down after a specified period of time, set Idle Time-Out to zero (0).

4. Click OK.

Limiting Request Queues

When hundreds or thousands of new requests pour into an application pool's request queue, the IIS server can become overloaded and overwhelmed. To prevent this from occurring, you can limit the length of the request queue. Once a queue limit is set, IIS checks the queue size each time before adding a new request to the queue. If the queue limit has been reached, IIS rejects the request and sends the client an HTTP Error 503: Service Unavailable message.

> **REAL WORLD** The standard limit for the default application pool is 1000 requests. On a moderately sized server with few applications configured, this might be a good choice. However, on a server with multiple CPUs and lots of RAM, this value might be too low. On a server with limited resources or many applications configured, this value might be too high. Here, you might want to use a formula of Memory Size in Megabytes × Number of CPUs × 10 / Number of Configured Applications to determine the size of the average request queue.
>
> This is meant to be a guideline to give you a starting point for consideration and not an absolute rule. For example, on a server with two CPUs, 2048 MB of RAM, and 24 configured applications, the size of the average request queue limit would be around 1,700 requests. You might have some applications configured with request queue limits of 1,000 and others with request queue limits of 2,000. However, if the same server had only one configured application, you probably wouldn't want to configure a request queue limit of 10,000 or more.

To configure the request queue limit, follow these steps:

1. In IIS Manager, expand the node for the server you want to work with, and then click the Application Pools node.

2. On the Application Pools page, click the application pool you want to work with, and then click Advanced Settings.

3. Perform one of the following:

- To specify and enforce a request queue limit, set the Queue Length to the desired limit.
- To remove the request queue limit, set the Queue Length option to zero (0).

4. Click OK.

> **NOTE** Requests that are already queued remain queued even if you change the queue limit to a value that's less than the current queue length. The only consequence here would be that new requests wouldn't be added to the queue until the current queue length is less than the queue limit.

Deleting IIS Application Pools

If you find that you no longer need an application pool, you can remove it by following these steps:

1. In IIS Manager, expand the node for the server you want to work with, and then click the Application Pools node.

2. On the Application Pools page, click the application pool you want to remove, and then in the Actions pane, click Remove.

3. When prompted to confirm that you want to remove the application, click Yes.

With the IIS command-line administration tool, you can delete an application pool by using the Delete AppPool command. Sample 3-4 provides the syntax and usage.

SAMPLE 3-4 Delete AppPool Syntax and Usage

Syntax
```
appcmd delete apppool [[/apppool.name:]"AppPoolName"]
```

Usage
```
appcmd delete apppool "CustServicesAppPool"
```

Chapter 4. Enhancing Web Server Security

As you've seen throughout this book, security features are integrated into many areas of Internet Information Services (IIS). In this chapter, you'll learn how to manage areas of Web server security that we have not yet discussed. Web servers have different security considerations from those of standard Windows Server configurations. On a Web server, you have three levels of security:

- **Windows security**   At the operating system level, you create user and group accounts, configure access permissions for files and directories, and set policies.
- **IIS security**   At the level of Internet Information Services (IIS), you set content permissions, authentication controls, and delegated privileges.
- **.NET security**   At the application level, you can control access to managed code applications by using the security features built into the Microsoft .NET Framework.

Windows security, IIS security, and .NET security can be completely integrated. The integrated security model allows you to use authentication based on user and group membership in addition to standard Internet-based authentication. It also allows you to use a layered permission model to determine access rights and permissions for applications and content. Before users can access files and directories, you must ensure that the appropriate users and groups have access at the operating system level. Then you must set IIS security permissions that grant permissions for content that IIS controls. Finally, you can use .NET Profile, .NET Users, and .NET Roles to manage top-level access to managed code applications.

Managing Windows Security

Before setting IIS security permissions, you use operating system tools to perform the following security tasks:

- Create and manage accounts for users and groups
- Configure access permissions for files and folders

- Set group policies for users and groups

Each of these topics is discussed in the sections that follow.

Working with User and Group Accounts

Windows Server 2008 and Windows Server 2008 R2 provide user accounts and group accounts. User accounts determine permissions and privileges for individuals. Group accounts determine permissions and privileges for multiple users.

IIS User and Group Essentials

You can set user and group accounts at the local computer level or at the domain level. Local accounts are specific to an individual computer and aren't valid on other machines or in a domain unless you specifically grant permissions. Domain accounts, on the other hand, are valid throughout a domain, which makes resources in the domain available to the account. Typically, you'll use specific accounts for specific purposes:

- Use local accounts when your IIS servers aren't part of a domain or you want to limit access to a specific computer.
- Use domain accounts when the servers are part of a Windows domain and you want users to be able to access resources throughout that domain.

User accounts that are important on IIS servers include:

- **Local System**   By default, all standard IIS services log on using the local system account. This account is part of the Administrators group on the Web server and has all user rights on the Web server. If you configure application pools to use this account, the related worker processes have full access to the server system, which may present a serious security risk.
- **Local Service**   A limited-privilege account that grants access to the local system only. The account is part of the Users group on the Web server and has the same rights as the Network Service account, except that it is limited to the local computer. Configure application pools to use this account when worker processes don't need to access other servers.

- **Network Service** By default, all applications log on using the network service account. When IIS is using out-of-process session state management, the ASP.NET State Service also uses this account by default. This account is part of the Users group on the Web server and provides fewer permissions and privileges than the Local System account (but more than the Local Service account). Specifically, processes running under this account can interact throughout a network by using the credentials of the computer account.
- **IUSR_*ComputerName*** Internet guest account used by anonymous users to access Internet sites. The account grants anonymous users limited user rights and is also known as the *anonymous user identity*.

When you install IIS, the IIS_IUSRS group is also created. If you use a specific user identity for an application pool, you must make this identity a member of the IIS_IUSRS group to ensure that the account has appropriate access to resources. See the section "Configuring Application Pool Identities" in Chapter 2, "Managing Applications and Application Pools," for details on configuring the application pool identity.

You can make changes to these accounts if necessary. For added security, you can configure IIS to use different accounts from the standard accounts provided. You can also create additional accounts.

Managing the IIS Service Logon Accounts

The standard IIS services use the local system account to log on to the server. Using the local system account allows the services to run system processes and perform system-level tasks. You really shouldn't change this configuration unless you have very specific needs or want to have strict control over the IIS logon account's privileges and rights. If you decide not to use this account, you can reconfigure the logon account for an IIS service by completing the following steps:

1. In the Computer Management console, in the left pane, connect to the IIS server whose services you want to manage.

2. Expand the Services And Applications node by clicking the plus sign (+) next to it, and then choose Services.

3. In the right pane, right-click the service you want to configure, and then choose Properties.

4. Click the Log On tab, as shown in Figure 4-1.

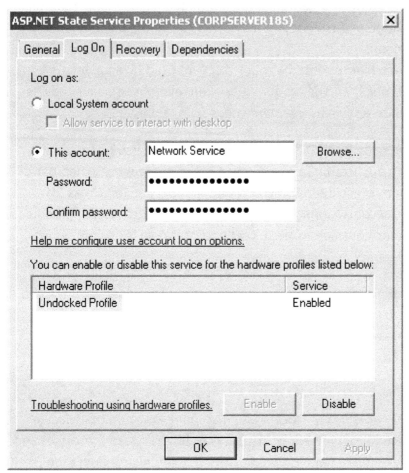

FIGURE 4-1 Use the Log On tab to configure the service logon account.

5. Choose one of the following:

- If the service should log on using the system account (the default for most services), select Local System Account.
- If the service should log on using a specific user account, select This Account. Be sure to type an account name and password in the appropriate fields. Click the Browse button to search for a user account if necessary.

6. Click OK.

Managing the Internet Guest Account

You manage the Internet Guest account at the IIS security level and at the Windows security level. At the IIS security level, you specify the user account to use for anonymous access. Normally, you manage anonymous access at the server or site level, and all related files and directories inherit the settings you use. You can change this behavior for individual files and directories as necessary.

To change the configuration of the anonymous user account for an entire server or another configuration level, complete the following steps:

1. In IIS Manager, navigate to the level of the configuration hierarchy you want to manage, and then double-click Authentication.

2. On the Authentication page, in the main pane, click Anonymous Authentication, and then in the Actions pane, click Edit.

3. The IUSR_*ComputerName* account is the default Internet guest account. Choose one of the following based on the user account you want to specify:

▪ If you want to specify a different user account, select Specific User, and then click Set. In the Set Credentials dialog box, type the user name for the account. Type and then confirm the account password, and then click OK twice.

▪ If you want to use the application pool identity rather than a specific user account, select Application Pool Identity, and then click OK.

NOTE When Anonymous Access is enabled, users don't have to log on using a user name and password. IIS automatically logs the user on using the anonymous account information provided for the resource. If Anonymous Authentication isn't listed as Enabled on the Authentication page, the resource is configured for named account access only. To enable anonymous access, click Anonymous Authentication, and then in the Actions pane, click Enable. However, you should do this only if you're sure that the resource doesn't need to be protected.

At the Windows security level, you perform all other account management tasks, including:

- Enabling or disabling accounts
- Unlocking the account after it has been locked out
- Changing group membership

Working with File and Folder Permissions

Every folder and file used by IIS can have different access permissions. You set these access permissions at the Windows security level. The sections that follow provide an overview of permissions. You'll learn the basics, including how to view and set permissions.

File and Folder Permission Essentials

The basic permissions you can assign to files and folders are summarized in Table 4-1. The basic permissions are created by combining special permissions, such as Traverse Folder and Execute File, into a single easily managed permission. If you want granular control over file or folder access, you can use advanced permissions to assign special permissions individually.

TABLE 4-1 File and Folder Permissions Used by Windows Server

Read	With folders, permits viewing and listing files and subfolders. With files, permits viewing or accessing the file's contents
Write	With folders, permits adding files and subfolders. With files, permits writing to a file
Read And Execute	With folders, permits viewing and listing files and subfolders and executing files; inherited by files and folders. With files, permits viewing and accessing the file's contents and executing the file.
List Folder Contents	With folders, permits viewing and listing files and subfolders and executing files; inherited by folders only.

Modify	With folders, permits reading and writing of files and subfolders; allows deletion of the folder. With files, permits reading and writing of the file; allows deletion of the file
Full Control	With folders, permits reading, writing, changing, and deleting files and subfolders. With files, permits reading, writing, changing, and deleting the file.

Whenever you work with file and folder permissions, you should keep the following in mind:

- Read is the only permission needed to run scripts. Execute permission applies only to executables.
- Read access is required to access a shortcut and its target.
- Giving a user permission to write to a file but not to delete it doesn't prevent the user from deleting the file's contents. A user can still delete the contents.
- If a user has full control over a folder, the user can delete files in the folder regardless of the permission of the files.

IIS uses the following users and groups to configure file and folder access:

- **Administrators** Allows administrators to access IIS resources.
- **Creator Owner** Allows the account that created a resource to access the resource.
- **System** Allows the local system to access the resource.
- **Users** Allows named accounts to access the resource (including the Local Service and Network Service accounts, which are user accounts).
- **IIS_IUSRS** Allows you to set specific permission for special identities that are members of the IIS_IUSRS group. To prevent malicious users from gaining access to files and modifying them, you can deny this account Full Control, Modify, and Write permission on important directories.

When you grant Read permission to these users and groups, anyone who has access to your Internet or intranet Web site will be able to access the files and folders. If you want to restrict access to certain files and folders, you should set specific user and group permissions and then use authenticated access rather than anonymous access. With authenticated access, IIS authenticates the user before granting access and then uses the Windows permissions to determine what files and folders the user can access.

As you evaluate the permissions, you might want to apply to files and folders used by IIS, refer to Table 4-2. This table provides general guidelines for assigning permissions based on content type.

TABLE 4-2 General Guidelines for Permissions Based on Content Type

CGI scripts and executables (.exe, .dll, .cmd)	Users (Execute), Administrators (Full Control), System (Full Control)
Dynamic content (.asp, .aspx, .vbs, .js, .pl)	Users (Read Only), Administrators (Full Control), System (Full Control)
Include files (.inc, .shtm, .shtml, .stm)	Users (Read Only, Deny Write), Administrators (Full Control), System (Full Control)
Static content (.txt, .rtf, .gif, .jpg, .jpeg, .htm, .html, .doc, .ppt, .xls)	Users (Read Only, Deny Write), Administrators (Full Control), System (Full Control)

Instead of setting permissions on individual files, you should organize content by type in subdirectories. For example, if your Web site used static, script, and dynamic content, you could create subdirectories called WebStatic, WebScripts, and WebDynamic. You would then store static, script, and dynamic content in these directories and assign permissions on a per-directory basis. Don't forget to consider whether it's prudent to specifically deny a permission, such as Full Control, Modify, or Write.

Viewing File and Folder Permissions

You view security permissions for files and folders in Windows Explorer or in IIS Manager by completing the following steps:

1. Open Windows Explorer or IIS Manager as appropriate. In Windows Explorer, right-click the file or folder you want to work with, and then select Properties. In IIS Manager, navigate to the site node or folder node you want to work with, and then in the Actions pane, click Edit Permissions.

2. You should now see the Properties dialog box for the file or folder you previously selected. On the General tab, be sure to note any NTFS attributes, such as Read only or Hidden, that are being applied, because you might need to change these.

3. Select the Security tab. In the Group Or User Names list box, select the user, computer, or group whose permissions you want to view. If check boxes in the Permissions For list are dimmed, it means that the permissions are inherited from a parent object.

Setting File and Folder Permissions

You can set permissions for files and folders by completing the following steps:

1. Open Windows Explorer or IIS Manager as appropriate. In Windows Explorer, right-click the file or folder you want to work with, and then select Properties. In IIS Manager, navigate to the site node or folder node you want to work with, and then in the Actions pane, click Edit Permissions.

2. In the Properties dialog box, select the Security tab, select a user, computer, or group, and then click Edit. This displays an editable version of the Security tab, as shown in Figure 4-2.

3. Users or groups that already have access to the file or folder are listed in the Group Or User Names list box. You can change permissions for these users and groups by doing the following:

- Select the user or group you want to change.
- Use the Permissions For list box to grant or deny access permissions.

> **NOTE** Inherited permissions are dimmed. If you want to override an inherited permission, select the opposite permission. For example, if, because of inheritance, a user is granted a permission you don't want that user to have, you could override the inheritance by explicitly denying the permission in the Permissions For list box.

4. Click Add to set access permissions for additional users, contacts, computers, or groups. This displays the Select Users, Computers, Or Groups dialog box. You can select computer accounts and configure their permissions only if you are a member of a domain.

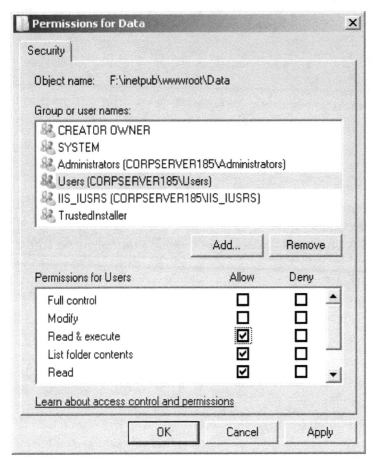

FIGURE 4-2 Use the Security tab to configure basic permissions for the file or folder.

5. In the Select Users, Computers, Or Groups dialog box, select the users, computers, or groups for which you want to set access permissions, and then click OK.

6. In the Group Or User Names list box, select the user, computer, or group you want to configure, and then use the fields in the Permissions For list box to allow or deny permissions. Repeat for other users, computers, or groups.

7. Click OK when you're finished.

Working with Group Policies

Group policies are another aspect of Windows security that you need to understand. You'll use group policies to automate key security administration tasks and to manage IIS resources more effectively. Group policies for sites, domains, and organizational units (OUs) can be configured only for computer, group, and user accounts that are part of a domain.

Group Policy Essentials

Group policies provide central control over privileges, permissions, and capabilities of users and computers. You can think of a policy as a set of rules that you can apply to multiple computers and to multiple users. Because computers can be a part of larger organizational groups, you can apply multiple policies. The order in which policies are applied is extremely important in determining which rules are enforced and which rules are not.

When multiple policies are in place, the policies are applied in the following order:

1. Local group policies that affect the local computer only
2. Site group policies that affect all computers that are part of the same site, which can include multiple domains
3. Domain polices that affect all computers in a specific domain
4. Organizational unit policies that affect all computers in an organizational unit
5. Child organizational unit policies that affect all computers in a subcomponent of an organizational unit

As successive policies are applied, the rules in those policies override the rules set in the previous policy. For example, domain policy settings have precedence over the local Group Policy settings. Exceptions allow you to block, override, and disable policy settings. A discussion of exceptions is outside the scope of this book.

Policy settings are divided into two broad categories: those that affect computers and those that affect users. Computer policies are applied during system startup. User policies are applied during logon.

Two graphical user interface (GUI) tools are provided for managing Active Directory Group Policy: Group Policy Object Editor and Group Policy

Management Console. Although both are used to manage Active Directory Group Policy, you can think of Group Policy Object Editor as a basic editor and Group Policy Management Console as an advanced editor. By using Group Policy Object Editor, you can view and configure policy settings for a specific Group Policy Object (GPO). By using Group Policy Management Console, you can view, configure, and manage policy settings for Group Policy Objects in any forest and domain to which you can connect and have appropriate administrator permissions. Management features in Group Policy Management Console enable you to import, export, back up, and restore GPOs. You can also use Group Policy Management Console to plan Group Policy changes and to determine how group policies are being applied to particular computers and users.

To use the Group Policy Object Editor and related features to access and use site, domain, and OU policies, complete the following steps:

1. For sites, open the Active Directory Sites and Services console to create a GPO that is linked to the site. For domains and OUs, open the Active Directory Users and Computers console to create a GPO that is linked to the domain or OU.

2. In the left pane of the appropriate Active Directory window, right-click the site, domain, or OU for which you want to create or manage Group Policy. Then on the shortcut menu, select Properties. The Properties dialog box opens.

3. In the Properties dialog box, click the Group Policy tab. You can now:

- **Create a new policy** To create a new policy, click New. Type a name for the policy, and then press Enter. Then click Edit to configure the new policy.
- **Edit an existing policy** To edit an existing policy, select the policy, and then click Edit. You can then edit the policy settings.
- **Change the priority of a policy** To change the priority of a policy, click the Up or Down button to change its position in the Group Policy Object Links list.

The Group Policy Management Console is included with Windows Server. To use the Group Policy Management Console and related features to access and work with site, domain, and OU policies, complete the following steps:

1. When you add the Group Policy Management feature using the Add Feature Wizard, the Group Policy Management Console is available on the Administrative Tools menu. Click Start, point to Administrative Tools, and then select Group Policy Management.

2. In the MMC, you'll see two top-level nodes: Group Policy Management (the label for the console root) and Forest (a node representing the forest to which you are currently connected). When you expand the Forest node, you'll then see the following nodes:

- **Domains**   Provides access to the policy settings for domains in the related forest. By default, you are connected to your logon domain and can add connections to other domains. If you expand a domain, you'll be able to access Default Domain Policy, the Domain Controllers OU (and the related Default Domain Controllers Policy), and Group Policy Objects defined in the domain.

- **Sites**   Provides access to the policy settings for sites in the forest. Sites are hidden by default.

- **Group Policy Modeling**   Provides access to the Group Policy Modeling Wizard, which you can use to help you plan policy deployment and simulate settings for testing purposes. The wizard also provides access to any saved policy models.

- **Group Policy Results**   Provides access to the Group Policy Results Wizard. For each domain to which you are connected, you have all the related Group Policy Objects and OUs available to work with in one location.

3. You can now:

- **Create a new policy**   Right-click the site, domain, or OU you want to work with, and then select Create And Link A GPO Here. In the New GPO dialog box, type a descriptive name for the new GPO, and then click OK. The GPO is now created and linked to the site, domain, or OU. Right-click the GPO, and then choose Edit. This opens the Group Policy Object Editor. You can then edit the policy settings.

- **Edit an existing policy**   Expand the site, domain, or OU node in which the related policy is stored. Right-click the policy, and then choose Edit. This opens the Group Policy Object Editor.

You manage local group policies for an individual computer by completing the following steps:

1. Click Start, point to All Programs, and then point to Accessories.
2. Right-click Command Prompt, and then select Run As Administrator.
3. At the command prompt, type **mmc**. This opens an empty Microsoft Management Console (MMC).
4. On the File menu, select Add/Remove Snap-In.
5. In the Add Or Remove Snap-In dialog box, under Available Snap-Ins, select Local Group Policy Object Editor, and then click Add.
6. By default, the editor works with the local computer's Group Policy Object (GPO), so you need only click Finish to accept this as the default.
7. Click OK. You can now manage the local policy on the selected computer.

> **TIP** There is another way to start the Group Policy Object Editor for the local computer: On the Start menu, click Run, in the Run box type **gpedit.msc**, and then press Enter.

Group policies for passwords, account lockout, and auditing are essential to your Web server's security. Guidelines for password policies are as follows:

- Set a minimum password age for all accounts. I recommend 2–3 days.
- Set a maximum password age for all accounts. I recommend 30 days.
- Set a minimum password length. I suggest the minimum be set at eight characters to start.
- Enable secure passwords by enforcing password complexity requirements.
- Enforce password history. I recommend using a value of 5 or more.

Guidelines for account lockout polices include the following:

- Set an account lockout threshold. In most cases accounts should be locked after five bad attempts.
- Set account lockout duration. In most cases you'll want to lock out accounts indefinitely.
- Reset the lockout threshold after 30–60 minutes.

Guidelines for auditing include the following:

- Audit system event success and failure
- Audit logon event success and failure
- Audit failed object access attempts
- Audit successful and failed policy changes
- Audit successful and failed account management
- Audit successful and failed account logon

Techniques for managing these policies are examined in the sections that follow.

Setting Account Policies for IIS Servers

You can set account policies by completing the following steps:

1. Access the group policy container you want to work with as described in the "Group Policy Essentials" section of this chapter. Expand the Computer Configuration node, then Windows Settings, then Security Settings, and finally, Account Policies.

2. You can now manage account policies. For domains, sites, and OUs, you'll have Password Policy, Account Lockout Policy, and Kerberos Policy nodes. For local computers, you'll have Password Policy and Account Lockout Policy nodes only.

3. To configure a policy, double-click its entry or right-click it and select Properties. This opens a Properties dialog box for the policy. Then do one of the following:

- For a local policy, the Properties dialog box will be different from that for a site, domain, or OU. Use the appropriate fields to configure the local policy. Skip the remaining steps; they apply to global group policies.
- For a site, domain, or OU, all policies are either defined or not defined— that is, they're either configured for use or not configured for use. A policy that isn't defined in the current container could be inherited from another container.

4. Select or clear the Define This Policy Setting check box to determine whether a policy is defined.

5. Policies can have additional fields for configuring the policy. Often, these fields have the following option buttons:

- **Enabled**   Turns on the policy restriction
- **Disabled**   Turns off the policy restriction

Setting Auditing Policies

Auditing is the best way to track what's happening on your IIS server. You can use auditing to collect information related to resource usage, such as file access, system logon, and system configuration changes. Whenever an action occurs that you've configured for auditing, the action is written to the system's security log, where it's stored for your review. You access the security log from Windows Event Viewer.

You can set auditing policies by completing the following steps:

1. Access the Group Policy container you want to work with as described in the "Group Policy Essentials" section in this chapter. Expand the Computer Configuration node, Windows Settings, Security Settings, and Local Policies. Then select Audit Policy.

2. You now have access to the following auditing options:

- **Audit Account Logon Events**   Tracks events related to user logon and logoff.
- **Audit Account Management**   Tracks account management. Events are generated anytime user, computer, or group accounts are created, modified, or deleted.
- **Audit Directory Service Access**   Tracks access to the Active Directory service. Events are generated whenever users or computers access the directory.
- **Audit Logon Events**   Tracks events related to user logon, logoff, and remote connections to network systems.
- **Audit Object Access**   Tracks system resource usage for files, directories, shares, printers, and Active Directory objects.
- **Audit Policy Change**   Tracks changes to user rights, auditing, and trust relationships.
- **Audit Privilege Use**   Tracks the use of user rights and privileges, such as the right to back up files and directories, but doesn't track system logon or logoff.

- **Audit Process Tracking**   Tracks system processes and the resources they use.
- **Audit System Events**   Tracks system startup, shutdown, and restart, in addition to actions that affect system security or the security log.

3. To configure an auditing policy, double-click its entry or right-click it and select Properties. This opens a Properties dialog box for the policy.

4. Select Define These Policy Settings, and then select the Success check box, the Failure check box, or both. Success logs successful events, such as successful logon attempts. Failure logs failed events, such as failed logon attempts.

5. Click OK when you're finished.

Managing IIS Security

After setting operating system security, use IIS security to set the Web server and execute permissions for content by:

- Configuring handler mappings
- Configuring authentication methods
- Setting authorization rules for application access
- Controlling access by IP address or Internet domain name
- Managing feature delegation and remote administration

Each of these topics is discussed in the sections that follow. When working with this myriad of security features, keep in mind that all these related features collectively determine whether IIS grants access to a particular client and user. For example, if the client IP address or domain name is denied access, a user won't be able to log in to get authenticated.

Configuring Handler Mappings for Applications

Handler mappings are used to specify the ISAPI extensions, CGI programs, IIS modules, and managed types that are available to handle incoming requests. Each type of content that IIS can work with has a specific handler mapping. A handler mapping identifies the module used to process requests for files with a specific file extension or a specific file name. IIS Setup creates handler mappings automatically when you install and enable related role services or modules.

To view the general handler mappings, in IIS, navigate to the level of the configuration hierarchy you want to manage, and then double-click the Handler Mappings feature. On the Handler Mappings page, shown in Figure 4-3, you'll see the configured handler mappings.

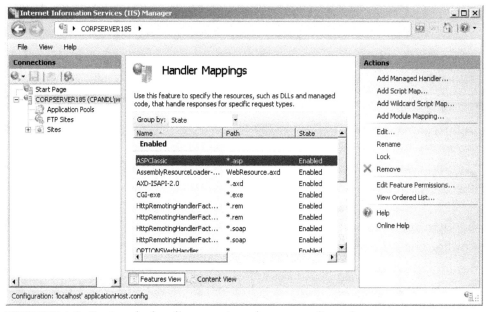

FIGURE 4-3 Review the handler mappings that are configured.

These handler mappings are listed by:

- **Name**   The name of the handler mapping.
- **Path**   The file extension or file name for which the handler will process a response.
- **State**   The current state as either Enabled or Disabled. If a handler requires a type of access that is not enabled in the access policy at that level, the handler is disabled.
- **Path Type**   The type of path to which the handler is mapped:

  - File, if the mapping applies to a file
  - Directory, if the mapping applies to a directory
  - Unspecified, if the mapping does not apply to a specific path type

- **Handler**   The module or managed type that responds to the request as specified in the mapping.
- **Entry Type**   The type of entry as either Local or Inherited.

You can configure and manage three general types of handler mappings:

- **Mappings for IIS modules**   Allow IIS to process specific requests through IIS modules configured on the Web server. For example, the PageHandlerFactory-ISAPI-2.0 handler mapping specifies that the IsapiModule handler process requests for .aspx files when IIS is using Classic mode.
- **Mappings for managed handlers**   Allow IIS to process specific requests through handlers written in managed code. For example, the PageHandlerFactory-Integrated handler mapping specifies that the System.Web.UI.PageHandlerFactory handler process requests for .aspx files when IIS is using Integrated mode.
- **Mappings for scripts and executables**   Allow IIS to process specific requests through ISAPI filters and extensions permitted to run on the Web server. For example, the ASPClassic handler mapping specifies that the IsapiModule handler process requests for .asp files.

> **NOTE**   Script maps provide backward compatibility with earlier versions of IIS. Executables must be written to the CGI specification, and dynamic link libraries must support the ISAPI extension interfaces. If you map a type of request to an .exe file, the CgiModule will load the associated executable when a request enters the server and it matches the handler mapping. If you map a type of request to a .dll file, IsapiModule will load the DLL when a request enters the server and it matches the handler mapping. For example, IIS includes a handler mapping for Active Server Pages (ASP). All requests for .asp files are processed by asp.dll, which is loaded by IsapiModule because asp.dll is an ISAPI extension.

You can create handler mappings by completing the following steps:

1. IIS Manager, navigate to the level of the configuration hierarchy you want to manage, and then double-click the Handler Mappings feature.

2. On the Handler Mappings page, click Add Managed Handler, Add Script Map, or Add Module Mapping as appropriate for the type of handler mapping you are creating.

> **NOTE** By default, when you add a managed handler, the handler will run only in application pools configured to use Integrated mode. To allow the new managed handler to be used in Classic mode, you must add the handler to the <httphandlers> section in the Web.config file.

3. In the Request Path text box, type a file name extension or file name with an extension for which you want the handler to process requests. File extensions don't have to have file type associations at the operating system level and can have more than three characters. If you wanted the handler to process all requests made for files with the extension .zip, type ***.zip**. Alternatively, if you want the handler to run all requests made for a specific file, type the file name and its extension, such as **Custom.zip**.

- For a managed handler, in the Type drop-down list, select the class type of the managed handler, such as System.Web.DefaultHttpHandler.
- For a module map, in the Module drop-down list, select the module that will process related requests, such as FastCgiModule.
- For a script map and optionally for a module map, in the Executable text box, specify the script or executable that will process related requests. Click the selection button to the right of the Executable text box to display the Open dialog box, which you can use to select the executable. The executable must be in a directory that's accessible to IIS, such as the *%SystemRoot%*\System32 or *%SystemRoot%*\System32\Inetsrv directory.

4. In the Name text box, type a descriptive name for the handler mapping.

5. Click the Request Restrictions button to open the Request Restrictions dialog box and specify additional, optional restrictions for the handler mapping. The Request Restrictions dialog box has two tabs:

- **Mapping** Use the settings on the Mapping tab to limit the ways the handler can be invoked. Select the Invoke Handler Only If Request Is Mapped To check box, and then choose File to limit the handler to file requests, Folder to limit the handler to folder requests, or File Or Folder to limit the handler to file or folder requests.

- **Verbs** Use the settings on the Verbs tab to limit the HTTP request types that can be used to invoke the handler. Either allow all HTTP verbs to be used, or specify a list of allowed HTTP verbs, such as GET, HEAD, POST, and DEBUG. For a detailed list of HTTP request types, refer to Table 1-1 in Chapter 1, "Running IIS Applications."
- **Access** Access policy, together with a handler's required access setting, determines whether a handler can run. The access policy for handlers can be set to grant read, write, script, and execute permissions. If a handler requires a permission that is not enabled in the access policy, the handler will be disabled, and unless there is another handler that can process the request, all requests that are processed by that handler will fail.

6. Click OK twice to close all open dialog boxes and create the handler mapping.

To configure access policy that specifies the type of access permissions allowed for handlers at the current configuration level, click Edit Feature Permissions, and then, in the Edit Feature Permissions dialog box, select the allowed permissions or clear the denied permissions in the Permissions list. When you select a permission check box in the Edit Feature Permissions dialog box, the State column on the Handler Mappings page displays Enabled for the handlers that are enabled by the selection. Similarly, when you clear a selection in the Edit Feature Permissions dialog box, the State column on the Handler Mappings page displays Disabled for the handlers that are disabled by the selection. You can preview the handlers that are enabled or disabled by viewing the Handler Mappings page. If you click OK, any changes you've made to permissions are saved. If you click Cancel instead of OK, any changes you've made are not saved.

You can edit, rename, or remove handler mappings by using the following techniques:

- To modify a handler mapping's settings, click the handler mapping you want to modify, and then click Edit. In the Edit dialog box, make the necessary changes, and then click OK.
- To rename a handler mapping, click the entry to select it, and then click Rename. Type the new name for the filter, and then press Enter.

- To remove a handler mapping that is no longer needed, click the entry you want to remove, and then click Remove. When prompted to confirm the action, click Yes.

Setting Authentication Modes

Authentication modes control access to IIS resources. You can use authentication to allow anonymous access to public resources, to create secure areas within a Web site, and to create controlled access to Web sites and applications. When authentication is enabled, IIS uses the account credentials supplied by a user to determine whether the user has access to a resource and to determine which permissions the user has been granted.

Understanding Authentication

The authentication modes available on a Web server depend on the authentication modules you've installed and enabled for use. A complete list of related modules is provided in Chapter 2 of *Web Server Administration: The Personal Trainer* but a basic list of authentication modes follows:

- **Anonymous authentication** With anonymous authentication, IIS automatically logs users on with an anonymous or guest account. This allows users to access resources without being prompted for user name and password information. Because the first request all browsers send to a Web server is for anonymous access, you must disable anonymous authentication at the appropriate configuration level if you want to restrict access to content.
- **ASP.NET Impersonation** With ASP.NET Impersonation, a managed code application can run as either the user authenticated by IIS or a designated account that you specify when configuring this mode.
- **Basic authentication** With basic authentication, users are prompted for logon information. When it's entered, this information is transmitted unencrypted (as clear text) across the network. If you've configured secure communications on the server as described in the "Working with SSL" section of Chapter 6, "Managing Certificates and SSL," you can require

clients to use Secure Sockets Layer (SSL). When you use SSL with basic authentication, the logon information is encrypted before transmission.

- **Active Directory Client Certificate authentication**   With Client Certificate authentication, IIS can map Active Directory client certificates for authentication across multiple servers. This lets IIS automatically authenticate clients without using other authentication methods. If you enable this mode, you cannot use IIS certificate mapping for any other sites hosted on the server.

- **Digest authentication**   With digest authentication, user credentials are transmitted securely between clients and servers. Digest authentication is a feature of HTTP 1.1 and uses a technique that can't be easily intercepted and decrypted. This feature is available only when IIS is configured on a server that is part of an Active Directory domain. The client is required to use a domain account.

- **IIS Client Certificate mapping authentication**   With IIS Client Certificate authentication, IIS can map client certificates for authentication across multiple servers. This lets IIS automatically authenticate clients without using other authentication methods. If you enable this mode, you cannot use Active Directory Client Certificate mapping for any other sites hosted on the server.

- **Integrated Windows authentication**   With integrated Windows authentication, IIS uses standard Windows security to validate the user's identity. Instead of prompting for a user name and password, clients relay the logon credentials that users supply when they log on to Windows. These credentials are fully encrypted without the need for SSL, and they include the user name and password needed to log on to the network. The only Web browsers that support Integrated Windows Authentication are versions of Internet Explorer.

- **ASP.NET Forms-based authentication**   With ASP.NET Forms-based authentication, you manage client registration and authentication at the application level instead of relying on the authentication mechanisms in IIS. As the mode name implies, users register and provide their credentials using a login form. By default, this information is passed as clear text. To avoid this, you should use SSL encryption for the login page and other internal application pages.

By default, only anonymous authentication is enabled for IIS resources. Anonymous authentication is enabled as part of the server core. You can apply authentication on a global or local basis. You configure global authentication modes via the server configuration level. You set local authentication modes at the site, application, directory, or file configuration level.

Before you start working with authentication modes, you should keep the following in mind:

- When you combine anonymous access with authenticated access, users have full access to resources that are accessible anonymously via the Internet guest account. If this account doesn't have access to a resource, IIS attempts to authenticate the user using the authentication techniques you've specified. If these authentication methods fail, the user is denied access to the resource.
- When you disable anonymous access, you're telling IIS that all user requests must be authenticated using the authentication modes you've specified. Once the user is authenticated, IIS uses the user's account credentials to determine access rights.
- When you combine basic authentication with integrated or digest authentication, Internet Explorer attempts to use integrated Windows authentication or digest authentication before using basic authentication. This means that users who can be authenticated using their current account credentials won't be prompted for a user name and password.

In addition, before you can use digest authentication, you must enable reversible password encryption for each account that will connect to the server using this authentication technique. IIS and the user's Web browser use reversible encryption to manage secure transmission and unencryption of user information. To enable reversible encryption, follow these steps:

1. To start Active Directory Users And Computers, click Start, point to Administrative Tools, and then click Active Directory Users And Computers.
2. Double-click the user name that you want to use with digest authentication.

3. On the Account tab, under Account Options, select Store Password Using Reversible Encryption, and then click OK.

4. Repeat steps 1–3 for each account that you want to use with digest authentication.

Enabling and Disabling Authentication

You can enable or disable anonymous access to resources at the server, site, application, directory, or file level. If you enable anonymous access, users can access resources without having to authenticate themselves (as long as the Windows permissions on the resource allow this). If you disable anonymous access, users must authenticate themselves before accessing resources. Authentication can occur automatically or manually depending on the browser used and the account credentials the user previously entered.

You can enable or disable authentication at a particular configuration level by completing the following steps:

1. In IIS Manager, navigate to the level of the configuration hierarchy you want to manage, and then double-click the Authentication feature.

2. On the Authentication page, shown in Figure 4-4, you should now see the available authentication modes. If a mode you want to use is not available, you'll need to install and enable the related module.

3. To enable or disable anonymous access, select Anonymous Authentication, and then click Enable or Disable as appropriate.

4. Select and then use the related Enable, Disable, and Edit links in the Actions pane to configure the authentication methods you want to use. Keep the following in mind:

- Disabling basic authentication might prevent some clients from accessing resources remotely. Clients can log on only when you enable an authentication method that they support.
- A default domain isn't set automatically. If you enable basic authentication, you can choose to set a default domain that should be used when no domain information is supplied during the logon process. Setting the default domain is useful when you want to ensure that clients authenticate properly.

- With basic and digest authentication, you can optionally specify the realm that can be accessed. Essentially, a *realm* is the DNS domain name or Web address that will use the credentials that have been authenticated against the default domain. If default domain and realm are set to the same value, the internal Windows domain name may be exposed to external users during the user name and password challenge/response.

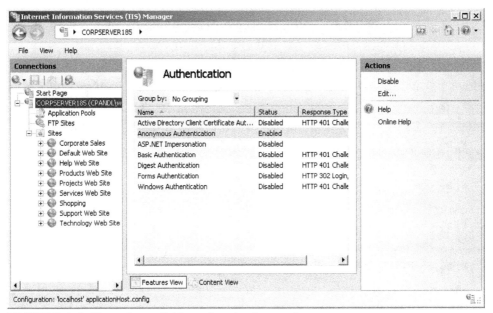

FIGURE 4-4 View the available authentication modes.

- With Windows authentication on IIS 7.5, you can use advanced settings to either accept or require extended protection. With extended protection, channel-binding data is encoded using a Channel Binding Token and service-binding data is encoded using a Service Principal Name.
- If you enable ASP.NET Impersonation, you can specify the identity to impersonate. By default, IIS uses pass-through authentication and the identity of the authenticated user is impersonated. You can also specify a specific user if necessary.
- If you enable forms authentication, you can set the login URL and cookies settings used for authentication. See the "FormsAuthenticationModule" section in the appendix, "Comprehensive IIS Module and Schema Reference," for details on the related options.

- If you enable passport authentication, all other authentication settings are ignored. As a result, the server will use this technique to authenticate only for the specified resource.

Setting Authorization Rules for Application Access

You can use authorization rules to control access to Web content. An authorization rule specifies which users, roles, and groups are allowed to or restricted from accessing content at a specific configuration level. The two types of authorization rules are:

- **Allow Authorization Rules**   Grants access to Web content at a specific configuration level
- **Deny Authorization Rules**   Denies access to Web content at a specific configuration level

To view the current authorization rules at a particular configuration level, navigate to the level of the configuration hierarchy you want to manage, and then double-click the Authorization Rules feature. On the Authorization Rules page, shown in Figure 4-5, you'll then see a list of applicable authorization rules listed by:

- **Mode**   Lists the type of rule as either Allow or Deny.
- **Users**   Lists the user types, names, or groups to which the rule applies.
- **Roles**   Lists the user roles to which the rule applies.
- **Verbs**   Lists the HTTP verbs to which the rule applies. Applicable only when a rule is limited to specific HTTP verbs.
- **Entry Type**   Lists the entry type as Local or Inherited.

FIGURE 4-5 Review the authorization rules for the selected configuration level.

You can set an Allow or Deny authorization rule by completing the following steps:

1. In IIS Manager, navigate to the level of the configuration hierarchy you want to manage, and then double-click the Authentication Rules feature.

2. On the Authorization Rules page, you should now see the currently configured authorization rules.

3. You can now set an authorization rule. To add an allow rule, click Add Allow Rule. To add a deny rule, click Add Deny Rule. Figure 4-6 shows the Add Allow Authorization Rule dialog box.

4. Use the options in the dialog box to specify the users to which the rule applies. With regard to users, these rules can be applied to:

- All users, meaning that both anonymous and authenticated users are either granted or denied access
- Anonymous users, meaning that all anonymous unauthenticated users are either granted or denied access
- Specified roles or user groups, meaning that authenticated users who are members of specific Windows roles and user groups are either granted or denied access

- Specified users, meaning that specific authenticated users are either granted or denied access

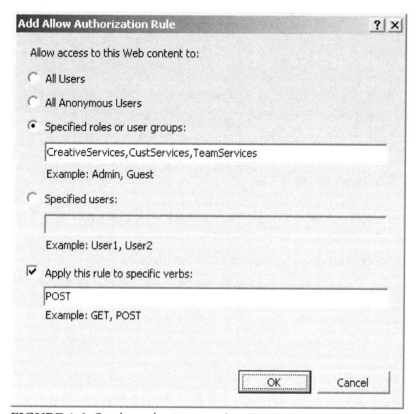

FIGURE 4-6 Set the authorization rule.

5. Authorization rules can be applied to all HTTP requests or to requests only with specific HTTP verbs, such as GET and POST. To apply the rule to specific HTTP verbs, select the Apply This Rule To Specific Verbs check box, and then type the verbs to use in a comma-separated list.

6. Click OK to set the rule.

You can edit or remove authorization rules by using the following techniques:

- To modify a rule's settings, click the authorization rule you want to modify, and then click Edit. In the Edit dialog box, make the necessary changes, and then click OK.

- To remove a rule that is no longer needed, click the entry you want to remove, and then click Remove. When prompted to confirm the action, click Yes.

Configuring IPv4 Address and Domain Name Restrictions

By default, IIS resources are accessible to all IPv4 addresses, computers, and domains, which present a security risk that might allow your server to be misused. To control use of resources, you might want to grant or deny access by IP Version 4 (IPv4) address, network ID, or domain. When you grant or deny access, keep the following in mind:

- Granting access allows a computer to make requests for resources but doesn't necessarily allow users to work with resources. If you require authentication, users still need to authenticate themselves.
- Denying access to resources prevents a computer from accessing those resources. Therefore, users of the computer can't access the resources—even if they could have authenticated themselves with a user name and password.

You can establish or remove restrictions globally at the server level and for individual sites, applications, and directories. The three types of restriction settings are:

- **General Restriction settings**   Determine whether unspecified clients are allowed or denied access and whether domain name restrictions are enabled or disabled. An unspecified client is a computer for which there is no other restriction rule.
- **Allow Restriction rules**   Grant access to a specific IP address, a range of IPv4 addresses, or a specific domain name.
- **Deny Authorization rules**   Deny access to a specific IP address, a range of IPv4 addresses, or a specific domain name.

IPv4 address ranges are set based on the IPv4 address for the network ID and the related subnet mask. With standard classful networks, the network ID is the .0 address for the network, such as 192.168.1.0. By default, domain name restrictions are disabled. The reason for this is that when you grant or deny access by domain, IIS must perform a reverse Domain Name System (DNS) lookup on each connection to determine whether the connection comes from the domain. These reverse lookups can severely increase response times for the first query each user sends to your site.

To view the current restriction rules at a particular configuration level, navigate to the level of the configuration hierarchy you want to manage, and then double-click the IPv4 And Domain Restrictions feature. On the IPv4 And Domain Restrictions page, shown in Figure 4-7, you'll see a list of applicable restriction rules listed by:

- **Mode**   Lists the type of rule as either Allow or Deny
- **Requestor**   Lists the specific IPv4 address, IPv4 address range, or domain to which the rule applies
- **Entry Type**   Lists the entry type as Local or Inherited

You can configure the general restriction settings by completing the following steps:

1. In IIS Manager, navigate to the level of the configuration hierarchy you want to manage, and then double-click the IPv4 And Domain Restrictions feature.

2. On the IPv4 And Domain Restrictions page, in the Actions pane, click Edit Feature Settings.

3. Set the restriction rule for unspecified clients, that is, clients that do not fall under any other restriction rule. To grant access to unspecified clients, set the Access For Unspecified Clients drop-down list to Allow. To deny access to unspecified clients, set the Access For Unspecified Clients drop-down list to Deny.

4. To allow domain name restrictions to be used in addition to IPv4 address restrictions, select the Enable Domain Name Restrictions check box.

5. Click OK to configure the restriction settings.

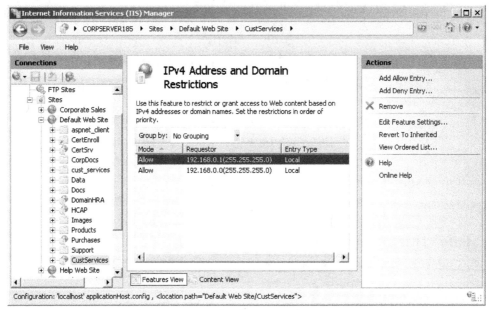

FIGURE 4-7 Review the restrictions for the selected configuration level.

You can set an allow or deny restriction by completing the following steps:

1. In IIS Manager, navigate to the level of the configuration hierarchy you want to manage, and then double-click the IPv4 And Domain Restrictions feature.

2. On the IPv4 And Domain Restrictions page, you should now see the currently configured IPv4 address and domain restrictions.

3. You can now specify a restriction. To add an allow restriction, click Add Allow Entry. To add a deny restriction, click Add Deny Entry. Figure 4-8 shows the Add Allow Restriction Rule dialog box.

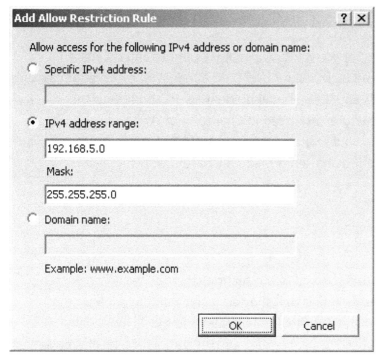

FIGURE 4-8 Create a restriction rule.

4. Create the Allow Access or Deny Access list. The settings you can specify for each option are as follows:

- For a single computer, select Specific IPv4 Address, and then type the IPv4 address for the computer, such as **192.168.5.50**.
- For groups of computers, select IPv4 Address Range, and then type the subnet address, such as **192.168.0.0**, and the subnet mask, such as **255.255.255.0**.
- For a domain name, select Domain Name, and then type the fully qualified domain name (FQDN), such as **eng.microsoft.com**. (Domain name restrictions must be enabled.)

5. Click OK to create the rule.

To remove a rule that is no longer needed, click the entry you want to remove, and then click Remove. When prompted to confirm the action, click Yes.

Managing Feature Delegation and Remote Administration

The Web Management Service (WMSVC) enables remote and delegated management of IIS using IIS Manager based on either Windows credentials only or Windows credentials and IIS Manager credentials. In addition to the Management Service feature, discussed in Chapter 3 of *Web Server Administration: The Personal Trainer*, you can use the following IIS features to control the way delegation and remote administration works:

- IIS Manager Users
- IIS Manager Permissions
- Feature Delegation

Each of these features is discussed in the sections that follow. When working with these features, keep in mind that they are used with IIS Manager for the purposes of delegation and remote administration. For local logon, any administrator user can use IIS Manager for administration of a local Web server. Furthermore, any user with direct access to content and configuration files can manipulate those files as appropriate for the file system permissions they've been granted.

Creating and Configuring IIS Manager User Accounts

The IIS Manager Users feature allows you to create accounts for individuals that act as Web site or Web application administrators when using IIS Manager for remote administration. When you specify an IIS manager, you set the permitted user name and password for the user, creating an IIS Manager account. You can then manage this account in IIS Manager. Options are available for enabling, disabling, and removing accounts as and for changing account passwords.

By default, IIS Manager permissions are based on Windows credentials. If you want to allow IIS Manager accounts to also be used, you must enable this option by completing the following steps:

1. In IIS Manager, select the server node, and then double-click Management Service.

2. On the Management Service page, the Identity Credentials options control whether IIS Manager accounts can be used. Do one of the following:

- If the Management Service is currently running and the Windows Credentials Or IIS Manager Credentials option is not selected, in the Actions pane, click Stop. Select the Windows Credentials Or IIS Manager Credentials option, click Apply, and then click Start.
- If the Management Service is not running and has not been configured, see Chapter 3 of *Web Server Administration: The Personal Trainer*.

You can configure IIS managers only at the server configuration level. To create and configure IIS managers, follow these steps:

1. In IIS Manager, select the server node, and then double-click the IIS Manager Users feature.
2. On the IIS Manager Users page, you should now see the currently configured IIS managers listed by user name and account status.
3. To create an IIS manager, in the Actions pane, click Add User. In the Add User dialog box, type the desired user name for the account. Type and confirm the account password, and then click OK.
4. You can work with IIS manager accounts by using the following techniques:

- To change an account password, click the user name you want to modify, and then click Change Password. In the Change Password dialog box, type and confirm the account password, and then click OK.
- To disable an account so that it cannot be used, click the user name, and then click Disable.
- To enable an account, click the user name, and then click Enable.
- To remove an account that is no longer needed, click the user name that you want to remove, and then click Remove. When prompted to confirm the action, click Yes.

Configuring IIS Manager Permissions

IIS Manager permissions control who can perform remote administration in IIS Manager. You configure IIS Manager permissions for individual sites, applications, or directories. Any permissions you apply at the site, application, or directory level also automatically apply to all lower configuration levels.

To grant a user permission to manage IIS remotely using IIS Manager, follow these steps:

1. In IIS Manager, select the configuration level below the server node for which you are configuring remote administration, and then double-click the IIS Manager Permissions feature.

2. On the IIS Manager Permissions page, you should now see a list of users who have been delegated remote administration privileges in IIS Manager. To see only users with permissions for a selected site, click Show Only Site Users.

3. In the Actions pane, click Allow User. In the Allow User dialog box, choose one of the following options:

    - **Windows**   Choose Windows if you want to configure permissions based on a Windows account.
    - **IIS Manager**   Choose IIS Manager if you want to configure permissions based on an IIS Manager account.

4. Click Select. Use the dialog box provided to choose the account to use, and then click OK.

To deny a user permission to manage IIS remotely using IIS Manager, follow these steps:

1. In IIS Manager, select the configuration level below the server node for which you are configuring remote administration, and then double-click the IIS Manager Permissions feature.

2. On the IIS Manager Permissions page, you should now see a list of users who have been delegated remote administration privileges in IIS Manager. To see only users with permissions for a selected site, click Show Only Site Users.

3. Click the user account that should no longer have administration permissions at or below the selected level, and then click Deny User.

Configuring Feature Delegation

Feature Delegation settings configure the delegation state at the server level or for individual sites for lower configuration levels in IIS Manager. These settings also determine the state of the related section in the applicationHost.config file. To configure Feature Delegation for all sites on a server, you configure feature delegation at the server level. To configure Feature Delegation for all application and directories within a site, you configure feature delegation at the site level.

As shown in Figure 4-9, each feature, with two noted exceptions, has one of the following delegation states:

- **Read/Write**   Enables remote administrators to view and change the feature. It also unlocks the configuration section in the applicationHost.config file, allowing settings for this feature to be read from and written to web.config files.
- **Read Only**   Enables remote administrators to view but not change the feature. It also locks the configuration section in the applicationHost.config file, preventing settings for this feature to be read from and written to web.config files.
- **Not Delegated**   Prevents remote administrators from viewing or changing the feature. Also locks the configuration section in the applicationHost.config file, preventing settings for this feature to be read from and written to Web.config files.

With the .NET Roles and .NET Users features, you'll see the delegation state specified as either Configuration Read/Write or Configuration Read Only. These settings work the same as Read/Write and Read Only but are distinguished from other features because configuration information can come not only from configuration files, but also from a database.

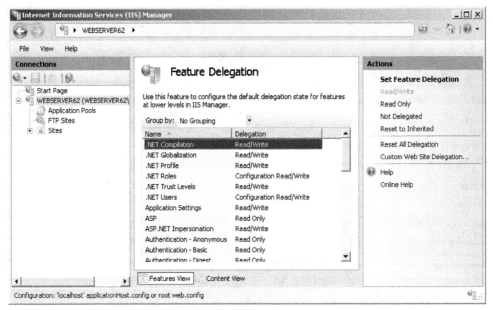

FIGURE 4-9 View the feature delegation state.

You can configure the delegation state by completing the following steps:

1. Open IIS Manager. To configure the delegation state at the server level for all lower configuration levels, select the server node, and then double-click Feature Delegation. To configure the delegation state of an individual site, select the server node, double-click Feature Delegation, and then in the Actions pane, click Custom Web Site Configuration. On the Feature Delegation or Custom Web Site Delegation page, you should now see the delegation state for each feature in IIS Manager.

2. You can now use the following techniques to manage delegation:

   - To change the delegation state, select the feature you want to work with, and then configure the Actions pane options to set the delegation state as Read/Write, Read Only, Configuration Read/Write, Configuration Read Only, or Not Delegated.
   - When you are working with the Custom Web Site Delegation page, you can reset a feature to its inherited value by selecting the feature and then clicking Reset To Inherited.
   - To reset the delegation state for all IIS features to their original state (as per the default value in schema), click Reset All Delegation.

Chapter 5. Using Active Directory Certificate Services

Active Directory Certificate Services and Secure Sockets Layer (SSL) provide an extra layer of security for your Web server. You use Certificate Services and SSL to protect sensitive information such as passwords, credit card numbers, or payment information. Certificate Services and SSL protect sensitive information by encrypting the data sent between client browsers and your server. *Encryption* is the process of encoding information by using a mathematical algorithm that makes it difficult for anyone other than the intended recipient to view the original information.

Internet Information Services (IIS) transfers encrypted data to a client browser by using the SSL protocol. With SSL, servers and clients can use certificates to provide proof of identity prior to establishing a secure connection. Once a connection is established, clients and servers use the secure SSL channel to transfer information. This information is encrypted using a technique that the clients and servers can interpret to extract the original information.

Understanding SSL

IIS supports SSL protocol version 3. SSL 3 enables encrypted data transfers between client browsers and Web servers. The sections that follow provide an overview on how SSL works and how it's used.

Using SSL Encryption

As stated previously, encryption is the process of encoding information by using a mathematical algorithm that makes it difficult for anyone other than the intended recipient to view the original information. The encryption algorithm uses a mathematical value, called a *key*, to scramble the data so that the key must be used to recover the data.

Many techniques are available for encrypting information so that it can be exchanged. Some encryption techniques use a combination of public and private keys—the public key can be shared and the private key can't. Some encryption techniques use shared secret keys that are transferred between authenticated systems. SSL uses a technique called *public key encryption*, which combines private, public, and shared secret (session) keys.

In public key encryption, there are three keys:

- A public key that's available to any application that requests it
- A private key that's known only to its owner
- A session key that's created using public and private key data

IIS uses the public key encryption component in SSL to establish sessions between clients and servers. You should use SSL whenever you want to provide additional protection for data that's transferred between clients and servers. Some specific instances in which you might want to use Certificate Services and SSL follow:

- When you remotely manage the Web server by using the Administration Web site or operator administration pages
- When your Web site has secure areas that contain sensitive company documents
- When your Web site has pages that collect sensitive personal or financial information from visitors
- When your Web site processes orders for goods or services and you collect credit or other personal information from customers

With SSL, users connect to Web pages by using a secure Uniform Resource Locator (URL) that begins with *https://*. The *https* designator tells the browser to try to establish a secure connection with IIS. SSL connections for Web pages are made on port 443 by default, but you can change the port designator as necessary. As you set out to work with SSL, keep in mind that you can't use host headers with SSL. With SSL, Hypertext Transfer Protocol (HTTP) requests are encrypted, and the host header name within the encrypted request can't be used to determine the correct site to which a request must be routed.

After the client browser contacts the server by using a secure URL, the server sends the browser its public key and server certificate. Next, the client and server negotiate the level of encryption to use for secure communications. The server always attempts to use the highest level of encryption it supports. Once the encryption level is established, the client browser creates a session key and uses the server's public key to encrypt this information for transmission. Anyone intercepting the message at this point wouldn't be able to read the session key—only the server's private key can decrypt the message.

The IIS server uses its private key to decrypt the message sent by the client. The SSL session between the client and the server is now established. The session key can be used to encrypt and decrypt data transmitted between the client and server.

To recap, secure SSL sessions are established using the following technique:

1. The user's Web browser contacts the server by using a secure URL.
2. The IIS server sends the browser its public key and server certificate.
3. The client and server negotiate the level of encryption to use for the secure communications.
4. The client browser encrypts a session key with the server's public key and sends the encrypted data back to the server.
5. The IIS server uses its private key to decrypt the message sent by the client, and the session is established.
6. Both the client and the server use the session key to encrypt and decrypt transmitted data.

Using SSL Certificates

Not reflected in the previous discussion is the way in which SSL uses certificates. You can think of a certificate as an identity card that contains information needed to establish the identity of an application or user over a network. Certificates enable Web servers and users to authenticate one another before establishing a connection. Certificates also contain keys needed to establish SSL sessions between clients and servers.

In most cases certificates used by IIS, Web browsers, and Certificate Services conform to the X.509 standard. For this reason, they're often referred to as X.509 certificates. Different versions of the X.509 standard have been issued (see

RFC 3280 for more information on this standard), and these versions have been revised from time to time. Two types of X.509 certificates are used:

- Client certificates, which contain identifying information about a client
- Server certificates, which contain identifying information about a server

Certificate authorities issue both types of certificates. A *certificate authority (CA)* is a trusted agency responsible for confirming the identity of users, organizations, and their servers and then issuing certificates that confirm these identities. Before issuing a client certificate, CAs require that you provide information that identifies you, your organization, and the client application you're using. Before issuing a server certificate, CAs require that you provide information that identifies your organization and the server you're using.

When you're choosing CAs to create your server certificates, you have several options. If you use Certificate Services, your organization can act as its own CA. When you act as your own CA, you use the following process to enable SSL on your Web server:

1. Install Active Directory Certificate Services on a server in the domain, and then generate the root CA certificate.
2. Generate a certificate request file for each Web site on your server that has a unique name, and then use the certificate request files to create server certificates for your Web sites.
3. Install the certificates and then enable SSL on each applicable Web site.
4. Client browsers won't recognize and trust your root CA certificate. To get browsers to trust the root CA, the user must install the certificate in the browser's authorities store.
5. Initiate SSL connections by using URLs that begin with *https://.*

Instead of using your own CAs, you can use third-party CAs—and there's an advantage to doing so. The third-party authority can vouch for your identity, and dozens of vendors are already configured as trusted CAs in Web browsers. In most versions of Microsoft Internet Explorer, you can obtain a list of trusted authorities by completing the following these general steps:

1. On the Tools menu, select Internet Options. The Internet Options dialog box appears.
2. On the Content tab, click Certificates. The Certificates dialog box appears.
3. On the Trusted Root Certification Authorities tab. you should now see a list of trusted root CAs.

When you use a trusted third-party authority, you follow a different procedure on your Web server to enable SSL than when you act as your own root CA:

1. Create a certificate request file for each Web site on your server that has a unique name.
2. Submit the certificate request files to a trusted third-party authority such as Verisign. The CA will process the requests and send you certificates.
3. Complete the certificate request by installing the certificate, and then enable SSL on each applicable Web site.
4. Client browsers initiate SSL sessions by using a secure URL beginning with *https://*.

Regardless of whether you act as your own CA or use a trusted CA, you still must manage the server certificates, and you use Active Directory Certificate Services to do this. Server certificates can expire or be revoked, if necessary. For example, if your organization is an Internet service provider (ISP) that issues its own certificates, you might want your customers' server certificates to expire annually. This forces customers to update their certificate information at least once a year to ensure that it's current. You also might want to revoke a certificate when a customer cancels service.

Understanding SSL Encryption Strength

An SSL session's encryption strength is directly proportional to the number of bits in the session key. This means that session keys with a greater number of bits are considerably more difficult to crack and, thus, are more secure.

The most commonly used encryption levels for SSL sessions are 40-bit, 128-bit, and 256-bit. Encryption at the 40-bit level is adequate for most needs, including e-commerce. Encryption at the 128-bit level provides added protection for e-commerce. Encryption at the 256-bit level provides superior protection for sensitive personal and financial information. Most versions of Windows Server shipped in the United States are configured with 256-bit encryption.

Don't confuse the encryption level for SSL sessions (the strength of the session key expressed as bits) with the encryption level for SSL certificates (the strength of the certificate's public and private keys expressed as bits). Most encryption keys (public and private) have a bit length of 512 or higher. When a user attempts to establish an SSL session with your Web server, the user's browser and the server use the bit length of their encryption keys to determine the strongest level of encryption possible. If the encryption keys use 512 bits, the level of encryption is set to 40 bits. If the encryption keys use 1024 bits, the level of encryption is set to 128 bits. If the encryption keys use 2048 bits, the level of encryption is set to 256 bits. Other key bit lengths and encryption levels are available.

Working with Active Directory Certificate Services

Active Directory Certificate Services allows you to issue and revoke digital certificates. You can use these certificates to enable SSL sessions and to authenticate the identity of your intranet, extranet, or Internet Web site.

Understanding Active Directory Certificate Services

Active Directory Certificate Services is a Windows service that runs on a designated certificate server. Certificate servers can be configured as one of four types of CAs:

- **Enterprise root CA**   The certificate server at the root of the hierarchy for a Windows domain. It's the most trusted CA in the enterprise and must be a member of the Active Directory service and have access to it.
- **Enterprise subordinate CA**   A certificate server that will be a member of an existing CA hierarchy. It can issue certificates but must obtain its own CA certificate from the enterprise root CA.

- **Stand-alone root CA**   The certificate server at the root of a non-enterprise hierarchy. It's the most trusted CA in its hierarchy and doesn't need access to Active Directory.
- **Stand-alone subordinate CA**   A certificate server that will be a member of an existing non-enterprise hierarchy. It can issue certificates but must obtain its own CA certificate from the stand-alone root CA in its hierarchy.

Certificate servers aren't required to be dedicated to Active Directory Certificate Services and can be the same servers you use for Web publishing. However, it's a good idea to designate specific servers in your domain that will act as certificate servers and to use these servers only for that purpose.

REAL WORLD   To safeguard the root CA from malicious users, you should create multiple levels in the CA hierarchy. For example, in an enterprise, you'd set up an enterprise root CA and then set up one or more enterprise subordinate CAs. You'd then issue certificates to users and computers only through the subordinate CAs. This safeguard should help ensure that the root CA's private key can't be easily compromised.

Once you install Active Directory Certificate Services on a computer, you're limited in what you can and can't do with the computer. Specifically, you can't do the following:

- You can't rename a computer that has Certificate Services installed.
- You can't change the domain membership of a computer that has Certificate Services installed.

You manage Certificate Services by using a Microsoft Management Console (MMC) snap-in called the Certificate Authority snap-in and a Web-based Active Server Pages (ASP) application that can be accessed in a standard Web browser. In the snap-in, you have full control over Certificate Services. The Web-based application, on the other hand, is used primarily to retrieve Certificate Revocation Lists (CRLs), to request certificates, and to check on pending certificates. You can access the Web-based application from the following URL: *http://hostname/certsrv*.

Figure 5-1 shows the Certification Authority snap-in's main window. As you can see, five containers are under the root authority. These containers are used as follows:

- **Revoked Certificates** Contains all certificates that have been issued and then revoked.
- **Issued Certificates** Contains all certificates that have been approved and issued by the Certificate Services administrator.
- **Pending Requests** Contains all pending certificate requests for this CA. If you're an administrator on the certificate server, you can approve requests by right-clicking them and selecting Issue. The default configuration is to process requests automatically, which means that no administrator involvement is required.
- **Failed Requests** Contains any declined certificate requests for this CA. If you're an administrator on the certificate server, you can deny requests by right-clicking them and selecting Deny.

> **NOTE** The label for the root node of the snap-in is set to the name of the CA. In the example, the CA name is Corporate Root CA.

- **Certificate Templates** Contains a set of certificate templates that are configured for different intended purposes. These templates provide basic rules for the various types of certificates. To install additional certificate templates, right-click Certificate Templates, select New, and then click Certificate Template To Issue. (Certificate Templates are available only with enterprise root and subordinate CAs.)

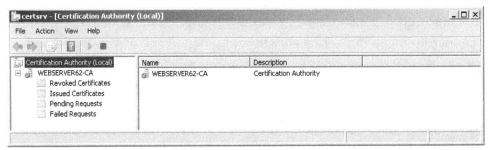

FIGURE 5-1 Use the Active Directory Certificate Services snap-in to manage Certificate Services.

Installing Active Directory Certificate Services

If the server isn't running IIS and you want to be able to retrieve CRLs to request certificates or to check on pending certificates through a browser, you must install IIS prior to installing Active Directory Certificate Services. To install Active Directory Certificate Services, complete the following steps:

1. Log on to the certificate server by using an account with Administrator privileges or, if you're creating an enterprise CA, Enterprise Administrator privileges.

2. Start Server Manager by clicking the Server Manager icon on the Quick Launch toolbar or by clicking Start, pointing to Administrative Tools, and then clicking Server Manager.

3. In Server Manager, in the left pane, select the Roles node, and then scroll down until you see the details section for the role you want to manage. In the details section for the role, click Add Role Services. This starts the Add Role Services Wizard. If the Before You Begin page appears, click Next.

4. On the Select Role Services page, select Active Directory Certificate Services, and then click Next. Read the introductory message, and then click Next.

5. The Certificate Authority role service is selected by default. Select these additional role services to install as necessary: Certificate Authority Web Enrollment and Online Certificate Status Protocol.

6. On the Specify Setup Type page, select the setup type as enterprise or stand-alone, and then click Next.

7. On the Specify CA Type page, specify the CA type as either root CA or subordinate CA.

8. All CAs must have a private key to generate and issue certificates. On the Setup Private Key page, select Create A New Private Key, and then click Next.

9. Use the settings on the Configure Cryptography For CA page to select a cryptographic provider, hash algorithm, and bit length for the CA's private key. Ensure that your selections are appropriate for the CA's intended use. If you are unsure, accept the default settings. Click Next when you are ready to continue.

10. On the Configure CA Name page, type the common name for the CA, such as **Corporate Root CA**. As necessary, set the distinguished name suffix for the CA name, and then click Next.

11. On the Set Validity Period page, set the CA certificate's expiration date. Most CA certificates are valid for at least five years. Click Next.

12. Specify the storage location for the configuration database and log. By default, the certificate database and log are stored in the *%SystemRoot%*\System32\CertLog folder. Click Next.

> **TIP** If hundreds or thousands of users use your CA, you might want the database and log files to be stored on separate drives. By placing these files on separate drives, you can improve the CA's performance and responsiveness. In all cases the database and log files should be on NTFS volumes. This ensures that the security permissions can be set to restrict access to these files by user account.

13. Click Install to complete the process. When the installation completes, click Close. If you installed Certificate Services on a computer running IIS, you can configure these services for Web access (as described in the section "Accessing Certificate Services in a Browser," immediately following).

Accessing Certificate Services in a Browser

When you install Certificate Services on a computer running IIS, the default (or primary) Web site is updated so that you can perform key certificate tasks through a Web browser. These tasks include:

- Retrieving CRLs
- Requesting certificates
- Checking on pending certificates

The structures that make Web-based requests possible are files configured for use in the two following virtual directories:

- **CertSrv** Contains files necessary for Web-based access to Certificate Services. It is located in *%SystemRoot%*\System32\CertSrv by default. This directory is set up as a pooled application called CertSrv.

- **CertEnroll**   Contains files necessary for controlling Certificate Services. It is located in *%SystemRoot%*\System32\CertSrv\CertEnroll by default.

> **TIP**   If these directories aren't available for some reason, you can create virtual directories that map aliases to their physical locations. At a command prompt, type certutil –vroot. The command-line utility Certutil creates the necessary virtual directories for you and maps them to their default locations.

Once you've configured Web-based access to Certificate Services, you can access these services by typing **http://*hostname*/certsrv/**, where *hostname* is the Domain Name System (DNS) or NetBIOS name of the host server, such as *ca.microsoft.com* or CASrvr. Figure 5-2 shows the main page for Certificate Services.

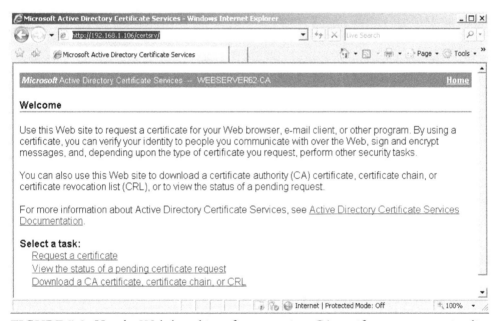

FIGURE 5-2   Use the Web-based interface to retrieve CA certificates or revocation lists, to request certificates, or to check on pending certificates.

Starting and Stopping Certificate Services

Active Directory Certificate Services runs as a Windows service on the certificate server. You can stop and start this service on a local system by completing the following steps:

1. In Administrative Tools, click Certification Authority to open the Certification Authority snap-in.
2. Right-click the root node for the CA, and then select All Tasks.
3. Select Stop Service to stop Certificate Services.
4. Select Start Service to start Certificate Services.

You can stop and start services on a remote system by completing the following steps:

1. In Administrative Tools, click Certification Authority to open the Certification Authority snap-in.
2. Right-click the Certification Authority node, and then on the shortcut menu, select Retarget Certification Authority. The Certification Authority dialog box appears.
3. Select Another Computer, type the name of the computer to which you want to connect, and then click Finish. You can also type the server's Internet Protocol (IP) address or fully qualified domain name (FQDN), or you can click Browse to search for the computer.
4. In the Certification Authority snap-in, right-click the root node for the CA, and then select All Tasks.
5. Select Stop Service to stop Certificate Services.
6. Select Start Service to start Certificate Services.

Backing Up and Restoring the CA

If your organization publishes its own CA, you should back up the CA information routinely. Backing up the CA information ensures that you can recover critical CA data, including:

- CA private key and certificate
- CA configuration information
- CA log and pending request queue

You can perform two types of backups through the Certification Authority snap-in:

- **Standard**   Creates a full copy of certificate database, logs, and pending request queues.
- **Incremental**   Creates a partial copy of certificate database, logs, and pending request queues. This copy contains only the changes since the last standard backup.

In a very large CA implementation, you can perform incremental backups of the database, logs, and queues by selecting Perform Incremental Backups. To use incremental backups, you must do the following:

1. First perform a standard backup.
2. Perform successive incremental backups at later dates.

When you use incremental backups, you must also restore incrementally. To do this, complete the following steps:

1. Stop Certificate Services.
2. Restore the last standard backup.
3. Restore each incremental backup in order.
4. Start Certificate Services.

Creating CA Backups

To back up the CA information on your certificate server, complete the following steps:

1. Create a folder that Certificate Services can use to store the backup information. This directory must be empty, and you should create it on the local machine where Certificate Services is installed.
2. Start the Certification Authority snap-in, right-click the root node for the CA, choose All Tasks, and then select Back Up CA. This starts the Certification Authority Backup Wizard.

> **NOTE**   Certificate Services must be running when you back up the CA. If the service isn't running, you'll see a prompt asking you if you want to start the service. Click OK.

3. Click Next, and then select the items you want to back up, as shown in Figure 5-3. The options are:

- Private Key And CA Certificate
- Certificate Database And Certificate Database Log

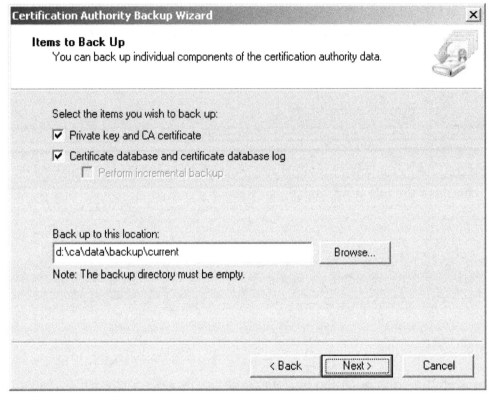

FIGURE 5-3 Specify the certification items that you want to back up.

4. If this is an incremental backup, select Perform Incremental Backup. Incremental backups can be performed only when backing up the certificate database and log.

5. In the Back Up To This Location field, type the file path to the backup folder, or click Browse to search for this folder. If you specify a folder that doesn't exist, you'll be given the option of creating it.

6. Click OK or Next. Type and then confirm a password that will be used to protect the private key and CA certificate files.

7. Click Next, and then click Finish. The wizard creates a backup of the selected data.

Recovering CA Information

If you ever need to recover the CA information, you can do this by completing the following steps:

1. The Certificate Services can't be running when you restore the CA. In the Certification Authority snap-in, right-click the root node for the CA, choose All Tasks, and then select Stop Service.

2. Right-click the root node a second time, choose All Tasks, and then select Restore CA. This starts the Certification Authority Restore Wizard.

3. Click Next, and then select the items you want to restore. The options are:

- Private Key And CA Certificate
- Certificate Database And Certificate Database Log

4. In the Restore From This Location field, type the file path to the backup folder, or click Browse to search for this folder. You should always restore the last complete backup before restoring any incremental backups.

5. Click Next. Type the password used to protect the CA files, and then click Next again.

6. Click Finish. The wizard restores the selected data and starts the Certificate Services service.

Configuring Certificate Request Processing

Unlike previous versions of Certificate Services, the version shipping with IIS is configured for autoenrollment by default. This means that authorized users can request a certificate, and the CA automatically processes the certificate request so that the user can immediately install the certificate.

If you want to view or change the default request processing policy, follow these steps:

1. In Administrative Tools, click Certification Authority to open the Certification Authority snap-in.

2. Right-click the CA node, and then select Properties. The Properties dialog box appears.

3. On the Policy Module tab, click Properties.

4. If you want to process requests manually, select "Set The Certificate Request Status To Pending. The Administrator Must Explicitly Issue The Certificate."

5. If you want the CA to process requests automatically, select Follow The Settings In The Certificate Template, If Applicable. Otherwise, Automatically Issue The Certificate.

6. Click OK twice.

Approving and Declining Pending Certificate Requests

If you've configured the CA so that certificates must be manually processed, you'll find that pending certificate requests are displayed in the Certification Authority snap-in's Pending Requests container.

You can approve pending requests by completing the following steps:

1. In Administrative Tools, click Certification Authority to open the Certification Authority snap-in.

2. Select the Pending Requests container. You will see a list of pending requests if there are any.

3. Right-click the request that you want to approve, choose All Tasks, and then select Issue.

4. Certificate Services generates a certificate based on the request and places this certificate in the Issued Certificates container.

5. Certificates are valid for one year. After this period they must be renewed.

You can decline pending certificate requests by doing the following:

1. In Administrative Tools, click Certification Authority to open the Certification Authority snap-in.

2. Select the Pending Requests container. You should see a list of pending requests.

3. Right-click the request that you want to decline, choose All Tasks, and then select Deny.

4. When prompted to confirm the action, select Yes.

> **CAUTION** Denied requests are moved to the Failed Requests container and can't be restored. The user must resubmit a new request.

Generating Certificates Manually in the Certification Authority Snap-In

Once you've issued a certificate, you can manually create the certificate file that you need to install. To do this, complete the following steps:

1. In Administrative Tools, click Certification Authority to open the Certification Authority snap-in.

2. Select the Issued Certificates container. You should see a list of certificates issued by this root CA, if any.

3. Right-click the certificate that you want to generate, and then select Open. The Certificate dialog box appears.

4. On the Details tab, select Copy To File. The Certificate Export Wizard opens. Click Next.

5. Select the Base-64 Encoded X.509 (.CER) export file format, and then click Next.

6. Specify the name of the file you want to export. Be sure to use .cer as the file extension. Click Browse if you want to use the Save As dialog box to set the file location and name.

7. Click Next, and then click Finish. After the Certificate Export Wizard confirms that the certificate was successfully exported, click OK. You can now install the certificate file as described in the "Processing Pending Requests and Installing Site Certificates" section of Chapter 6.

Revoking Certificates

Server certificates are valid for one year and can be revoked if necessary. Typically, you revoke a certificate when there's a change in the site's status or when the customer for whom you issued the certificate cancels the service subscription. To revoke a certificate, complete the following steps:

1. In Administrative Tools, click Certification Authority to open the Certification Authority snap-in.

2. Select the Issued Certificates container. You should see a list of issued certificates.

3. Right-click the certificate that you want to revoke, choose All Tasks, and then select Revoke Certificate. The Certificate Revocation dialog box appears.

4. In the Reason Code drop-down list, select a reason for the revocation, and then click Yes. The CA marks the certificate as revoked and moves it to the Revoked Certificates container.

By default, CAs publish CRLs weekly and CRL changes daily. You can change this setting through the Revoked Certificates Properties dialog box by performing the following steps:

1. In Administrative Tools, click Certification Authority to open the Certification Authority snap-in.

2. Right-click the Revoked Certificates container, select Properties, and then in the CRL Publication Interval fields, set a new interval for publishing the CRL and CRL changes. Then click OK.

Reviewing and Renewing the Root CA Certificate

The root CA certificate is valid for the period that was specified when the certificate was created. To view the expiration date or to review the certificate properties, complete the following steps:

1. In Administrative Tools, click Certification Authority to open the Certification Authority snap-in.

2. Right-click the root node for the CA, and then select Properties. This displays the Root CA Properties dialog box.

3. On the General tab, click View Certificate.

4. Use the Certificate dialog box to review the root CA certificate's properties, including the valid from and to dates.

The root CA certificate is usually valid for five years. If you're approaching the end of the five-year period, you should renew the certificate. You should also renew the root CA certificate if one of the following situations exists:

- The signing key is compromised.
- A program requires a new signing key to be used with a new certificate.
- The current CRL is too big and you want to move some of the information to a new CRL.

When you renew the root CA certificate, you can generate new public and private keys. Do this if the key has been compromised or a new key is required.

To renew the root CA certificate, complete the following steps:

1. Log on locally to the CA server.
2. Right-click the root node for the CA again, choose All Tasks, and then select Renew CA Certificate.
3. If prompted to stop Certificate Services, click Yes. Certificate Services can't be running when you renew the CA. The Renew CA Certificate dialog box appears.
4. In the Renew CA Certificate dialog box, select Yes if you want to generate a new public and private key pair. Otherwise, select No.
5. Click OK. Certificate Services is restarted automatically and a new certificate is issued.

Chapter 6. Managing Certificates and SSL

Web servers and clients can use SSL certificates to provide proof of identity prior to establishing secure connections. Once secure connections are established, web servers and client use the secure channel to transfer encrypted information. Generally, certificates used by IIS and browser clients conform to the X.509 standard.

Creating and Installing Certificates

You have two options for creating and installing certificates. You can use your own Certificate Services to generate your certificates, or you can use a trusted third-party authority. When you use Certificate Services, you manage the certificate creation, expiration, and revocation process. When you create certificates through trusted third-party authorities, you let the trusted authority manage the certificate creation, expiration, and revocation process. Either way, the basic tasks you need to perform to create and install a certificate are as follows:

1. Create a certificate request.
2. Submit the request to the authority of your choice or to your own root authority.
3. When you receive the response from the authority, process the pending request and install the certificate.
4. Ensure that SSL is enabled and that secure communications are configured properly.

Creating Certificate Requests

Each Web site hosted on your Web server needs a separate certificate if you want SSL to work properly. The first step in the certificate creation process is to generate a certificate request.

You can generate a self-signed certificate request by following these steps:

1. In IIS Manager, select the server node, and then double-click the Server Certificates feature.

2. On the Server Certificates page, you'll see a list of certificates that the Web server can use. In the Actions pane, click Create Self-Signed Certificate.

3. In the Specify Friendly Name dialog box, type a friendly name for the certificate, such as Default Web Site, and then click OK to create the self-signed certificate.

You can generate a certificate request to submit to CAs by completing the following steps:

1. In IIS Manager, select the server node, and then double-click the Server Certificates feature.

2. On the Server Certificates page, you'll see a list of certificates that the Web server can use. In the Actions pane, click Create Certificate Request.

3. Set the following properties as shown in Figure 6-1:

- **Common Name** Sets your Web site's common name. When the certificate is used on an intranet (or internal network), the common name may be one word, and it can also be the server's NetBIOS name, such as CorpIntranet. When the certificate will be used on the Internet, the common name must be a valid DNS name, such as *www.microsoft.com*.
- **Organization** Sets your company's legal name, such as Microsoft Corporation.
- **Organizational Unit** Sets the division in your company responsible for the certificate, such as Technology Department.

> **NOTE** Third-party authorities will use the organization name, the site's common name, and the geographical information you supply to validate your request for a certificate. If you don't type this information correctly, you won't be issued a certificate.

- **City/Locality** Type the city or locality in which your company is located.
- **State/Province** Type the full name of the state or province in which your company is located.
- **Country/Region** Select the country or region for your company.

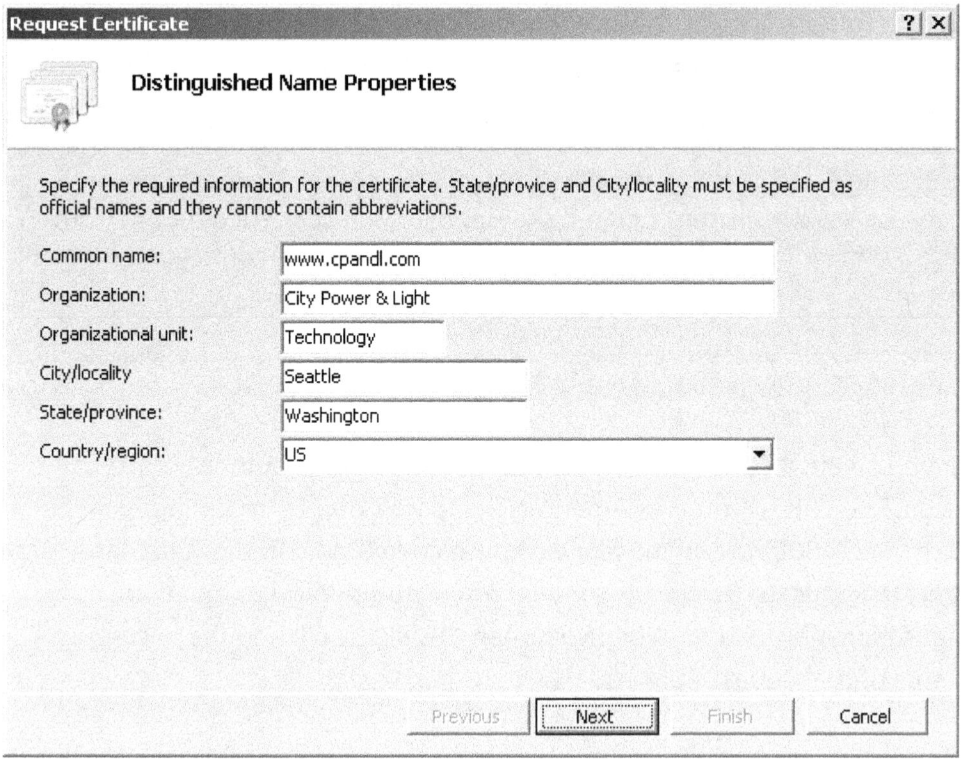

FIGURE 6-1 Specify the name properties for the certificate.

> **CAUTION** Don't use abbreviations when typing geographic data. Some authorities won't accept abbreviated geographic information, and you'll have to resubmit your request.

4. Click Next.

5. Use the options on the Cryptographic Service Provider Properties page to select a cryptographic provider, hash algorithm, and bit length for the certificate's private key. Ensure that your selections are appropriate for the certificate's intended use. If you are unsure, accept the default settings. Click Next when you are ready to continue.

6. You need to specify the file name and path for the certificate request file, such as C:\certreq.txt. Type a new path, or click the selection button to select a path and file name in the Specify Save As File Name dialog box.

7. Click Finish to complete the request generation process.

> **REAL WORLD** The common name is typically composed of *Host + Domain Name*, such as *www.microsoft.com* or *products.microsoft.com*.

Certificates are specific to the common name that they have been issued to at the Host level. The common name must be the same as the Web address you'll be accessing when connecting to a secure site. For example, a certificate for the domain *microsoft.com* will receive a warning if accessing a site named *www.microsoft.com* or *services.microsoft.com* because *www.microsoft.com* and *services.microsoft.com* are different from *microsoft.com*. You'd need to create a certificate for the correct common name.

Submitting Certificate Requests to Third-Party Authorities

After you create a CSR, you can submit it to a third-party authority such as Verisign. The CSR is stored as American Standard Code of Information Interchange (ASCII) text in the file you specified in Step 6 in the "Creating Certificate Requests" section. It contains your site's public key and your identification information. When you open this file, you'll find the encrypted contents of the request, such as:

```
--BEGIN NEW CERTIFICATE REQUEST--
MIXCCDCCAnECAQAwczERMA8GA1UEAxMIZW5nc3ZyMDExEzARBgNVBAsTClRlY2hu
b2xvZ3kxEzARBgNVBAoTCkRvbWFpbi5Db20xEjAQBgNVBAcTCVZhbmNvdXZlcjET
MBEGA3UECBMKV2FzaGluZ3RvbjELMAkGA1UEBhMCVVMwgZ8wDQYJKoZIhvcNAQEB
BQADgY0AMIGJAoGBALElbrvIZNRB+gvkdcf9b7tNns24hB2Jgp5BhKi4NXc/twR7
C+GuDnyTqRs+C2AnNHgb9oQkpivqQNKh2+N18bKU3PEZUzXH0pxxjhaiT8aMFJhi
3bFvD+gTCQrw5BWoV9/Ff5Ud3EF5TRQ2WJZ+JluQQewo/mXv5ZnbHsM+aLy3AgMB
AAGgggFTMBoGCisGAQQBgjcNAgMxDBYKNS4wLjIxOTUuMjA1BgorBgEEAYI3AgEO
MScwJTAOBgNVHQ8BAf8EBAMCBPAwEwYDVR0lBAwwCgYIKwYWWQUHAwEwgf0GCisG
AQQBgjcNAgIxge4wgesCAQEeWgBNAGkAYwByAG8AcwBvAGYAdAAgAFIAUwBBACAA
UwBDAGgAYQBuAG4AZQBsACAAQwByAHkAcAB0AG8AZwByAGEAcABoAGkAYwAgAFAA
cgBvAHYAaQBkAGUAcgDObiQBfE24DPqBwFplR15/xZDY8Cugoxbyymtwq/tAPZ6dz
Pr9Zy3MNnkKQbKcsbLR/4t9/tWJIMmrFhZonrx12qBfICoiKUXreSK89OILrLEto
1frm/dycoXHhStSsZdm25vszv827FKKk5bRW/vIIeBqfKnEPJHOnoiG6UScvgA8Q
fgAAAAAVVAAAMA0GCSqGSIb3DQEBBQUAA4GBAFZc6K4S04BMUnR/8Ow3J/MS3TYi
HAvFuxnjGOCefTq8Sakzvq+uazUO3waBqHxZ1f32qGr7karoD+fq8dX27nmh0zpp
RzlDXrxR35mMC/yP/fpLmLb5lsxOt1379PdS4trvWUFkfY93/CkUi+nrQt/uZHY3
NOSThxf73VkfbsE3
--END NEW CERTIFICATE REQUEST--
```

Most CAs require you to submit the certificate request as part of a formal site registration process. In this registration process you'll be asked to submit the request file in an e-mail message or through an online form. When using e-mail, you simply attach the request file to the message and send it. When using an online form, you can copy the entire text of the request—including the BEGIN and END statements—to the clipboard and paste this into the online form. You can use Microsoft Notepad to do this. Or you might be able to browse for the file to insert and let the server paste the data into the form for you.

After the CA reviews your certificate request, the CA either approves or declines it. If the CA approves the request, you'll receive an e-mail message with the signed certificate attached or a notice to visit a location where you can retrieve the signed certificate. The certificate is an ASCII text file that you can view in Notepad, and it can be decrypted only with the private key you generated previously. As before, the contents of the file are encrypted and include BEGIN and END statements, as in this example:

```
--BEGIN CERTIFICATE--
MXXCWjCCAgQCEDlpyIenknxBt43eUZ7JF9YwDQYJK oZIhvcNAQEEBQAwgakxFjAU
BgNERAoTDVZlcmlTaWduLCBJbmMxRzBFBgNVBAsTP nd3dy52ZXJppc2lnbi5jb20v
cmVwb3NpdG9yeS9UZXN0Q1BTIEluY29ycC4gQnkgU mVmLiBMaWFiLiBMVEQuMUYw
RAYDVQQLEz1G45IgVmVyaVNpZ24gYXV0aG9yaXplZ CB0ZXN0aW5nIG9ubHkuIeev
IGFzc3VyYW5jZXMgKEM345MxOTk3MB4XDTAwMTEwN zAwMDAwMFoXDTAwMTEyMTIz
NTk1OVowczELMAkGA1UEBhMCVVMxEzARBgNVBAgTC ldhc2hpbmd0b24xEjAQBgNV
BAcUCVZhbmNvdXZlcjETMBEGA1UEChQKRG9tYWluL kNvbTETMBEGA1UECxQKVGVj
aG5vbG9neTERMA8GA1UEAxQIZW5nc3ZyQWEwgZ8wD QYJKoZIhvcNAQEBBQADgY0A
MIGJAoGBALElbrvIZNRB+gvkdcf9b7tNns24hB2Jgp5BhKi4NXc/ twR7C+GuDnyT
qRs+C2AnNHgb9oQkpivqQNKh2+N18bKU3PEZUzXH0 prtyhaiT8aMFJhi3bFvD+gT
CQrw5BWoV9/Ff5Ud3EF5TRQ2WJZ+JluQQewo/ mXnTZnbHsM+aLy3AgMBAAEwDQYJ
KoZIhvcNAQEEBQADQQCQIrhq5UmsPYzwzKVHIiLDD nkYunbhUpSNaBfUSYdvlAU1
Ic/37OrdN/E1ZmOut0MbCWIXKr0Jk5q8F6Tlbqwe
--END CERTIFICATE—
```

Save the certificate file to a location that you can access when using IIS Manager. You should use .cer as the file extension. Then process and install the certificate as described in the "Processing Pending Requests and Installing Site Certificates" section of this chapter.

Submitting Certificate Requests to Certificate Services

After you create a CSR, you can submit it to Active Directory Certificate Services by using the Web-based interface. To do this, complete the following steps:

1. The CSR is stored as ASCII text in the file you specified in Step 6 in the "Creating Certificate Requests" section. Open this file in Notepad and copy the entire text of the request, including the BEGIN and END statements, to the clipboard (press Ctrl+A and then press Ctrl+C).

2. You're now ready to submit the request to Certificate Services. Start your Web browser, and then type in the Certificate Services URL, such as ***http://ca.microsoft.com/certsrv/***. You should see the main page for Certificate Services. If you don't, you might not have configured Web access correctly.

3. Select Request A Certificate.

4. On the Request A Certificate page, select Advanced Certificate Request.

5. Select Submit A Certificate Request Using A Base-64-Encoded … Request. This option tells Certificate Services that you're going to submit a request that's Base64-encoded.

6. Paste the request into the Saved Request field (press Ctrl+V).

7. Click Submit. If you've completed this process correctly, the final page shows you that your request has been received and is pending approval by the CA. If there's a problem with the request, you'll see an error page telling you to contact your administrator for further assistance. On the error page you can click Details to get more information on the error. You might need to re-create the certificate request or go back to ensure that you haven't accidentally inserted additional spacing or characters in the request submission.

8. If you're also the CA, you can use the Certification Authority snap-in to handle the request. See the "Approving and Declining Pending Certificate Requests" section of Chapter 5.

Once the request has been approved, use the Web-based interface to retrieve the signed certificate. To do this, complete the following steps:

1. Start your Web browser, and then type in the Certificate Services URL, such as ***http://ca.microsoft.com/certsrv/***.

2. Click View The Status Of A Pending Certificate Request.

3. You should see a list of pending requests. Requests are listed with a description and a date/time stamp. Click the request for the site you want to work with.

> **NOTE** If you can't access the certificate file online, you can have the certificate administrator generate the certificate manually. See the "Generating Certificates Manually in the Certification Authority Snap-In" section of Chapter 5.

4. If a certificate has been issued for the request, you should see a page stating that the certificate you requested was issued to you. On this page, select Base 64 Encoded, and then click Download Certificate.

5. You should see a File Download dialog box. Click Save.

6. Use the Save As dialog box to select a save location for the certificate file, click Save, then Close. You should use .cer as the file extension. Then process and install the certificate as described in the section "Processing Pending Requests and Installing Site Certificates," immediately following.

> **TIP** The default save location is the Downloads subfolder in your user data folder. I recommend placing all certificate files and requests in a common folder on the Web server's local file system. You should safeguard this folder so that only administrators have access.

Processing Pending Requests and Installing Site Certificates

Once you receive the certificate back from the authority, you can install it by completing the following steps:

1. In IIS Manager, select the server node, and then double-click the Server Certificates feature.

2. On the Server Certificates page, you'll see a list of certificates that the Web server can use. In the Actions pane, click Complete Certificate Request.

3. Type the path and file name to the certificate file returned by the authority, or click the selection button to search for the file.

4. Type a friendly name for the certificate, such as Default Web Site.

5. Click OK. Check the SSL configuration, and manage the certificate as necessary.

Working with SSL

Installing a site certificate automatically enables SSL so that it can be used, but you might need to change the default settings. You'll need to configure and troubleshoot SSL as necessary.

Configuring SSL Ports

Once you install a certificate on a Web site, you can use a site's bindings to change the SSL port the site uses. To add a binding for SSL, follow these steps:

1. In IIS Manager, navigate to the Sites node by double-clicking the icon for the computer you want to work with, and then double-clicking Sites.
2. In the left pane, select the node for the site you want to work with.
3. In the Actions pane, click Bindings. In the Site Bindings dialog box, you'll see a list of the site's current bindings.
4. Click Add. In the Add Site Binding dialog box, select HTTPS as the Type.
5. Port 443 is used for SSL by default. As necessary, change the port value in the appropriate text box.
6. On the SSL Certificate list, select the SSL certificate the site should use. Click OK, and then click Close.

Chapter 6, "Configuring Web Sites and Directories," in *Web Server Administration: The Personal Trainer* provides a more detailed discussion about site bindings. A site can have multiple SSL identities (meaning that the site can answer on different SSL ports). The SSL port configured in the Web Site tab is the one the site responds to by default. All other SSL ports must be specified in the browser request. For example, if you configure SSL for ports 443, 444, and 445, a request for *https://yoursite/* is handled by port 443 automatically, but you must specify the other ports to use them, such as *https://yoursite:445/*.

Adding the CA Certificate to the Client Browser's Root Store

Most root CA certificates issued by third-party CAs are configured as trusted CAs in Web browsers. However, if you're acting as your own CA or are using a self-signed certificate, client browsers won't recognize and trust your certificate. To get browsers to trust the certificate, the user must install the certificate in the browser's authorities store.

To install the certificate, complete the following steps:

1. Connect to your site by using a secure URL that begins with *https://*.

2. The user's browser displays a security alert stating that there's a problem with the site's security certificate.

3. On the Certificate Error page, click the Continue To This Web Site link. The alert appears because the user hasn't chosen to trust your root CA or you are using a self-signed certificate.

4. When you continue to the site, a Certificate Error option appears to the right of the address field (see Figure 6-2). Click Certificate Error to display a related error dialog box, and then click View Certificates. The Certificate dialog box appears.

5. The General tab information should state that the CA Root certificate isn't trusted. To enable trust, click Install Certificate.

FIGURE 6-2 Note the certificate error that is being highlighted by Internet Explorer.

6. This starts the Certificate Import Wizard. Click Next.

7. Choose Automatically Select The Certificate Store Based On The Type Of Certificate, and then click Next.

8. Click Finish. The default settings allow the browser to select the certificate store based on the type of certificate.

9. Click OK in response to the successful import message that appears, and then click OK to close the Certificate dialog box. The user shouldn't see the original security alert again.

Confirming that SSL Is Correctly Enabled

Secure connections can be established only when the browser connects to the server by using a secure URL beginning with *https://*. Browsers display a warning if any embedded content (such as images) on a secure Web page are retrieved using an insecure (*http://*) connection. This warning tells users that some of the content on the page is insecure and asks them if they want to continue.

Once you've enabled SSL on your server, you should confirm that SSL is working and that the encryption level is set properly. To confirm that SSL is working in Internet Explorer, complete these steps:

1. Access your Web site by using a secure URL beginning with *https://*. In Internet Explorer 7 or later, the background of address bar turns green and a padlock icon appears to the right of the address bar to indicate that an SSL session has been established. If this does not happen, the SSL session wasn't established.

2. Right-click anywhere on the Web page, and then select Properties. This displays a Properties dialog box, which provides summary information on the Web page.

3. Click Certificates, and then on the Details tab, scroll down to display details concerning the certificates and the level of encryption used.

Resolving SSL Problems

If SSL isn't working, ensure that you've installed the server certificate on the correct Web site and that you've enabled SSL on the site. These steps should resolve a server-based SSL problem.

If the encryption level isn't what you expected, you should check to ensure that the browser supports the encryption level you're using. If a browser supports

256-bit encryption and the encryption level in use according to the browser's Properties dialog box is 128-bit, the problem is the server certificate. The server certificate must be upgraded to 256-bit encryption.

In Internet Explorer, check encryption support by completing the following steps:

1. On the Help menu, select About Internet Explorer.
2. The Cipher Strength field shows the level of encryption supported. You must have 256-bit support to establish a 256-bit session. After viewing the encryption level, click OK.
3. On the Tools menu, select Internet Options. In the Internet Options dialog box, select the Advanced tab.
4. Scroll down through the Advanced options until you see the Security heading. Ensure that Use SSL 3.0 is selected, and then click OK.

Ignoring, Accepting, and Requiring Client Certificates

Client certificates allow users to authenticate themselves through their Web browser. You might want to use client certificates if you have a secure external Web site, such as an extranet. If a Web site accepts or requires client certificates, you can configure client certificate mappings that permit access control to resources based on client certificates. A client certificate mapping can be mapped to a specific Windows account using a one-to-one mapping, or it can be mapped based on rules you specify.

By default, IIS doesn't accept or require client certificates. You can change this behavior. Keep in mind that *accepting* client certificates isn't the same as *requiring* client certificates. When a site requires client certificates, the site is secured for access using SSL only and can't be accessed using standard HTTP. When a site accepts client certificates rather than requiring them, the site can use either HTTP or Hypertext Transfer Protocol Secure (HTTPS) for communications.

To configure client certificate usage, follow these steps:

1. In IIS Manager, select the Web site you want to manage, and then double-click the SSL Settings feature.

2. If you want to require SSL (and preclude the use of insecure communications), select Require SSL. Optionally, you can also select Require 128-Bit SSL if your server has a 128-bit encryption installed and enabled.

3. Under Client Certificates, select the Ignore, Accept, or Require option as necessary, and then click Apply to save your settings.

> **NOTE** You can require client certificates only when secure SSL communications are also required. Because of this, you must select the Require SSL check box when you want to require client certificates. If you want to map client certificates to Windows user accounts, enable Active Directory Client Certificate Authentication at the server level.

Requiring SSL for All Communications

In some cases you'll want to create sites that can be accessed using only secure communications. You can do this by requiring SSL and prohibiting the use of insecure communications. To require SSL for communications with a Web site, follow these steps:

1. In IIS Manager, select the Web site you want to manage, and then double-click the SSL Settings feature.

2. If you want to require SSL (and preclude the use of insecure communications), select Require SSL. Optionally, you can also select Require 128-Bit if your server has a 128-bit encryption installed and enabled. Click Apply to save your settings.

Chapter 7. Performance Tuning, Monitoring, and Tracing

Monitoring, performance tuning, and tracing are essential parts of Web administration. You monitor servers to ensure that they're running smoothly and to troubleshoot problems as they occur. You tune the performance of servers to achieve optimal performance based on the current system resources and traffic load. When you have problems that cannot be resolved by performance tuning or diagnosed through standard monitoring, you can use tracing to get detailed diagnostic information about failed requests that allows you to track a request from its start, through individual filter and module notifications, to its end. With the addition of performance statistics, authentication and authorization details, and internal tracing of Microsoft ASP.NET pages, failed request tracing is the definitive power tool for determining the exact cause of request failure whether you are developing or deploying new applications, Web pages, or Web sites.

Monitoring IIS Performance and Activity

Windows Server 2008 and Windows Server 2008 R2 include several tools that you can use to monitor Internet Information Services (IIS). The key tools are the Performance Monitor, Reliability Monitor, Microsoft Windows event logs, and the IIS access logs. You'll often use the results of your monitoring to optimize IIS. Monitoring IIS isn't something you should do haphazardly. You need to have a clear plan—a set of goals that you hope to achieve. Let's look at some reasons that you might want to monitor IIS and the tools you can use to do this.

Why Monitor IIS?

Troubleshooting performance problems is a key reason for monitoring. For example, users might be having problems connecting to the server, and you might want to monitor the server to troubleshoot these problems. Here, your goals would be to track down the problem by using the available monitoring resources and then to solve it.

Another common reason for wanting to monitor IIS is to use the results to improve server performance. Improving server performance can reduce the need for costly additional servers or additional hardware components, such as CPUs and memory. This allows you to squeeze additional processing power out of the server and budget for when you really must purchase new servers and components.

To achieve optimal performance, you must identify performance bottlenecks, maximize throughput, and minimize the time it takes for Web applications to process user requests. You achieve this by:

- Monitoring memory and CPU usage and taking appropriate steps to reduce the load on the server, as necessary. Other processes running on the server might be using memory and CPU resources needed by IIS. Resolve this issue by stopping nonessential services and moving support applications to a different server.
- Resolving hardware issues that might be causing problems. If slow disk drives are delaying file reads, work on improving disk input/output (I/O). If the network cards are running at full capacity, install additional network cards for performing activities such as backups or load balancing.
- Optimizing Web pages and applications running on IIS. You should test Web pages and IIS applications to ensure that the source code performs as expected. Eliminate unnecessary procedures and optimize inefficient processes.

Unfortunately, there are often tradeoffs to be made when it comes to resource usage. For example, as the number of users accessing IIS grows, you might not be able to reduce the network traffic load, but you might be able to improve server performance by optimizing Web pages and IIS applications.

> **TIP** Don't overlook the value of IIS failed request tracing in your optimization efforts for dynamic pages. In a failed request trace, the Performance View shows the exact duration of each step in the request handling process, and other views can also provide important clues about processing delays.

Getting Ready to Monitor

Before you start monitoring IIS, you should establish baseline performance metrics for your server. To do this, measure server performance at various times and under different load conditions. You can then compare the baseline performance with subsequent performance to determine how IIS is performing. Performance metrics that are well above the baseline measurements might indicate areas where the server needs to be optimized or reconfigured.

After you establish the baseline metrics, you should formulate a monitoring plan. A comprehensive monitoring plan involves the following steps:

1. Determine which server resources should be monitored to help you accomplish your goal.
2. Set filters to reduce the amount of information collected.
3. Configure performance counters to measure the resource usage.
4. Log the usage data so that it can be analyzed.
5. Analyze the usage data and replay the data as necessary to find a solution.

These procedures are examined later in this chapter in the "Monitoring IIS Performance and Reliability" section. Although in most cases you should develop a monitoring plan, there are times when you might not want to go through all these steps to monitor IIS. In this case, use the steps that make sense for your situation.

The primary tools you'll use to monitor IIS are:

- **Windows Performance Monitor**   Configure counters to watch resource usage over time. Use the usage information to gauge the performance of IIS and determine areas that can be optimized.
- **Windows Reliability Monitor**   Tracks changes to the system and compares them to changes in system stability, thus giving you a graphical representation of the relationship between changes in the system configuration and changes in system stability.
- **IIS Access logs**   Use information in the access logs to find problems with pages, applications, and IIS. Entries logged with a status code beginning

with a 4 or 5 indicate a potential problem. Access logs can be written in several different formats, including IIS log file format, National Center for Supercomputing Applications (NCSA) Common Log File Format, and World Wide Web Consortium (W3C) Extended Log File Format.

- **Windows Event logs** Use information in the event logs to troubleshoot system-wide problems, including those from the operating system, IIS, and other configured applications. The primary logs you'll want to work with are the System, Security, and Application event logs.

Detecting and Resolving IIS Errors

IIS records errors in three locations: the IIS access logs, the Windows event logs, and the failed request trace logs. In the access logs, you'll find information related to missing resources, failed authentication, and internal server errors. In the event logs, you'll find IIS errors, failed authentication, IIS application errors, and errors related to other applications running on the server. In the failed request trace logs, you'll find detailed diagnostic traces of specific types of failed requests.

Examining the Access Logs

Access logs are created when you enable logging as discussed in Chapter 9 of *Web Server Administration: The Personal Trainer*. Every time someone requests a file from a site, an entry goes into the access log, making the access log a running history of resource requests. Because each entry has a status code, you can examine entries to determine the success or failure of a request. Failed requests have a status code beginning with a 4 or 5.

The most common error you'll see is a 404 error, which indicates that a resource wasn't found at the expected location. You can correct this problem by:

- Placing the file in the expected location.
- Renaming the file if the current name is different than expected.
- Modifying the linking file to reflect the file's correct name and location.

If you want to find the access log for a particular site, select the node for the server you want to manage in IIS Manager. If the server you want to use isn't listed, connect to it. In the main pane, the Logging feature is listed under IIS when you group by area. Double-click Logging to open this feature. You should now see the current top-level logging configuration.

The Directory field shows the base directory for this site's access logs. The default base directory is *%SystemDrive%*\Inetpub\Logs\LogFiles. You'll find the site's logs in a subdirectory of the base directory. Typically, subdirectories for sites are named W3SVC*N* where *N* is the index number of the service or a random tracking value. An example of such a subdirectory name is W3CSVC1.

The current log is the file in this subdirectory with the most recent date and time stamp. All other logs are archive files that could be moved to a history directory.

Now that you know where the log files are located for the site, you can search for errors in the log file. Because logs are stored as either American Standard Code of Information Interchange (ASCII) text or Unicode Transformation Format 8 (UTF-8), one way to do this would be to open a log in Microsoft Notepad or another text editor and search for error codes, such as 404. Another way to search for errors would be to use the FIND command from a command-prompt window to search the log files. At an elevated command prompt, you could search for 404 errors in any log file within the current directory by using the following command:

```
find "404" *
```

Once you identify missing files, you can use any of the previously recommended techniques to resolve the problem.

> **NOTE** I use the term *elevated command prompt* to refer to a command prompt being run with administrator credentials. To run a command prompt as an administrator, click Start, point to All Programs and then Accessories, right-click Command Prompt, and then select Run As Administrator. When prompted, provide consent for elevation by clicking Continue or providing the appropriate administrator credentials. Then click OK.

Examining the Windows Event Logs

Windows event logs provide historical information that can help you track down problems with services, processes, and applications. The Windows Event Log service controls the events that are tracked. When this service is started, user actions and resource usage events can be tracked through the event logs. Two general types of log files are used:

- **Windows logs** Logs that the operating system uses to record general system events related to applications, security, setup, and system components
- **Application and service logs** Logs that specific applications and services use to record application-specific or service-specific events

You access the Windows event logs by completing the following steps:

1. Click Start, point to Administrative Tools, and then select Event Viewer. This starts Event Viewer.

2. As shown in Figure 7-1, Event Viewer displays logs for the local computer by default. If you want to view logs on a remote computer, right-click Event Viewer in the console tree (left pane), and then select Connect To Another Computer. In the Select Computer dialog box, type the name of the computer you want to access, and then click OK.

> **TIP** You can connect to another server also by using alternate credentials. To do this, select the Connect As Another User check box, and then click Set User. After you select or type the account name to use in the form *DOMAIN\UserName*, such as CPANLD\WilliamS, type the account password, and then click OK.

3. You can now work with the server's event logs in the following ways:

- To view all errors and warnings for all logs, expand Custom Views, and then select Administrative Events. In the main pane you should now see a list of all warning and error events for the server.
- To view all errors and warnings for a specific server role, expand Custom Views, expand ServerRoles, and then select the role to view. In the main pane you should now see a list of all warning and error events for the selected role.

- To view events in a specific log, expand the Windows Logs node, the Applications And Services Logs node, or both nodes. Select the log you want to view, such as Application or System.

4. Use the information in the Source column to determine which service or process logged a particular event.

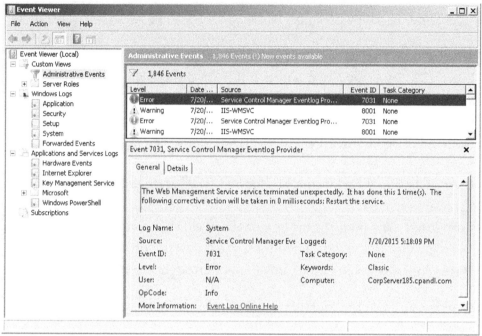

FIGURE 7-1 Event Viewer displays events according to their source.

Entries in the main pane of Event Viewer provide a quick overview of when, where, and how an event occurred. To obtain detailed information on an event, review the details provided on the General tab in the lower portion of the main window. The event level or keyword precedes the date and time of the event. Event levels include:

- **Information** An informational event, which is generally related to a successful action.
- **Audit Success** An event related to the successful execution of an action.
- **Audit Failure** An event related to the failed execution of an action.
- **Warning** A warning. Details for warnings are often useful in preventing future system problems.

- **Error**   An error, such as the failure of a service to start.

> **NOTE**   Warnings and errors are the two key types of events that you'll want to examine closely. Whenever these types of events occur and you're unsure of the cause, review the detailed event description.

In addition to level, date, and time logged, the summary and detailed event entries provide the following information:

- **Source**   The application, service, or component that logged the event
- **Event ID**   Generally a numeric identifier for the specific event, which could be helpful when searching knowledge bases
- **Task Category**   The category of the event, which is almost always set to None but is sometimes used to further describe the related action, such as a process or a service
- **User**   The user account that was logged on when the event occurred, if applicable
- **Computer**   The name of the computer on which the event occurred
- **Description**   In the detailed entries, a text description of the event
- **Data**   In the detailed entries, any data or error code output by the event

The sources you'll want to look for include those summarized in Table 7-1.

TABLE 7-1 Key Event Sources for Tracking IIS Issues

.NET Runtime	Microsoft .NET Framework service
.NET Runtime Optimization Service	Microsoft .NET Framework optimization processes
Active Server Pages (ASP)	Applications and ASP engines
ASP.NET	ASP.NET State Service and other ASP.NET processes
CertificateServicesClient	Authorization and authentication through the Certificate Services client
CertificationAuthority	Certificate Authorities (CAs)
Hostable Web Core	Web Management Service
IISADMIN	IIS Admin Service

IIS-IISManager	Management and configuration processes performed in IIS Manager
IISInfoCtrs	IIS information counters
IIS-W3SVC-PerfCounters	World Wide Web Service performance counters
IIS-W3SVC-WP	World Wide Web Service worker processes
MSDTC	Microsoft Distributed Transaction Coordinator service
MSDTC Client	Client processes when using MS DTC

If you want to see a particular type of event, you can filter the log by completing the following steps:

1. In Event Viewer, select the log you want to work with.

2. In the Actions pane or on the Action menu, click Filter Current Log. This opens the dialog box shown in Figure 7-2.

3. From the Logged drop-down list, select the included time frame for logged events. You can choose to include events from the Last Hour, Last 12 Hours, Last 24 Hours, Last 7 Days, or Last 30 Days.

4. Select the desired Event Level check boxes to specify the level of events to include. Select Verbose to get additional detail.

5. From the Event Source drop-down list, select the event sources to include, such as .NET Runtime and Active Server Pages, and then click OK.

6. You should now see a filtered list of events. Review these events carefully and take steps to correct any problems that exist. To clear the filter and see all events for the log, in the Actions pane, click Clear Filter.

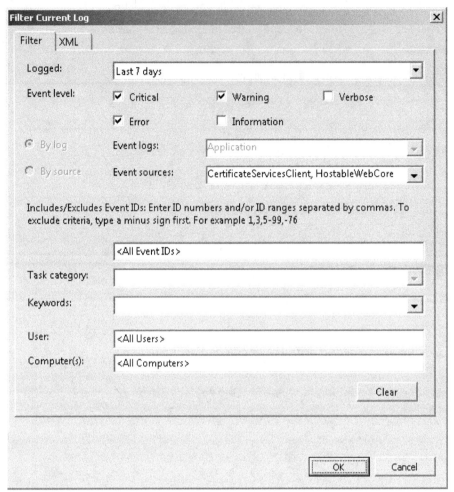

FIGURE 7-2 You can filter logs so that only specific events are displayed.

Examining the Trace Logs

Trace logs allow you to track a failed request from its start, through internal IIS notifications and authentication requests, to its end. Because tracing failed requests can degrade a server's performance, you should enable failed request tracing only when you need to perform detailed diagnostics for troubleshooting. Once you've diagnosed an issue, you should then disable failed request tracing.

Tracing Failed Requests

Failed request tracing is designed to help administrators and developers more easily identify and track failed requests. In previous versions of IIS, you could check for certain HTTP error codes in the IIS logs to identify failed requests, but you could not easily get detailed trace information that would help resolve related issues. With IIS 7.0 and IIS 7.5, request traces can be logged automatically when an error code is generated or when the time taken for a request exceeds a specified duration. For general tracing for debugging or other purposes, you can also configure general tracing on a per-URL basis.

To perform traces, the HTTP Tracing role service must be installed and enabled on the IIS server. Although you can configure the types of failed requests to trace globally for all Web sites and applications on a server, you enable and configure failed request tracing at the site level. Unlike other types of logging, each failed request is stored in a separate file in the logging directory.

Because trace files are named sequentially, starting with FR000001.xml, the file for the most recent failed request is the one with the highest numeric suffix and the most recent date and time stamp. Also in the trace directory is an XSL style sheet (FREB.xsl) that specifies the formatting for trace files when displayed in a Web browser, such as Internet Explorer.

You control the way tracing works by instituting Failed Request Tracing Rules. In IIS Manager, you can view the currently configured trace rules for a server, site, virtual directory, or application by selecting the node for the level you want to manage and then in the main pane, double-clicking Failed Request Tracing Rules. When you are working with failed request tracing rules, as shown in Figure 7-3, rules listed as Local are created at the level you selected. Rules listed as Inherited are created at a higher level.

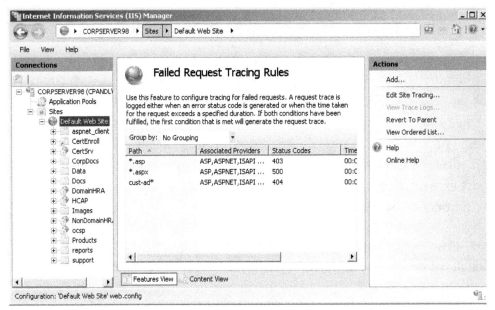

FIGURE 7-3 You can review the currently configured trace rules by using the Failed Request Tracing feature.

IIS traces a request whenever the trace rule criteria are reached. With each trace rule, you must specify precisely the types of failures to track according to the following criteria:

- **Path**   The URL path to trace, which can contain one wildcard at most and must be within the context of the level at which the definition is enabled. For example, you could use the path *.aspx to trace failed requests for ASP.NET pages, or you could use the path page* to trace failed requests for any type of document whose name begins with page, such as page1.asp, paged.aspx, or pages.htm.
- **Condition**   The conditions under which a request should be traced, including event severity (Error, Critical Error, or Warning), HTTP status code, and Time Taken. For general tracing, you can also trace information and other non-error events.
- **Trace Provider**   The functional area for tracing according to the provider that traces a request, including ASP, ASP.NET, ISAPI extension, and WWW server.

Failed requests can be traced through one or more of the following providers:

- **ASP**   Traces the failed request through Active Server Pages (*%Windir%*\System32\Inetsrv\Asp.dll). Use this provider when you want to trace the start and completion of ASP requests.
- **ASP.NET**   Traces the failed request through ASP.NET (*%SystemRoot%*\Microsoft.NET\Framework\v2.0.50727\Aspnet_isapi.dll or *%SystemRoot%*\Microsoft.NET\Framework\v2.0.50727\Webengine.dll). Use this provider when you want to see transitions into and out of managed code. This includes requests for .aspx pages and any other request processed through managed modules, such as forms-based authentication for static content.
- **ISAPI Extension**   Traces the failed request through ISAPI extension for ASP.NET (*%SystemRoot%*\Microsoft.NET\Framework\v2.0.50727\Aspnet_filter.dll). Use this provider when you want to trace the transition of a request into and out of an ISAPI extension process.
- **WWW Server**   Traces the failed request through the IIS server core. Use this provider when you want to trace requests through IIS worker processes.

When you specify a provider to use, you can set the tracking verbosity as:

- **General**   Trace general information about a request.
- **Critical Errors**   Trace critical errors related to a request.
- **Errors**   Trace standard errors related to a request.
- **Warnings**   Trace warnings related to a request.
- **Information**   Trace information events related to a request.
- **Verbose**   Trace all available information and errors related to a request.

By using ASP.NET, you can specify the area within managed modules to trace as any combination of the following:

- **Infrastructure**   Traces the failed request through ASP.NET infrastructure. Use when you want to trace events that are related primarily to entering and leaving various parts of the ASP.NET infrastructure.
- **Module**   Traces the failed request through HTTP pipeline-related modules, managed modules, or both. Use when you want to trace events that are logged when a request enters and leaves HTTP pipeline and/or managed modules.

- **Page** Traces page load, trace write, and trace warn events for failed requests. Use when you want to generate trace events that correspond to specific ASP.NET page–related events.
- **AppServices** Traces the failed request through application services. Use when you want to trace events logged as part of the application services functionality.

By using WWW Server, you can specify the area within the IIS server core to trace as any combination of the following:

- **Authentication** Traces the failed request through authentication-related modules. Use when you want to trace authentication attempts, including the name of the authenticated user, the authentication method, and the results of the authentication attempt.
- **Security** Traces the failed request through system security. Use when you want to trace events when requests are rejected by the server for security-related reasons, such as when a client is denied access to a resource because of insufficient permissions.
- **Filter** Traces the failed request through the IsapiFilterModule, the RequestFilteringModule, or both. Use when you want to determine how long it takes an ISAPI filter to process requests.
- **StaticFile** Traces the failed request through the StaticFile module. Use when you want to trace how long it takes requests for static files to be completed or to see how filters might be changing requests.
- **CGI** Traces the failed request through the CgiModule. Use when a request is made for a CGI file and you want to trace execution through the CgiModule.
- **Compression** Traces the failed request through the StaticCompressionModule or the DynamicCompressionModule. Use when a response is compressed and you want to trace execution through these compression-related modules.
- **Cache** Traces the failed request through cache-related modules. Use when you want to generate trace events for cache operations associated with a request.

- **RequestNotifications** Traces the failed request through the RequestMonitorModule. Use when you want to capture all request notifications from start to completion.

Enabling and Configuring Failed Request Tracing

You can enable and configure failed request tracing for a site by completing the following steps:

1. In IIS Manager, select the node for the server you want to manage. If the server you want to use isn't listed, connect to it.

2. In the main pane, when you group by area, the Failed Request Tracing Rules feature is listed under IIS. Double-click Failed Request Tracing Rules to open this feature. You should now see the currently set rules for failed request tracing (if any). Rules listed as Local, under Entry Type, are set for the site you selected. Rules listed as Inherited are set at the server level.

3. In the Actions pane, click Edit Site Tracing. This displays the Failed Request Tracing Settings dialog box shown in Figure 7-4.

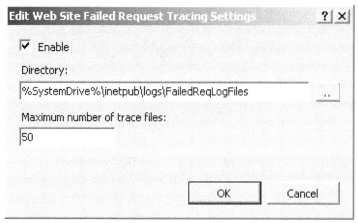

FIGURE 7-4 You can enable and configure failed request tracing as necessary for advanced diagnostics.

4. If trace logging is currently disabled, all logging options are unavailable and cannot be selected. To enable trace logging select the Enable checkbox in the Failed Request Tracing Settings dialog box.

5. By default, trace log files are located in a subdirectory under *%SystemDrive%*\ Inetpub\Logs\FailedReqLogfiles. If you want to change

the default logging directory, in the Directory field, type the directory path, or click the selection button to look for a directory that you want to use.

6. Unlike other types of logging, each failed request is stored in a separate file in the logging directory. Type a value in the Maximum Number Of Trace Files text box to specify the maximum number of trace files to store at one time, and then click OK to save your settings.

> **REAL WORLD**   When the maximum value is reached, IIS deletes an old trace file before creating a new one. The default maximum number of trace files is 50. Although you should rarely perform live tracing on a production server (because doing so could degrade performance considerably), you may need to raise this value on a busy enterprise server to ensure that files are available for the types of failed requests you want to track.

Creating and Managing Trace Rules

You can create a trace rule by completing the following steps:

1. In IIS Manager, access the Failed Request Tracing Rules feature for the server, site, virtual directory, or application you want to manage.

2. In the Actions pane, click Add. This starts the Add Failed Request Tracing Rule Wizard.

3. As shown in Figure 7-5, specify the type of content to trace as one of the following, and then click Next:

- All Content (*)   Configures tracing for all file requests that match the rule criteria.
- ASP.NET   Configures tracing for all ASP.NET file requests that match the rule criteria and have the .aspx file extension.
- ASP   Configures tracing for all ASP file requests that match the rule criteria and have the .asp file extension.
- **Custom**   Configures tracing based on the value entered, which can contain, at most, one wildcard character. The valid characters are A–Z, a–z, +, –, ., / and the wildcard character (*).

TIP Trace rules must be unique. You can create only one trace rule for *, *.aspx, and *.asp. You can create only one trace rule for each unique custom trace path.

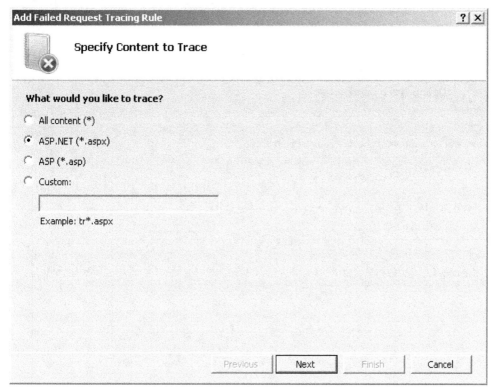

FIGURE 7-5 Specify the type of content to trace.

4. As shown in Figure 7-6, specify one or more of the following conditions under which IIS should trace a request, and then click Next:

- **Status Code(s)** Select the related check box, and then type the HTTP status codes and substatus code combinations to trace. Use a period between an HTTP status code and its optional substatus code. Use a comma to separate multiple entries. A request meets this condition if it causes IIS to generate any one of the listed status codes.
- **Time Taken (In Seconds)** Select the related check box, and then type a Time Taken value in seconds. A request meets this condition if it takes longer to process the response than the specified value. This condition must be selected with another condition.

- **Event Severity**   Select the related check box, and then choose a severity level of events to trace. The severity levels you can choose from are Error, Critical Error, and Warning. A request meets this condition if it causes IIS to generate one or more events with the specified severity level. This condition must be selected with another condition.

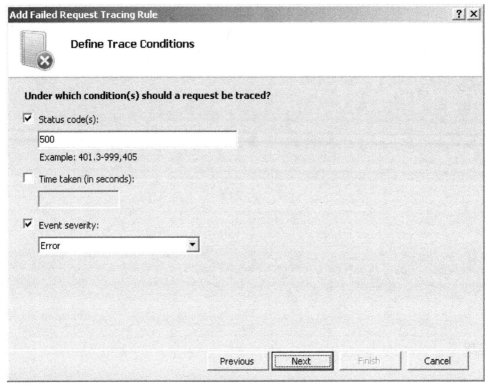

FIGURE 7-6 Specify the conditions that trigger a trace.

5. As shown in Figure 7-7, specify the providers to trace by selecting or clearing providers.

6. To select a provider, select its check box. Then in the Verbosity drop-down list, you can set the types of related events to trace, or you can elect to trace all related events for that provider. The Verbosity drop-down list is designed so that when you select a level, all preceding levels in the list are included. For example, if you select Errors, General and Critical Errors are also included because they precede General in the list. The default level is Verbose, which as the last level in the list, includes all the others.

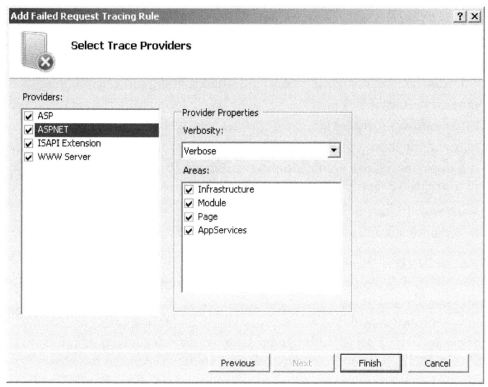

FIGURE 7-7 Specify the providers to trace.

The Verbosity drop-down list contains the following levels:

- **General**   Includes general informational events that provide context information for the request activity, such as GENERAL_REQUEST_START (which logs the URL and the verb for the request) and GENERAL_REQUEST_END (which logs the bytes sent and bytes received), HTTP status code, and substatus code generated. General includes GENERAL_, FILTER_, and MODULE_ that do not contain warnings or errors. It does not include other notification or informational events, such as those that begin with PRE_BEGIN_, NOTIFY_, or AUTH_.
- **Critical Errors**   Includes critical error events that provide information about actions that cause a process to end or that are about to cause a process to end. As a result of critical errors, IIS generally stops processing a request.
- **Errors**   Includes general errors that provide information about components that encounter an error when running and cannot continue to

process requests. As a result of general errors, IIS usually stops processing a request.

- **Warnings**   Includes warning events that provide information about components that encounter a warning when running but can continue to process requests.
- **Information**   Includes informational events that provide general information about requests. Information includes all informational events but does not include notification events, such as those that begin with PRE_BEGIN_ or NOTIFY_.
- **Verbose**   Includes all events and notifications to provide detailed information about requests from start to finish.

> **REAL WORLD**   To get a complete picture of a request from start to finish, you'll need to use the Verbosity level of Verbose. However, as you track additional types of events and notifications, IIS generates more and more information about a request, resulting in increasing resource usage. For example, on a server with most role services enabled, IIS generated 115–175 KB of data for a failed request at a Verbose level. On the other hand, with a Warnings level (which includes General, Critical Errors, Errors, and Warnings) IIS generated trace files of 8–12 KB. And with an Information level (which includes General, Critical Errors, Errors, Warnings, and Information) IIS generated trace files of 29–52 KB.

7. When you select the ASPNET or WWW Server provider in the Areas section, select the check box(es) for the specific areas to track. By default, all areas are selected.

8. Click Finish to create the trace rule.

To edit an existing trace rule, in the main pane, click the rule, and then in the Actions pane, select Edit. To remove a trace rule, in the main pane, select Remove, and then click Yes to confirm that you want to remove the rule. If you remove a rule at a level lower than the one for which it was originally set, you delete the rule only at that level of the configuration hierarchy.

Monitoring IIS Performance and Reliability

Performance tuning is as much an art as it is a science. You often tune performance based on trial and error. You adjust the server, monitor the server's performance over time, and then gauge the success of the updated settings. If things aren't working as expected, you adjust the settings again. In an ideal world, while tuning server performance, you'd have staging or development servers that are similar in configuration to your production servers. Then once you've made adjustments that worked in staging, you could configure these changes on the production servers.

Using the Reliability And Performance Console

The Reliability And Performance Monitor console is the tool of choice for performance tuning. To access a stand-alone console, click Start, point to Administrative Tools, and then click Reliability And Performance Monitor. In Server Manager, you can access this tool as a snap-in under the Diagnostics node. Double-click the Diagnostics node to expand it, then double-click the Reliability And Performance node. With the Reliability And Performance node selected, you see an overview of resource usage. As shown in Figure 7-8, the resource usage statistics are broken down into four categories:

- **CPU Usage**   The summary details show the current CPU utilization and the maximum CPU utilization. If you expand the CPU entry below the graph (by clicking the options button), you'll see a list of currently running executables including name, process ID, description, number of threads used, current CPU utilization, and average CPU utilization.
- **Disk Usage**   The summary details show the number of kilobytes per second being read from or written to disk and the highest percentage usage. If you expand the Disk entry below the graph (by clicking the options button), you'll see a list of currently running executables that are performing or have performed I/O operations including name, process ID, description, file being read or written, number of bytes being read per minute, number of bytes being written per minute, I/O priority, and the associated disk response time.

- **Network Usage** The summary details show the current network bandwidth utilization in kilobytes and the percentage of total bandwidth utilization. If you expand the Network entry below the graph (by clicking the options button), you see a list of currently running executables that are transferring or have transferred data on the network, including name, process ID, IP address being contacted, number of bytes being sent per minute, number of bytes received per minute, and total bytes sent or received per minute.

- **Memory Usage** The summary details show the current memory utilization and the number of hard faults occurring per second. If you expand the Memory entry below the graph (by clicking the options button), you'll see a list of currently running executables including name, process ID, hard faults per minute, commit memory in kilobytes, working set memory in kilobytes, shareable memory in kilobytes, and private (non-shareable) memory in kilobytes.

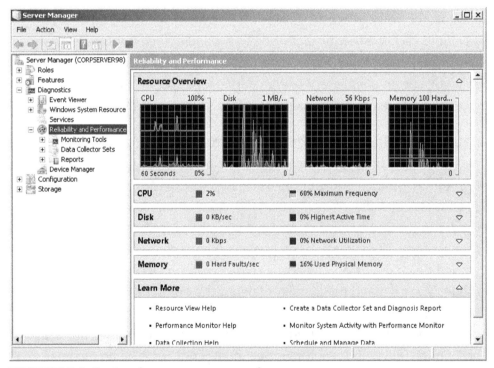

FIGURE 7-8 Review the resource usage on the server.

In the Reliability And Performance Monitor console, you'll find two additional tools under Monitoring tools:

- Performance Monitor
- Reliability Monitor

Performance Monitor graphically displays statistics for the set of performance parameters you've selected for display. These performance parameters are referred to as *counters*. When you install IIS on a system, Performance Monitor is updated with a set of counters for tracking IIS performance. You can further update these counters when you install additional services and add-ons for IIS.

As Figure 7-9 shows, Performance Monitor creates a graph depicting the counters you're tracking. The update interval for this graph is configurable but is set to 1 second by default. As you'll see when you work with Performance Monitor, the tracking information is most valuable when you record performance information in a log file so that it can be replayed. Also, you can use Performance Monitor to configure alerts that send messages when certain events occur, such as when an automatic IIS restart is triggered.

The Reliability And Performance Monitor console also includes Reliability Monitor, shown in Figure 7-10. Reliability Monitor tracks changes to the server and compares them to changes in system stability. In this way, you can see a graphical representation of the relationship between changes in the system configuration and changes in system stability. By recording software installation, software removal, application failures, hardware failures, Windows failures, and key events regarding the configuration of the server, you can see a timeline of changes in both the server and its reliability, and then you can use this information to pinpoint changes that are causing problems with stability. For example, if you see a sudden drop in stability, you can click a data point and then expand the related data set, such as Application Failures or Hardware Failures, to find the specific event that caused the drop in stability.

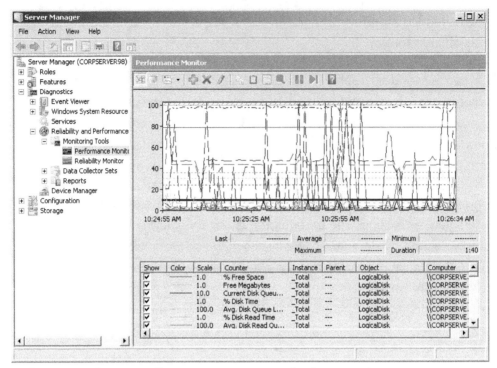

FIGURE 7-9 Review performance measurements for the server.

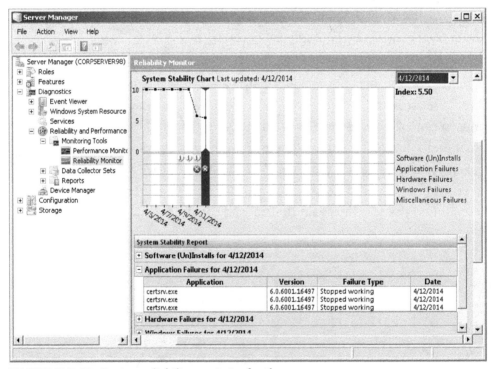

FIGURE 7-10 Review reliability statistics for the server.

Windows Server 2008 and later also include Data Collector Sets and Reports. Data Collector Sets allow you to specify sets of performance objects and counters that you want to track. Once you've created a Data Collector Set, you can easily start or stop monitoring of the performance objects and counters included in the set. In a way, this makes Data Collector Sets similar to the performance logs used in earlier releases of Windows. However, Data Collector Sets are much more sophisticated. A single data set can be used to generate multiple performance counters and trace logs. You can also:

- Assign access controls to manage who can access collected data.
- Create multiple run schedules and stop conditions for monitoring.
- Use data managers to control the size of collected data and reporting.
- Generate reports based on collected data.

In the Reliability And Performance Monitor console, you can review currently configured Data Collector Sets and reports under the Data Collector Sets and Reports nodes respectively. You'll find data sets and reports that are user-defined and system-defined. User-defined data sets are created by users for general monitoring and performance tuning. System-defined data sets are created by the operating system to aid in automated diagnostics.

Choosing Counters to Monitor

The Performance Monitor tool displays information only for counters you're tracking. IIS counters are related to different IIS services; several hundred IIS counters are available in total. Counters are organized into object groupings. For example, all ASP-related counters are associated with the Active Server Pages performance object. You'll also find object counters for other services. A list of the main IIS-related counter objects follows:

- **ASP.NET** Object counters for general tracking of ASP.NET applications, application requests, and worker processes
- **ASP.NET Applications** Object counters for tracking the ASP.NET application queue and other specific ASP.NET application counters
- **ASP.NET State Service** Object counters for tracking ASP.NET sessions

- **Active Server Pages**   Object counters for ASP scripts and applications running on the server
- **HTTP Service, HTTP Service Request Queues, HTTP Service URL Groups** Object counters for URLs, cached URLs, HTTP requests, and other HTTP-related functions of IIS
- **Internet Information Services Global**   Object counters for all Internet services (WWW, FTP, SMTP, NNTP, and so on) running on the server
- **Web Service**   Object counters for the World Wide Web Publishing Service
- **Web Service Cache**   Object counters that provide detailed information on the cache used by the Web service, including cache for metadata, files, memory, and Uniform Resource Identifiers (URIs)

The easiest way to learn about these counters is to read the explanations available in the Add Counters dialog box. Start the Performance Monitor tool, then on the toolbar, click the Add button, and then in the Available Counters list, expand an object. Select the Show Description check box, and then scroll through the list of counters for this object.

> **TIP**   Multiple versions of ASP.NET can be installed. As a result, the ASP.NET and ASP Applications counter objects have version-specific instances. Use the counter objects for the specific ASP.NET versions you want to track.

When Performance Monitor is monitoring a particular object, it can track all instances of all counters for that object. Instances are individual occurrences of a particular counter; multiple occurrences can exist. For example, when you track counters for the Web Service object, you often have a choice of tracking all Web site instances or specific Web site instances. Following this, if you configured CorpWeb, CorpProducts, and CorpServices sites, you could use Web Service counters to track a specific Web site instance or multiple Web site instances.

To select which counters you want to monitor, complete the following steps:

1. In the Reliability And Performance Monitor console, expand Monitoring Tools, and then select Performance Monitor.

2. Performance Monitor has several views and view types. Ensure that you are viewing current activity by clicking the View Current Activity button on the toolbar or pressing Ctrl+T. To switch between the view types (Line, Histogram Bar, and Report), click the Change Graph Type button or press Ctrl+G.

3. To add counters, on the toolbar, click Add, or press Ctrl+I. This displays the Add Counters dialog box.

4. In the Select Counters From Computer list box type the Universal Naming Convention (UNC) name of the IIS server you want to work with, such as **\\ENGSVR01**, or choose <Local computer> to work with the local computer.

> **NOTE** You'll need to be at least a member of the Performance Monitor Users group in the domain or the local computer to perform remote monitoring. When you use performance logging, you'll need to be at least a member of the Performance Log Users group in the domain or the local computer to work with performance logs on remote computers.

5. In the Available Counters pane, Performance Objects are listed alphabetically. If you select an object by clicking it, all related counters are selected. If you expand an object entry, you can see all the related counters and can then add individual counters by selecting them, and then clicking Add. For example, you could expand the entry for the Active Server Pages object and then select Requests Failed Total, Requests Not Found, Requests Queued, and Requests Total counters.

6. When you select an object or any of its counters, you see the related instances. Choose All Instances to select all counter instances for monitoring. Or select one or more counter instances to monitor. For example, you could select instances of Anonymous Users/Sec for individual Web sites or for all Web sites.

7. When you've selected an object or a group of counters for an object and the object instances, click Add to add the counters to the graph. Repeat Steps 5 to 7 to add other performance parameters. Click OK when you're finished.

> **TIP** Don't try to chart too many counters or counter instances at once. You'll make the display too difficult to read, and you'll use system resources—namely, CPU time and memory—that might affect server responsiveness.

Tuning Web Server Performance

Now that you know how to monitor your Web servers, let's look at how you can tune the operating system and hardware performance. I'll examine the following areas:

- Memory usage and caching
- Processor utilization
- Disk I/O
- Network bandwidth and connectivity

Monitoring and Tuning Memory Usage

Memory is often the source of performance problems, and you should always rule out memory problems before examining other areas of the system. One of the key reasons memory can be such a problem has to do with caching. Caching improves performance by returning a processed copy of a requested Web page from cache, resulting in reduced overhead on the server and faster response times. IIS 7.0 and IIS 7.5 support several levels of caching, including output caching in user mode and output caching in kernel mode. When kernel-mode caching is enabled, cached responses are served from the kernel rather than from IIS user mode, giving IIS an extra boost in performance and increasing the number of requests IIS can process. Improperly configured caching settings, however, can degrade performance either by using too much memory on a server with a relatively small amount of free memory or using too little memory on a server with a relatively large amount of free memory.

The configuration of the HttpCacheModule controls the way output caching works for static files and non-managed code. OutputCacheModule provides output caching for managed code. IIS uses cache in other ways as well. FileCacheModule is used to cache file handles. TokenCacheModule is used to cache security tokens for password-based authentication. UriCacheModule is used to cache URL-specific server state information. In addition to the detailed references for these modules in the appendix, "Comprehensive IIS Module and Schema Reference," you'll find more information on server output caching in Chapter 2, "Managing Applications and Application Pools."

A server's physical and virtual memory configuration can also present a problem. Adding memory when there's a caching or virtual memory problem on the server won't solve performance problems. Because of this, you should always check for memory, caching, and virtual memory problems at the same time. Table 7-2 provides an overview of counters that you'll want to track to uncover memory, caching, and virtual memory (paging) bottlenecks. The table is organized by issue category.

TABLE 7-2 Uncovering Memory-Relasted Bottlenecks

Physical and virtual memory usage	Memory\Available Kbytes is the amount of physical memory available to processes running on the server. Memory\Committed Bytes is the amount of committed virtual memory. If the server has very little available memory, you might need to add memory to the system. In general, you want the available memory to be no less than 5 percent of the total physical memory on the server. If the server has a high ratio of committed bytes to total physical memory on the system, you might also need to add memory. In general, you want the committed bytes value to be no more than 75 percent of the total physical memory.
Memory caching	Memory\Cache Bytes represents the total size of the file system cache. Internet Information Services Global\Current File Cache Memory Usage represents the current memory used by the IIS file cache. Internet Information Services Global\File Cache Hits % represents the ratio of cache hits to total cache requests and reflects how well the settings for the IIS file cache are working. A site with mostly static files should have a very high cache hit percentage (70–85 percent). Internet Information Services Global\File Cache Flushes tells you how quickly IIS is flushing files out of cache. If flushes are occurring too quickly, you might need to increase the time-to-live value for cached objects (ObjectCacheTTL). If flushes are occurring too slowly, you might be wasting memory and might need to decrease the time-to-live value for cached objects.

Memory page faults	A page fault occurs when a process requests a page in memory and the system can't find it at the requested location. If the requested page is elsewhere in memory, the fault is called a *soft page fault*. If the requested page must be retrieved from disk, the fault is called a *hard page fault*. Most processors can handle large numbers of soft faults. Hard faults, however, can cause significant delays. Page Faults/sec is the overall rate at which the processor handles all types of page faults. Pages Input/sec is the total number of pages read from disk to resolve hard page faults. Page Reads/sec is the total disk reads needed to resolve hard page faults. Pages Input/sec will be greater than or equal to Page Reads/sec and can give you a good idea of your hard page fault rate. If there is a large number of hard page faults, you might need to increase the amount of memory or reduce the cache size on the server. Memory used by IIS can be controlled by modifying cache settings.
Memory paging	These counters track the number of bytes in the paged and nonpaged pool. The paged pool is an area of system memory for objects that can be written to disk when they aren't used. The nonpaged pool is an area of system memory for objects that can't be written to disk. If the paged pool's size is large relative to the total amount of physical memory on the system, you might need to add memory to the system. If the nonpaged pool's size is large relative to the total amount of virtual memory allocated to the server, you might want to increase the virtual memory size.

Monitoring and Tuning Processor Usage

The CPU does the actual processing of information on your server. As you examine a server's performance, you should focus on the CPUs after memory bottlenecks have been eliminated. If the server's processors are the performance bottleneck, adding memory, drives, or network connections won't overcome the problem. Instead, you might need to upgrade the processors to faster clock speeds or add processors to increase the server's processing capacity. You could also move processor-intensive applications, such as Microsoft SQL Server, to another server.

Before you decide to upgrade or add CPUs, you should rule out problems with memory and caching. If signs still point to a processor problem, you should monitor the performance counters discussed in Table 7-3. Be sure to monitor these counters for each CPU installed on the server.

Table 7-3 Uncovering Processor-Related Bottlenecks

Thread queuing	System\Processor Queue Length displays the number of threads waiting to be executed. These threads are queued in an area shared by all processors on the system. If this counter has a sustained value of 10 or more threads, you'll need to upgrade or add processors.
CPU usage	Processor\% Processor Time displays the percentage of time the selected CPU is executing a non-idle thread. You should track this counter separately for all processor instances on the server. If the % Processor Time values are high while the network interface and disk I/O throughput rates are relatively low, you'll need to upgrade or add processors.
ASP performance	Active Server Pages\Request Wait Time, Active Server Pages\Requests Queued, Active Server Pages\Requests Rejected, and Active Server Pages\Requests/sec indicate the relative performance of IIS when working with ASP. Active Server Pages\Request Wait Time is the number of milliseconds the most recent request was waiting in the queue. Active Server Pages\Requests Queued is the number of requests waiting to be processed. Active Server Pages\Requests Rejected is the total number of requests not executed because there weren't resources to process them. Active Server Pages\Requests/sec is the number of requests executed per second. In general, you don't want to see requests waiting in the queue, and, if requests are queuing, the wait time should be very low. You also don't want to see requests rejected because resources aren't available. Consider and treat these problems relative to the number of requests handled per second. You might notice some variance under peak loads. To resolve these issues you might need to upgrade or add processors.

> **REAL WORLD**   In many cases a single server might not be sufficient to handle the network traffic load. If that happens, you might need to scale your site across multiple servers. For example, you could replicate the site to additional servers and then distribute the traffic across these servers by using a load balancer. If you already have a multiple-server Web farm, you could add Web servers.

Monitoring and Tuning Disk I/O

With today's high-speed disks, the disk throughput rate is rarely the cause of a bottleneck. That said, however, accessing memory is much faster than accessing disks. So if the server has to do a lot of disk reads and writes, the server's overall performance can be degraded. To reduce the amount of disk I/O, you want the server to manage memory very efficiently and page to disk only when necessary. You monitor and tune memory usage as discussed previously in the "Monitoring and Tuning Memory Usage" section of this chapter.

Beyond the memory tuning discussion, you can monitor some counters to gauge disk I/O activity. Specifically, you should monitor the counters discussed in Table 7-4.

Table 7-4 Uncovering Drive-Related Bottlenecks

Overall drive performance	Use PhysicalDisk\% Disk Time in conjunction with Processor\% Processor Time and Network Interface\Bytes Total/sec. If the % Disk Time value is high and the processor and network connection values aren't high, the system's hard disk drives might be creating a bottleneck. Be sure to monitor % Disk Time for all hard disk drives on the server.
Disk I/O	Use PhysicalDisk\Disk Writes/sec; PhysicalDisk\Disk Reads/sec; PhysicalDisk \Avg. Disk Write Queue Length; PhysicalDisk\Avg. Disk Read Queue Length; Physical Disk\Current Disk Queue Length. The number of writes and reads per second tells you how much disk I/O activity there is. The write and read queue lengths tell you how many write or read requests are waiting to be processed. In general, you want there to be very few waiting requests. Keep in mind that the request delays are proportional to the length of the queues minus the number of drives in a redundant array of independent disks (RAID) set.

> **NOTE** Counters for physical and logical disks might need to be enabled before they're available. To enable these objects, run the following commands at a command prompt:
>
> **Diskperf -yd** for physical disks
>
> **Diskperf -yv** for logical disks

> **NOTE** For complete information on Diskperf syntax, switches, and parameters, run **Diskperf -?**.

Monitoring and Tuning Network Bandwidth and Connectivity

No other factor weighs more in a visitor's perceived performance of your Web site than the network that connects your server to the visitor's computer. The delay, or *latency*, between the time a request is made and the time it's received can make all the difference. If there's a high degree of latency, it doesn't matter if you have the fastest server on the planet. The user experiences a delay and perceives that your Web site is slow.

Generally speaking, the latency experienced by the user is beyond your control. It's a function of the type of connection the user has and the route the request takes through the Internet to your server. Your server's total capacity to handle requests and the amount of bandwidth available to your servers are factors under your control, however. Network bandwidth availability is a function of your organization's connection to the Internet. Network capacity is a function of the network cards and interfaces configured on the servers.

A typical network card is equipped to handle a 100-megabit-per-second (Mbps) or 1,000 Mbps (1 Gigabit) connection with fair efficiency, which is much more traffic than the typical site experiences and much more traffic than the typical server can handle. Because of this, your organization's bandwidth availability is typically the limiting factor. If you have a shared T1 for all Internet activity, your servers are sharing the 1.544 Mbps connection with all other Internet traffic. If you have a dedicated T1 for your Web servers, your servers have 1.544 Mbps of bandwidth availability. If you have multiple T1s or a T3, the bandwidth available to your servers could range from 3 Mbps to 45 Mbps.

To put this in perspective, consider that the number of simultaneous connections your network can handle is relative to the speed of the connection, the average size of the data transferred per connection, and the permitted transfer time. For example, if you have a T1, the typical data transfer per connection (for a dial-up connection) is 50 kilobits per second (Kbps), and transfer time allowable is 15 seconds, your connection could handle 30 data transfers per second (1,544 Kbps / 50 Kbps) or 450 simultaneous transfers within 15 seconds (30 data transfers * 15 seconds).

On the other hand, if you have a T3, the typical data transfer per connection is 250 Kbps, and allowable transfer time is 15 seconds, your connection could handle 180 data transfers per second (45,000 Kbps/ 250 Kbps) or 2,700 simultaneous transfers within 15 seconds (180 data transfers * 15 seconds).

TIP Your network card's capacity can be a limiting factor in some instances. Most servers use 100/1000 network cards, which can be configured in many ways. Someone might have configured a card for 100 Mbps instead of 1000 Mbps, or the card might be configured for half duplex instead of full duplex. If you suspect a capacity problem with a network card, you should always check the configuration. Duplex settings on datacenter network equipment may be a factor as well, so be sure to confirm switch settings with your network administrator.

REAL WORLD A T1 connection is a useful example for many commercial sites. Larger commercial sites are typically co-located at a hosting service and might have a connection speed to the Internet of 100 Mbps or greater. If this is the case for your site, keep in mind that some devices configured on your network might restrict the permitted bandwidth. For example, your company's firewall might be configured so that it allows only 50 Mbps for Web, 20 Mbps for FTP, and 10 Mbps for SMTP.

As your organization moves to 1 and 10 Gbps connections from 100 Mbps connections, you'll also want to look closely at physical wiring. Older ethernet cables won't properly support 1 Gbps or 10 Gbps connections and can limit bandwidth severely simply because they aren't designed for gigabit networking.

To determine the throughput and current activity on a server's network cards, you can check the following performance counters:

- Network Interface\Bytes Received/sec
- Network Interface\Bytes Sent/sec
- Network Interface\Bytes Total/sec
- Network Interface\Current Bandwidth

If the total bytes-per-second value is more than 50 percent of the total capacity under average load conditions, your server might have problems under peak load conditions. You might want to ensure that operations that take a lot of network bandwidth, such as backups, are performed on a separate interface card. Keep in mind that you should compare these values in conjunction with PhysicalDisk\% Disk Time and Processor\% Processor Time. If the process time and disk time values are low but the network values are very high, there might be a capacity problem.

IIS provides several ways to restrict bandwidth usage and to improve bandwidth-related performance. These features are as follows:

- **Bandwidth throttling** You can restrict bandwidth usage by enabling bandwidth throttling and limiting the maximum number of allowable connections. Bandwidth throttling restricts the total bandwidth available to a service or to individual sites. Because users will be denied service when the bandwidth limits are exceeded, you should enable these features only when you're sure that this setting is acceptable. Before you restrict bandwidth, you should monitor the network interface object counters discussed earlier in this chapter. If these counters indicate a possible problem, restricting bandwidth is one answer.
- **Connection limitations** Connection limitations restrict the total number of allowable connections to a service. Because users might be denied service when these values are exceeded, you should enable these features only when you're sure that this setting is acceptable. Before you restrict the number of connections to a server, you should monitor the network interface object counters discussed earlier in this chapter. If these counters indicate a possible problem, connection limitation is one answer.
- **HTTP compression** With HTTP compression enabled, the Web server compresses files before sending them to client browsers. File compression reduces the amount of information transferred between the server and the client, which in turn can reduce network bandwidth usage, network capacity, and transfer time. For HTTP compression to work, it must be enabled, and the client browser must support HTTP 1.1. Although most current browsers support HTTP 1.1 and have the feature enabled by default, older browsers might not support HTTP 1.1. Older browsers will still be able

to retrieve files from your site, but they won't be taking advantage of HTTP compression. Before you enable compression, you should monitor the current processor usage on the server. HTTP compression adds to the overhead on the server, which means that it will increase overall processor utilization. If your site uses dynamic content extensively and process utilization (% Processor Time) is already high, you might want to upgrade or add processors before enabling HTTP compression.

> **MORE INFO** For additional details, see Chapter 6 and Chapter 7 in *Web Server Administration: The Personal Trainer.*

Strategies for Improving IIS Performance

In this section I examine strategies you can use to improve the performance of IIS. The focus of this section is on improving the overall responsiveness of IIS and not the underlying server hardware.

Removing Unnecessary Applications and Services

One of the most obvious ways to improve IIS performance is to remove resource drains on the server. Start by removing applications that might be affecting the performance of IIS, including:

- SQL Server
- Microsoft Exchange Server
- File and print services
- UNIX services

If necessary, move these applications and services to a separate server. This will give IIS more resources to work with. For applications that you can't move, see if there's a way to run the applications only during periods of relatively low activity. For example, if you're running server backups daily, see if you can schedule backups to run late at night when user activity is low.

System services are another area you can examine to see if there are unnecessary resource drains. Every service running on the server uses resources that can be used in other ways. You should stop services that aren't necessary and set them to start manually. Before you stop any service, you should check for dependencies to ensure that your server isn't adversely affected.

If you have dedicated IIS servers, remove roles, roles services, and features that aren't required.

Optimizing Content Usage

Your server's responsiveness is tied directly to the content you're publishing. You can often realize substantial performance benefits by optimizing the way content is used. IIS can handle both static and dynamic content. Although static content is passed directly to the requesting client, dynamic content must be processed before it can be passed to the client. This places a resource burden on the server that you can reduce by using static content.

> **NOTE** I'm not advocating replacing all dynamic content with static content. Dynamically generated content is a powerful tool for building highly customized and full-featured sites. However, if there are places where you're using dynamic content for no specific reason, you might want to rethink this strategy.

When you use static content, keep in mind that you should set expire headers whenever possible. Expire headers allow the related files to be stored in the client's cache, and this can greatly improve performance on repeat visits when the original content hasn't changed. For details on setting expire headers, see Chapter 7 in *Web Server Administration: The Personal Trainer*.

With dynamic content, you should limit your use of Common Gateway Interface (CGI) applications. CGI applications require more processor and memory resources than their Internet Server Application Programming Interface (ISAPI), Active Server Pages (ASP), and ASP.NET counterparts. Because of this, you should replace or convert CGI applications with or to ISAPI, ASP, or ASP.NET. An alternate is to install FastCGI—a more robust version of CGI that is available as an add-on module for IIS.

Whenever you work with ISAPI, ASP, or ASP.NET applications, try to push as much of the processing load onto the client as possible. This reduces the server resource requirements and greatly improves application responsiveness. One example of pushing processing to the client is to use client-side scripting to evaluate form submissions before data is sent to the server. This technique reduces the number of times information is sent between the client and the server; therefore, it can greatly improve the application's overall performance.

To improve content-related performance, you might also want to do the following:

- **Analyze the way content is organized on your hard disk drives**.　In most cases you should keep related content files on the same logical partitions of a disk. Keeping related files together improves IIS file caching.
- **Defragment your drives periodically**.　Over time, drives can become fragmented, and this decreases read/write performance. To correct this, defragment your server's drives periodically. Many defragmentation tools allow you to automate this process so that you can configure a scheduled job to automatically defragment drives without needing administrator intervention.
- **Reduce the size of content files**.　The larger the file size, the more time it takes to send the file to a client. If you can optimize your source Hypertext Markup Language (HTML) or ASP code and reduce the file size, you can increase your Web server's performance and responsiveness. Some of the biggest bandwidth users are multimedia files. Compress image, video, or audio files by using an appropriate compression format whenever possible.
- **Store log files on separate disks from content files**.　Logging activity can reduce the responsiveness of a busy server. One way to correct this is to store access logs on a different physical drive from the one storing your site's content files. In this way, disk writes for logging are separate from the disk reads or writes for working with content files, which can greatly improve the overall server responsiveness.
- **Log only essential information**.　Trying to log too much information can also slow down a busy server. By using the World Wide Web Consortium (W3C) extended logging format, you can reduce logging overhead by logging only the information that you need in order to generate reports and by removing logging for nonessential information. With any type of logging, you can reduce logging overhead by organizing different types of

content appropriately and then disabling logging on directories containing content whose access doesn't need to be logged. For example, you could place all your image files in a directory called Images and then disable logging on this directory.

> **MORE INFO** Techniques for configuring logging are discussed in Chapter 9 of *Web Server Administration: The Personal Trainer*. If your organization has large IIS installations running dozens or hundreds of IIS sites per server, you should consider using centralized binary logging, which is also discussed in that chapter.

Optimizing ISAPI, ASP, and ASP.NET Applications

Improperly configured and poorly optimized applications can be major resource drains on an IIS server. To get the most from the server, you need to optimize the way applications are configured. Do the following to optimize applications:

- **Enable type library caching.** IIS can cache type libraries used by applications in memory. This allows frequently used type libraries to be accessed quickly. You can control caching with the *enableTypelibCache* attribute of the *system.webServer/asp/cache* element.
- **Manage application buffering and flushes appropriately.** Application buffering allows all output from an application to be collected in the buffer before being sent to the client. This cuts down on network traffic and response times. However, users don't receive data until the page is finished executing, which can give the perception that a site isn't very responsive. You can control application buffering by using the *BufferingOn* attribute of the *system.webServer/asp* element.
- **Disable application debugging.** Application debugging slows IIS performance considerably. You should use debugging only for troubleshooting. Otherwise, you should disable debugging. You can control debugging by using the *appAllowClientDebug* and *appAllowDebug* attributes of the *system.webServer/asp* element.
- **Optimize application performance.** You can configure ASP and ASP.NET applications to shut down idle processes, limit memory leaks and outages, and rapidly detect failures. For more information, see Chapter 3.

- **Manage session configuration appropriately.** As the usage of your server changes, so should the session management configuration. By default, session management is enabled for all applications. If your applications don't use sessions, however, you're wasting system resources. Instead of enabling sessions by default, you should disable sessions by default and then enable sessions for individual applications. You can control sessions with the *allowSessionState*, *keepSessionIdSecure*, *max*, and *timeout* attributes of the *system.webServer/asp/session* element.

- **Set a meaningful session time-out.** The session time-out value is extremely important in determining the amount of resources used in session management. Set this value accurately. Sessions should time out after an appropriate period. Configure session time-out by using the *timeout* attribute of the *system.webServer/asp/session* element.

- **Set appropriate script and connection time-out values.** ASP scripts and user connections should time out at an appropriate interval. By default, ASP scripts time out after 90 seconds and user connections are queued indefinitely (but checked every 3 seconds to make sure they're still valid). Zombie scripts and open connections use resources and can reduce the server's responsiveness. To reduce this drain, set appropriate time-outs based on the way your site is used. You can control script and connection time-outs by using the *scriptTimeout*, *queueConnectionTestTime*, *queueTimeout*, and *requestQueueMax* attributes of the *system.webServer/asp/limits* element.

Optimizing IIS Caching, Queuing, and Pooling

IIS uses many memory-resident caches and queues to manage resources. If you make extensive use of dynamic content or have a heavily trafficked site, you should optimize the way these caches and queues work for your environment. You might want to do the following:

- **Consider changing application pool queue length.** Whenever requests for applications come in, the HTTP listener (Http.sys) picks them up and passes them to an application request queue. To prevent large numbers of requests from queuing up and flooding the server, each application request queue has a default maximum amount of concurrent requests. If this value doesn't meet your needs, you can modify it by using the *queueLength* attribute of the *system.applicationHost/applicationPools* element's *add* collection. In most cases you'll want to set this value to the maximum number of connection requests you want the server to maintain.

- **Consider changing the maximum processor threads for ASP.** By default, IIS limits to 25 the maximum number of work threads per processor that IIS can create to handle ASP requests. You can use the *processorThreadMax* attribute of the *system.webServer/asp/limits* element to increase or decrease this value as appropriate.

- **Consider changing the maximum worker processes for application pools.** By default, IIS limits to 1 the maximum number of work processes that IIS can create to handle ASP requests for an application pool. If this value doesn't meet your needs, you can modify it by using the *maxProcesses* attribute of the *system.applicationHost/applicationPools* element's *add* collection.

- **Consider changing the Output Cache settings.** By default, IIS uses up to 50 percent of the server's available physical memory. This value ensures that IIS works well with other applications that might be running on the server. If the server is dedicated to IIS or has additional memory available, you might want to increase this setting to allow IIS to use more memory. To control IIS file caching, you can use the *maxCacheSize* attribute of the *system.webServer/caching* element.

- **Consider changing the maximum cached file size.** By default, IIS caches only files that are 262,144 bytes or less in size. If you have large data files or multimedia files that are accessed frequently, you might want to increase this value to allow IIS to cache larger files. Keep in mind that with file sizes over this size you'll reach a point at which caching won't significantly improve performance. The reason for this is that with small files the overhead of reading from disk rather than the file cache is significant, but with large files the disk read might not be the key factor in determining overall performance. To control the maximum cached file size, you can use the *maxResponseSize* attribute of the *system.webServer/caching* element.

- **Consider adjusting the Time to Live (TTL) value for cached resources.** By default, IIS purges from cache any resources that haven't been requested within the last 30 seconds. If you have additional memory on the server, you might want to increase this value so that files aren't removed from cache as quickly. To control the TTL value for cached resources, you can use the *duration* attribute of the *add* collection for the *system.webServer/caching/profiles* element.

> **TIP**   If you have a dedicated server running only IIS, you might want to consider allowing resources to remain in cache until they are overwritten (due to *maxCacheSize* limits). In this case, you would set an unlimited duration by using a value of 00:00:00.

- **Consider modifying the ASP template cache.**   The ASP template cache controls the number of ASP pages that are cached in memory. By default, IIS will cache up to 2,000 files. This typically is enough on a site with lots of ASP content. Template cache entries can reference one or more entries in the ASP Script Engine Cache. To control template caching, you set the *maxDiskTemplateCacheFiles* attribute of the *system.webServer/asp/cache* element.

- **Consider modifying the script engine cache.**   The ASP Script Engine Cache is an area of memory directly accessible to the scripting engines used by IIS. As such, the preferred area for IIS to retrieve information from is the script engine cache. By default, the script engine cache can hold up to 250 entries. To control script engine caching, you set the *scriptEngineCacheMax* attribute of the *system.webServer/asp/cache* element.

Chapter 8. IIS Backup and Recovery

When you back up an Internet Information Services (IIS) server, you need to look at the IIS configuration in addition to the system configuration. This means that you must do the following:

- Save the IIS configuration whenever you change the properties of the IIS installation.
- Maintain several configuration backups as an extra precaution.
- Periodically back up the server by using a comprehensive backup procedure, such as the one outlined in this chapter.

Backing up an IIS server by using this technique gives you several recovery options. You can:

- Recover the IIS configuration settings for sites and virtual servers by using the IIS configuration backup you've created.
- Recover a corrupted IIS installation by reinstalling IIS and then recovering the last working IIS configuration.
- Restore the server, its data files, and its IIS configuration by recovering the system from archives.
- Perform a partial server restore to retrieve missing or corrupted files from archives.

The sections that follow examine backing up and recovering IIS server configurations and data files.

Backing Up the IIS Configuration

Backing up the IIS configuration is an important part of any Web administrator's job. Before you get started, take a moment to learn the key concepts that'll help you every step of the way.

Understanding IIS Configuration Backups

IIS configuration backups contain metadata that describes the configuration settings used by IIS modules, Web sites, applications, and virtual directories. IIS uses the metadata to restore values for all resource properties on a server. IIS also uses this information to maintain the run state of the server. Therefore, if you save the IIS configuration and then restore the configuration later, the IIS configuration settings are restored and the IIS resources are also returned to their original state.

I recommend that you create an IIS configuration backup every time you make IIS configuration changes and before you make major changes that affect the availability of resources. Because IIS has new configuration architecture, creating and managing IIS configuration backups is fundamentally different than with previous editions of IIS. Throughout this chapter, I'll refer to backups of IIS server configuration and content configuration simply as IIS configuration backups. However, the distinction between server configuration and content configuration is an important one.

Server configuration backups include:

- Automated backups of applicationHost.config created by IIS and stored in the configuration history under *%SystemDrive%*\Inetpub\History by default
- Administrator generated backups of the server's current configuration and running state stored under *%SystemRoot%*\System32\Inetsrv\Backup by default

IIS automatically creates a backup of applicationHost.config when you make configuration changes. This history captures the last 10 configuration changes made on the server in sequentially numbered CFGHISTORY subdirectories of *%SystemDrive%*\Inetpub\History. When you change the configuration, IIS does the following:

1. Deletes the oldest configuration history subdirectory under *%SystemDrive%*\Inetpub\History.
2. Creates a new configuration history subdirectory under *%SystemDrive%*\Inetpub\History.

3. Writes a copy of applicationHost.config to the newly created subdirectory.

As you continue to make configuration changes, IIS does not track every individual change. Instead, after the first configuration change, IIS stores the current configuration every 2 minutes. Thus, if you make a series of changes to the IIS configuration over a period of 10 minutes, IIS would track the configuration changes by creating up to five configuration history files.

As an IIS administrator, you can create backups of an IIS server's current configuration and running state. IIS stores these backups by default in a subdirectory of *%SystemRoot%*\System32\Inetsrv\Backup. Administrator-generated backups generally can include the following configuration files:

- **Administration.config**   Stores the current configuration for delegation and management
- **ApplicationHost.config**   Stores the current configuration and running state of the server plus all applications, application pools, and virtual directories created on the server
- **Mbschema.xml**   Stores the schema for the IIS 6 metabase
- **Metabase.xml**   Stores the IIS 6 metabase
- **Redirection.config**   Stores redirection configuration

> **NOTE**   IIS 7.0 and IIS 7.5 use the metabase only for backwards compatibility with FTP services as designed for IIS 6. Metabase files are stored as part of the configuration only when you've installed the IIS metabase compatibility and FTP Server role services.

Content configuration backups include copies of the Web.config files that modify the default configuration for Web site, application, and directory roots. Neither the automated IIS backup process nor the manual administrator backup process creates backup copies of Web.config files. Because of this, you must use a separate backup or copy process to create copies of Web.config files.

Assuming that you've installed the IIS server root under *%SystemDrive%*\Inetpub (per the default configuration), you can quickly obtain a list of all Web.config files used on a server by running the command-line script shown in Listing 8-1.

LISTING 8-1 Script for Web.config Files

```
@echo off
@title "Listing IIS web.config files to working.txt"
cls
color 07

echo *********************************************** > working.txt
echo "Listing of web.config files as of:" >> working.txt
date /t >> working.txt
echo *********************************************** >> working.txt
echo * >> working.txt
for /r %SystemDrive%\inetpub %%B in (web.config) do
(echo %%B >> working.txt)
echo Done...listing contents of working.txt...
echo *
type working.txt
echo *
```

Sample Output

```
**************************************************
"Listing of web.config files as of:"
Fri 12/21/2015
**************************************************
*
C:\inetput\wwwroot\web.config
C:\inetput\wwwroot\Sales\web.config
C:\inetput\wwwroot\Support\web.config
C:\inetput\wwwroot\Reports\web.config
*
```

The heart of this basic script is the following For loop:

```
for /r %SystemDrive%\inetpub %%B in (web.config) do (echo %%B >>
working.txt)
```

This For loop looks recursively in subdirectories of *%SystemDrive%*\Inetpub for instances of files named Web.config and then writes the full path of each file in turn to a text file in the current directory called working.txt. If you created the IIS server root in another location, simply substitute that location for

%SystemDrive%\Inetpub when running the script. %%B is an iteration variable that tracks the current working value. In this script, %%B tracks an instance of a file path where there's a Web.config file on the server.

The other statements in the script are there for aesthetics. They provide additional details on the command line and in the working file itself. Knowing this, you could also run the For loop at the command prompt by typing the following:

```
for /r %SystemDrive%\inetpub %B in (web.config) do (echo %B >>
working.txt)
```

> **NOTE**   See the syntax change for the iteration variable. You reference iteration variables in scripts by using %% notation and at a command line by using % notation.

IIS configuration backups can help you in many situations. You can:

- **Recover deleted resources**   References to all site, application pool, virtual directory, and application instances running on the server are stored with the configuration backup. If you delete a site, application pool, virtual directory, or application, you can restore the necessary resource references by restoring the configuration files.
- **Restore resource properties**   All configuration settings of sites, application pools, virtual directories, and applications are stored in the configuration backup. If you change properties, you can recover the previous IIS settings from backup.
- **Recover global settings and module configuration**   Global properties and module configuration settings are stored in configuration backups. This means that you can recover default settings for the server and modules from backup.
- **Rebuild a damaged IIS installation**   If the IIS installation is corrupted and you can't repair it through normal means, you can rebuild the IIS installation. You do this by uninstalling IIS, reinstalling IIS, and then using the configuration backup to restore the IIS settings. See the "Rebuilding Corrupted IIS Installations" section of this chapter for details.

Backup files created by IIS are simply copies of the original configuration files. This means that you can open them in a standard text editor to view or modify their settings as you would with any of the other configuration files.

Managing the IIS Configuration History

You can manage the way IIS creates automatic backups of configuration changes by running the IIS command-line administration tool's Set Config command and the configHistory section of the applicationHost.config file. The available attributes for this configuration section are:

- **Enabled** Controls whether configuration history tracking is turned on or off. By default, this attribute is set to True. To turn off configuration history tracking, set this attribute to False.

> **NOTE** Typically, you'd want to turn off the configuration history only when you are doing extensive testing or debugging of applications and don't want any of these changes tracked. When you are finished testing or debugging, you should re-enable configuration history.

- **Path** Sets the directory to which IIS writes configuration history. The default is *%SystemDrive%*\Inetpub\History.
- **maxHistories** Sets the maximum number of history files to track. The default is 10.
- **Period** Sets the interval at which IIS writes configuration history as you continue to make changes. The default interval is every 2 minutes.

> **NOTE** You can use maxHistories and Period to optimize history tracking for the way you work with IIS. For example, if you want to maintain more history information and find that you often modify history over extended periods, you may want to increase maxHistories and increase the write period. In this way, IIS will retain more history files and make fewer history files when you modify the running configuration over long periods.

Sample 8-1 provides the syntax and usage for working with configuration history. Note that period values are set in *hh:mm:ss* format where the *h* position is for hours, the *m* position is for minutes, and the *s* position is for seconds.

SAMPLE 8-1 Managing the Configuration History Syntax and Usage

Syntax

```
appcmd set config /section:configHistory
[/enabled: true|false] [/path: "DestPath"]
[/maxHistories: "NumHistories"]
[/period: "HH:MM:SS"
```

Usage to Modify History Tracking

```
appcmd set config /section:configHistory
/maxHistories: "25" /period: "00:05:00"
```

Usage to Disable History Tracking

```
appcmd set config /section:configHistory /enabled:false
```

Viewing IIS Configuration Backups

IIS stores configuration backups by default in the *%SystemDrive%*\Inetpub\History directory. Each subdirectory in this directory contains the files for a specific configuration backup. By using the IIS command-line administration tool, you can list configuration backups by running the List Backup command. Sample 8-2 provides the syntax and usage. As the syntax shows, you can list all backups or a specific backup. You list a specific backup to determine if that specific backup exists. Appcmd doesn't provide other details about a backup, however.

SAMPLE 8-2 List Backup Syntax and Usage

Syntax

```
appcmd list backup [/backup.name:] "BackupName"]
```

Usage

```
appcmd list backup
```

```
appcmd list backup "101207_583921"
```

Creating IIS Configuration Backups

Each IIS server has a configuration that must be backed up to ensure that IIS can be recovered in case of problems. You can create backups at the server, site, or virtual directory level.

At the server level, you create a configuration backup of all sites, application pools, applications, and virtual directories on the server by using the IIS command-line administration tool and the Add Backup command. Sample 8-3 provides the syntax and usage. If you do not provide a backup name, AppCmd generates a name using a date time stamp that tracks the year, month, date, and time to the second, such as 20150415T143535.

SAMPLE 8-3 Add Backup Syntax and Usage

Syntax
```
appcmd add backup [/name:"BackupName"]
```

Usage
```
appcmd add backup

appcmd add backup /name:"10-12-08_CurrentSet"
```

After you back up the IIS configuration, you should also back up the content configuration, that is, the individual Web.config files for sites, applications, and virtual directories. Listing 8-1 provides a script for listing each Web.config file on the server.

Removing IIS Configuration Backups

As you create configuration backups, you create more and more configuration backup subdirectories and files on the server. You can delete backups by removing the related subdirectories, which are stored by default under %SystemDrive%\Inetpub\History.

By using the IIS command-line administration tool, you can delete individual configuration backups by running the Remove Backup command. Sample 8-4 provides the syntax and usage. As the syntax shows, you must provide the name of the backup configuration to delete.

SAMPLE 8-4 Delete Backup Syntax and Usage

Syntax

```
appcmd delete backup [/backup.name:]"BackupName"
```

Usage

```
appcmd delete backup

appcmd delete backup /backup.name:"10-12-08_CurrentSet"
```

Restoring IIS Server Configurations

You can restore IIS from backup configuration files. When you do this, the previous property settings and state are restored for all sites, application pools, applications, and virtual directories. Recovering the configuration won't repair a corrupted IIS installation. To repair a corrupted installation, follow the technique outlined in the "Rebuilding Corrupted IIS Installations" section of this chapter.

When you restore IIS from a backup configuration, the IIS command-line administration tool stops the server, copies the backup configuration files over the existing configuration files, and then starts the server. IIS then loads the current run state from these files on startup. Stopping and then starting IIS is a precaution to ensure that the full state of the server is reset. If AppCmd did not stop and start the server, some settings that require restart would not be applied until you manually restarted the server process. For example, if the access log settings in the backup configuration are different from those in the running configuration, the restored access log settings are applied only when the server process is restarted.

> **TIP** Restoring the IIS configuration doesn't' restore content configuration, which may include additional settings that need to be restored. Thus, to restore the configuration fully, you many need to copy the backup Web.config files to their original locations.

By using the IIS command-line administration tool, you can restore a configuration backup by running the Restore Backup command. Sample 8-5 provides the syntax and usage. As the syntax shows, you must provide the name of the backup configuration to restore. Optionally, you can specify whether AppCmd stops the server before restoring the configuration. Because stopping and starting the server causes all server processes to be recycled, this could cause issues with user sessions and applications.

SAMPLE 8-5 Restore Backup Syntax and Usage

Syntax

```
appcmd restore backup [/backup.name:]"BackupName" [/stop:true|false]
```

Usage

```
appcmd restore backup "10-12-08_CurrentSet"
```

```
appcmd restore backup "10-12-08_CurrentSet" /stop:false
```

Rebuilding Corrupted IIS Installations

A corrupt IIS installation can cause problems with your IIS sites, application pools, applications, and virtual directories. Resources might not run. IIS might not respond to commands. IIS might freeze intermittently. To correct these problems, you might need to rebuild the IIS installation. Rebuilding the IIS installation is a lengthy process that requires a complete outage of the server. The outage can last from 5 to 15 minutes or more.

You rebuild a corrupt IIS installation by completing the following steps:

1. Log on locally to the computer on which you want to rebuild IIS. Make sure to use an account with Administrator privileges.

2. Create a new backup of the server configuration and content configuration by using the techniques discussed previously in this chapter.

3. Start Server Manager by clicking the Server Manager icon on the Quick Launch toolbar or by clicking Start, pointing to Administrative Tools, and then clicking Server Manager.

4. In Server Manager, right-click the Roles node, and then select Remove Roles. This starts the Remove Roles Wizard.

5. On the Remove Server Roles page, Setup selects the currently installed roles. To remove a role, clear the related check box. When you are finished selecting roles to remove, click Next, and then click Remove.

6. In Server Manager, right-click the Roles node, and then select Add Roles. This starts the Add Roles Wizard.

7. On the Select Server Roles page, Setup makes the currently selected roles dimmed so that you cannot select them. To add a role, select it in the Roles list. When you are finished selecting roles to add, click Next, and then click Install.

8. Restore the server configuration by using the IIS command-line administration tool and the Restore Backup command. This restores the IIS server configuration.

9. Restore the content configuration by copying the Web.config files to the appropriate locations.

Backing Up and Recovering Server Files

Windows Server 2008 and Windows Server 2008 R2 provide a utility called Windows Server Backup for creating server backups. You use Windows Server Backup to perform common backup and recovery tasks. Other features include startup and recovery options and a facility for making recovery disks.

> **NOTE**   The focus of this book is on IIS administration and not Windows Server administration. A full discussion of backup, recovery, and troubleshooting the operating system is beyond the scope of this book.

Turning on the Backup Feature

Windows Server Backup is provided as an add-on component for the operating system. In earlier versions of Microsoft Windows, you use the Add/Remove Windows Components application of Add Or Remove Programs to add or remove operating system components. In Windows Server, operating system components are considered Windows features that can be turned on or off rather than added or removed.

To turn on the Backup feature, follow these steps:

1. Start Server Manager by clicking the Server Manager icon on the Quick Launch toolbar or by clicking Start, pointing to Administrative Tools, and then clicking Server Manager.

2. In Server Manager, select the Features node to view a list of installed features. If Windows Server Backup is not listed as an installed feature, click Add Features. This starts the Add Features Wizard.

3. Under Features, select the Windows Server Backup check box.

4. Click Next, and then click Install.

5. When the installation process finishes, click Close to close the Add Features Wizard.

You can now use Windows Server Backup on the server.

Working with Windows Server Backup

Once you've turned on the Windows Server Backup feature, you can access the related utility in several ways, including:

- Click Start, point to Administrative Tools, and then click Windows Server Backup.
- In Server Manager, expand the Storage node, and then select Windows Server Backup.

The first time you use Windows Server Backup, you may want to configure basic performance settings and create a backup schedule. Basic performance settings control whether Windows Server Backup performs full or incremental backups by default. A backup schedule allows you to configure Windows Server Backup to back up the server automatically according to a recurring schedule, such as once daily or twice daily. You also can back up a server manually.

To perform backup and recovery operations, you must have certain permissions and user rights. Members of the Administrators and Backup Operators groups have full authority to back up and restore any type of file, regardless of who owns the file and the permissions set on it. File owners and those that have been given control over files can also back up files, but only those that they own or those for which they have Read, Read And Execute, Modify, or Full Control permissions.

> **NOTE** Keep in mind that although local accounts can work only with local systems, domain accounts have domain-wide privileges. Therefore, a member of the local administrators group can work with files only on the local system, but a member of the domain administrators group can work with files throughout the domain.

Windows Server Backup can perform two general types of backups:

- Full
- Incremental

With a full (normal) backup, Windows Server Backup backs up all files that have been selected and then clears the archive bit. If a file is later changed, the operating system sets the archive bit to mark the file as needing backup. With full backups, you always have a full set of data, but the backup process takes longer than with incremental backups because you are backing up more data. When you run only full backups, you restore a server by restoring the most recent full backup.

With an incremental backup, Windows Server Backup backs up only files that have changed since the most recent full or incremental backup. Windows Server Backup determines that a file needs to be backed up incrementally based on the file having its archive bit set. With incremental backups, the first backup on the server will always be a full backup and then successive backups will be incremental backups. Because incremental backups back up only files that have changed since the most recent full or incremental backup, incremental backups are usually smaller than full backups and can therefore be created more quickly.

In most cases, you'll want to create full backups of a server at least once a week and then supplement this with daily incremental backups. Restoring a server from incremental backups can be much slower than restoring a server from a full backup. With incremental backups, you restore a server by restoring the most recent full backup and then restoring each incremental backup created since the most recent full backup. For example, you create a full backup on

Sunday and incremental backups Monday through Saturday. If the server fails on Friday, prior to creating Friday's incremental backup, you restore the server by applying Sunday's full backup and the incremental backups from Monday, Tuesday, Wednesday, and Thursday.

Although you can back up to shared volumes and DVD media manually, you will need a separate, dedicated hard disk for running scheduled backups. After you configure a disk for scheduled backups, the backup utilities automatically manage the disk usage and reuse the space of older backups when creating new backups. Once you schedule backups, you'll need to check periodically to ensure that backups are being performed as expected and that the backup schedule meets current needs.

Setting Basic Performance Options

By default, Windows Server Backup always performs a full backup of all physical drives on the server. Both internal and external drives are included in the backup as long as the drives are formatted as NTFS.

You can change the default settings so that Windows Backup Server performs incremental backups of all internal drives on the server or selectively performs a full or incremental backup depending on the drive. With full backups, you can perform a full Volume Shadow Copy Service (VSS)–based backup or a copy backup. With full VSS backups, VSS is used to perform block-level (image) backups, which ensures that the backup includes files that are being written to by the operating system or user processes, such as application data. When you perform a copy backup, application data is not included in the backup, and you then also must use a third-party backup utility to back up applications. With scheduled backups, Windows performs copy backups. With manual backups, you can specify whether you want to perform a full VSS or copy backups. Although Windows Server Backup does not currently enable you to specify that you want to perform a full backup weekly or monthly (for instance), and then incremental backups once or twice daily (for instance), this functionality probably will be added in a future service pack.

You can view or change the default options by completing the following steps:

1. In Server Manager, expand the Storage node, and then select Windows Server Backup.

2. In the Actions Pane or on the Action menu, select Configure Performance Settings. The Optimize Backup Performance dialog box appears.

3. Choose an appropriate default backup option. If you choose Custom, you can set the backup options and type for each supported drive. With a custom backup option, you also can exclude drives. However, drives that contain the operating system or applications must always be selected for backup.

4. Click OK to save the default settings.

Scheduling Server Backups

Scheduling a backup allows you to back up a server automatically according to a specified schedule. You create a backup schedule for a server by completing the following steps:

1. In Server Manager, expand the Storage node, and then select Windows Server Backup.

2. In the Actions Pane or on the Action menu, select Backup Schedule. When the Backup Schedule Wizard starts, click Next.

3. You can use the Select Backup Type page to perform either a full server backup, which includes all supported drives, or a custom server backup, in which some drives are excluded from the backup. Note that the size of the full backup is listed. To continue, do one of the following:

- To perform a full server backup of all supported drives to include both internal and external drives, select Full Server, and then click Next. Drives that are formatted as NTFS are included in the backup set. Drives that are formatted as FAT, FAT32, or another file system are not included in the backup set.
- To selectively backup drives, select Custom, and then click Next. On the Select Custom Backup Items page, select the check boxes for the drives you want to include and clear the check boxes for drives you want to exclude. You must always include drives that contain the operating system and applications.

4. On the Specify Backup Time page, specify how often you want to run backups. You can schedule backups to run once a day at a specified time or multiple times a day at specified times. Click Next.

> **TIP** When scheduling your backups, keep in mind that you typically will want to perform backups during off-peak times because the backup process could result in reduced responsiveness to user requests. Also keep in mind that a full backup of a server can take several hours to complete (as can incremental backups that include many gigabytes of data).

5. On the Select Destination Disk page, select the disk or disks for storing the backup, and then click Next. The Backup Schedule Wizard will check the format of the target disk or disks and reformat the disk or disks as necessary. When a disk is reformatted, all data on the disk is lost. When selecting target disks, keep the following in mind:

- If you choose multiple disks, Windows Server Backup creates multiple copies of the backup. Creating multiple backup copies allows you to store a backup on a disk directly connected to the server in addition to on a remote server or network storage device. Because a network storage device can be in a different physical location, this makes it easier to create and store backups off site to protect against natural disasters. Although being able to create multiple backup copies is a tremendous benefit, keep in mind that each additional backup copy creates an additional burden on the server, and you may need to monitor resource usage carefully during backup creation. In addition, to write backups to different physical locations efficiently, you may need to set up a dedicated backup network.
- The list of disks for backups includes both internal and external disks. Any disk connected to the server can be used for storing backups as long as the disk does not have system or application files. Only the most likely disk or disks for storing backups are listed for selection. To list other available disks, click Show All, select a check box for a disk to make it available for use, and then click OK.
- When selecting a disk to use for the backup, note the size of the disk in addition to the amount of space used. Note also the Backup Item Size and then Recommended Target Size details. Backup Item Size lists the total size of the backup. Recommended Target Size lists the recommended amount

of free space for creating the backup. The recommended amount of free space is more than the required free space to allow Windows Server Backup to create temporary working files and to ensure optimal performance. If a target disk has less free space than the recommended amount, the backup process will be less efficient and slower than usual.

6. If you are writing a backup to an external disk, you see the Label Destination Disk page and are prompted to label the disk so that it is identified as a backup disk. Click Next.

7. On the Confirmation page, review the backup schedule and details, and then click Finish. The server must be turned on at the scheduled run time for automated backups to work.

Backing up a Server

You can use the Backup Wizard to back up a server manually at any time by completing the following steps:

1. In Server Manager, expand the Storage node, and then select Windows Server Backup.

2. In the Actions Pane or on the Action menu, select Backup Once.

3. On the Backup Options page, choose Different Options, and then click Next.

4. On the Specify Backup Type page, you can choose to perform either a full server backup that includes all supported drives or a custom server backup in which some drives are excluded from the backup. To continue, do one of the following, and then click Next:

- To perform a full server backup of all supported drives to include both internal and external drives, select Full Server, and then click Next. Drives that are formatted as NTFS are included in the backup set. Drives that are formatted as FAT, FAT32, or another file system are not included in the backup set.
- To selectively back up drives, select Custom, and then click Next. On the Backup Items page, select the check boxes for the drives you want to include and clear the check boxes for drives you want to exclude. You must always include drives that contain the operating system and applications.

5. You can store the backup on a local drive or on a remote shared folder by using the following techniques. To continue, do one of the following, and then click Next:

- To store the backup on a local drive, select Local Drives, and then click Next. On the Select Backup Location page, on the Backup Location list, choose a backup location. When selecting a disk to use for the backup, note the size of the disk in addition to the amount of space used. Note also the Backup Item Size. The disk you select should have approximately 50 percent more free space than the backup item size. This allows Windows Server Backup to create temporary working files and ensures optimal performance. If a disk doesn't have additional free space, the backup process will be less efficient and slower than usual.
- To store the backup on a remote shared folder, select Remote Shared Folder, and then click Next. On the Specify Remote Folder page, type the UNC path to the remote shared folder, such as \\BackupServer26\Backup\WebServer85. The remote shared folder must be configured as an available network location.

6. On the Specify VSS Backup Type page, specify whether you want to perform a copy backup or a VSS full backup. Choose Copy Backup if you are using a separate backup utility to back up application data, such as that from Microsoft SQL Server. Otherwise, choose VSS Full Backup to fully back up the selected volumes, including all application data.

7. On the Confirmation page, review the backup schedule and details, and then click Backup. The Backup Once Wizard will then create a shadow copy of the drives you are backing up. This allows the wizard to back up files that are being written to by the operating system or user processes. Click Backup.

On the Backup Progress page, you'll see the status of the backup and the amount of data transferred. The backup is complete when the backup status reaches 100 percent. If you click Close, the backup will continue to run in the background, and you can review the final backup status for errors or other issues in Server Manager. Simply double-click the backup entry under Messages.

Protecting a Server Against Failure

Backing up a server is one way of protecting a server against failure. Windows Server has a built-in recovery feature that automatically runs if a server fails to start or experiences a fatal system error (also known as a STOP error). For some of these features to work, you may need the original Windows installation disk. Additionally, computer manufacturers increasingly are including recovery features as part of a comprehensive hardware option. These features can also be used to recover the operating system to a bootable state. If these features fail, Windows Server 2008 and Windows Server 2008 R2 provide other protection features, including:

- Startup and recovery options
- Recovery disks

The sections that follow discuss how to configure these recovery options.

Configuring Recovery Options

Startup and recovery options control the way Windows Server 2008 and Windows Server 2008 R2 start and handle failures. You can manage startup and recovery options by completing these steps:

1. Click Start, and then click Control Panel. In Control Panel, click System and Maintenance, and then click System.

2. In the System console, in the left pane, click Advanced System Settings. On the Advanced tab, under Startup and Recovery, click Settings. This opens the Startup and Recovery dialog box.

3. If the server has multiple bootable operating systems, you can set the default operating system by selecting one of the operating systems in the Default Operating System drop-down list. These options change the configuration settings that Windows Boot Manager uses.

4. At the startup of a computer with multiple bootable operating systems, Windows Server displays the startup configuration menu for 30 seconds by default. To boot immediately to the default operating system, clear the Time To Display List Of Operating Systems check box. To display the available options for a specific amount of time, select the Time To Display

List Of Operating Systems check box, and then set the desired time delay in seconds.

5. When the system is in a recovery mode and is booting, a list of recovery options might appear. To boot immediately using the default recovery option, clear the Time To Display Recovery Options When Needed check box. To display the available recovery options for a specific amount of time, select the Time To Display Recovery Options When Needed check box, and then set a time delay in seconds.

6. System Failure options control what happens when the system encounters a STOP error. The available options for the System Failure area are as follows:

- **Write an Event to the System Log**   Logs the error in the System log, which allows you to review the error later using the Event Viewer.
- **Automatically Restart**   Select this check box to have the system attempt to reboot when a fatal system error occurs.
- **Write Debugging Information**   Choose the type of debugging information to write to a dump file if a fatal error occurs. You can then use the dump file to diagnose system failures.
- **Dump File**   Sets the location for the dump file. The default dump locations are *%SystemRoot%*\Minidump for small memory dumps and *%SystemRoot%*\MEMORY.DMP for all other memory dumps.
- **Overwrite Any Existing File**   Ensures that any existing dump files are overwritten if a new STOP error occurs.

7. Click OK to save your settings.

The Windows Recovery Environment includes the following tools:

- **Windows Complete PC Restore**   Allows you to recover a server's operating system or perform a full system recovery. With an operating system or full system recovery, make sure your backup data is available and that you can log on with an account that has the appropriate permissions. With a full system recovery, keep in mind that existing data that was not included in the original backup will be deleted when you recover the system, including any in-use volumes that were not included in the backup.

- **Windows Memory Diagnostics Tools**   Allows you to diagnose a problem with the server's physical memory. Three different levels of memory testing can be performed: basic, standard, or exhaustive.

You can also access a command prompt. This command prompt gives you access to the command-line tools available during installation as well as to these additional programs:

- **On-screen Keyboard (x:\sources\setuposk.exe)**   Allows you to enter keystrokes using the on-screen keyboard.
- **Rollback wizard (x:\sources\rollback.exe)**   Normally the Rollback wizard starts automatically if Windows Setup encounters a problem during installation.
- **Startup Repair wizard (x:\sources\recovery\StartRep.exe)**   Normally this tool starts automatically on boot failure if Windows detects an issue with the boot sector, the boot manager, or the boot configuration data (BCD) store.
- **Startup Recovery Options (x:\sources\recovery\recenv.exe)**   Allows you to start the Startup Recovery Options wizard. If you previously entered the wrong recovery settings, you can provide different options.

You can recover a server's operating system or perform a full system recovery by following these steps:

1. Insert the recovery disc into the CD or DVD drive and turn on the computer. If needed, press the required key to boot from the disc. The Install Windows Wizard should appear.
2. Specify the language settings to use, and then click Next.
3. Click Repair Your Computer. Setup searches the hard disk drives for an existing Windows installation and then displays the results in the System Recovery Options Wizard. If you are recovering the operating system onto separate hardware, the list should be empty and there should be no operating system on the computer. Click Next.
4. On the System Recovery Options page, click Windows Complete PC Restore. This starts the Windows Complete PC Restore Wizard.

Recovering Files and Folders

You can recover files and folders from a backup by completing the following steps:

1. In Server Manager, expand the Storage node, and then select Windows Server Backup.

2. In the Actions Pane or on the Action menu, select Recover. The Recovery Wizard starts.

3. On the Getting Started page, choose This Server.

4. On the Select Backup Date page, note the earliest and latest available backup dates, and then use the calendar view provided to select a date for recovery. Click Next.

5. Backup copies are available for dates shown in bold in the calendar view. If there are multiple backup times on a date, select a specific backup from the Time drop-down list. Note the backup target and status of the selected backup. The target disk must be available online to recover files and applications.

6. On the Select Recovery Type page, select Files And Folders to recover specific files and folders from a backup, and then click Next.

7. On the Select Items To Recover page, expand the server, volume, and folder nodes to find the files and folders to recover. You can recover only one folder/file set at a time. When you select a folder by clicking it, the folder and all its related subfolders and files are selected for recovery. Click the folder you want to recover, such as Inetpub, and then click Next.

8. On the Specify Recovery Options page, use the Restore Destination options to choose the restore location and the click Next. The options are:

- **Original Location** Restores data to the location from which it was backed up.
- **Alternate Location** Restores data to a location that you designate, preserving the existing directory structure. After you select this option, type the folder path to use, or click Browse to select the folder path.

9. Select one of the following options to specify how you want to restore files, and then click Next:

- **Create Copies So I Have Both Versions Of The File Or Folder**   Select this option if you don't want to copy over existing files. With this option, you'll have copies of the recovered files in the recovery destination and will need to review the files to see which files you want to use. In most cases, you won't want to use this option if you are restoring multiple files to the original location, because this would cause many duplicate files to be created (and you'd probably need to use Windows Explorer to clean up all the duplicates).
- **Overwrite Existing Files With Recovered Files**   Select this option to replace all existing files on disk with files from the backup and to restore deleted files that do not otherwise exist at the recovery location. This option allows you to recover files and folders to a previous state (the state the files were in when the backup was created). Files that were deleted from the recovery location are also restored.
- **Don't Recover Any Existing Files And Folders**   Select this option to recover only files that do not exist at the recovery destination. This allows you to recover deleted files without overwriting existing files. If you accidentally removed files from a folder, this is a good option to use to recover only those accidentally removed files.

10. By default, Restore Security Settings is selected. This ensures that the Recovery Wizard restores the original security settings for files and folders. If you don't want to restore the original security settings, clear this check box. The Recovery Wizard will then use the default security settings for the recovery folder. Click Next

11. On the Confirmation page, review the items that will be recovered, and then click Finish. The Recovery Wizard will then recover the selected items. On the Recovery Progress page, you'll see the status of the recovery and the amount of data transferred for each item. Click Recover.

12. The recovery is complete when the recovery status reaches 100 percent. Click Close to finish the wizard.

Appendix A. Comprehensive IIS Module and Schema Reference

In IIS 6, the configuration of a Web server is stored in the metabase, which is formatted using Extensible Markup Language (XML). When you create a backup of the metabase in IIS 6, you back up the server configuration into XML files stored in the *%SystemRoot%*\System32\Inetsrv directory. The metabase files are not meant to be edited and instead are managed through the IIS 6 Manager.

Although IIS 7.0 and IIS 7.5 include IIS 6 metabase support, they do not use a metabase to store configuration information. Instead, IIS 7.0 and IIS 7.5 use a distributed configuration system with a single global configuration file, zero or more application-specific configuration files, and XML schema files that define the configuration elements, attributes, and the data that they can contain and provide precise control over exactly how you can configure IIS.

The global configuration file, Application.Host.config, is stored in the *%SystemRoot%*\System32\Inetsrv\Config directory. This file controls the global configuration of IIS. Application-specific configuration (Web.config) files can be stored in application directories to control the configuration of individual applications. Schema files define the exact set of configuration features and options that you can use within Application.Host.config and Web.config files. On a Web server, schema files are stored in the *%SystemRoot%*\System32\Inetsrv\Config\Schema directory. The three standard schema files are:

- **IIS_schema.xml**   Provides the IIS configuration schema

- **ASPNET_schema.xml**   Provides the Microsoft ASP.NET configuration schema

- **FX_schema.xml**   Provides the Microsoft .NET Framework configuration schema (beyond ASP.NET)

If you want to extend the configuration features and options available in IIS, you can do this by extending the XML schema. You can extend the schema by defining the desired configuration properties and the necessary section container in an XML schema file, placing this file in the

%SystemRoot%\System32\Inetsrv\Config\Schema directory, and then referencing the new section in the IIS global configuration file.

Working with IIS 7.0 and IIS 7.5 Modules

IIS features are componentized into more than 40 independent modules. Modules are either IIS native modules or IIS managed modules.

Introducing the Native Modules

A native module is a Win32 DLL that must be both installed and activated prior to use. The 32 native modules that ship with the IIS installation provide the core server functionality. As depicted in Figure A-1, this core functionality can be divided into several broad categories.

- **Application Development** Modules that provide features for application development and dynamic content

- **Common HTTP** Modules that provide common features for Hypertext Transfer Protocol (HTTP) and the Web server in general

- **Health and Diagnostics** Modules that provide features that help administrators track the health of the Web server and diagnose problems if they occur

- **Performance** Modules that provide features that can be used to improve performance and scale the server

- **Security** Modules that provide authentication, authorization, and filtering features

Configuration modules can be installed and made available for use:

- During initial setup of IIS

- By editing the Application.Host.config file or Web.config file as appropriate

- Using the graphical administration tool, IIS Manager

- Using the command-line administration tool, Appcmd.exe

Table A-1 provides an overview of specific IIS features, the related configuration modules, and the standard installation technique for each module. As the table shows, you can install most configuration modules by selecting a related feature during initial setup. Some modules are installed automatically as part of the core installation. Others can be installed only manually.

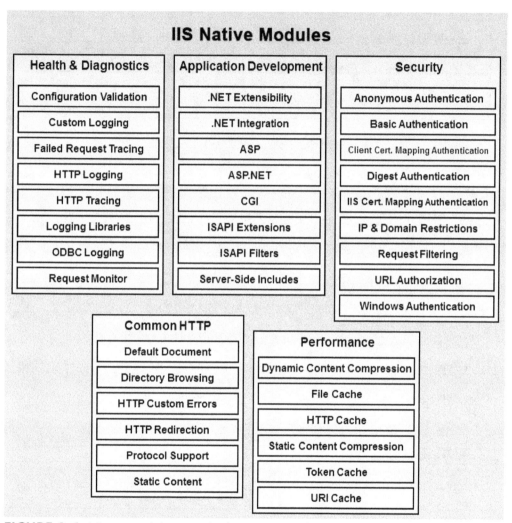

FIGURE A-1 Native modules provide the core server functionality.

TABLE A-1 Native Modules Shipped with IIS

COMMON HTTP FEATURES	
Default Document	DefaultDocumentModule; installed by feature selection
Directory Browsing	DirectoryListingModule; installed by feature selection
HTTP Custom Errors	CustomErrorModule; installed by feature selection
HTTP Redirection	HttpRedirectionModule; installed by feature selection
Protocol Support	ProtocolSupportModule; installed automatically as part of the core installation
Static Content	StaticFileModule; installed by feature selection

APPLICATION DEVELOPMENT FEATURES	
.NET Extensibility	IsapiModule; installed by feature selection
ASP	IsapiFilterModule; installed by feature selection
ASP.NET	IsapiFilterModule; installed by feature selection
CGI	CgiModule; installed by feature selection
Fast CGI	FastCgiModule; installed by feature selection
ISAPI Extensions	IsapiModule; installed by feature selection
ISAPI Filters	IsapiFilterModule; installed by feature selection
Server-Side Includes	ServerSideIncludeModule; installed by feature selection

HEALTH AND DIAGNOSTICS	
Configuration Validation	ConfigurationValidationModule; installed automatically as part of the core installation
Custom Logging	CustomLoggingModule; installed by feature selection
Failed Request Tracing	FailedRequestsTracingModule; installed by feature selection
HTTP Logging	HttpLoggingModule; installed by feature selection
HTTP Tracing	TracingModule; must be manually installed after setup

Logging Tools	CustomLoggingModule; installed by feature selection
ODBC Logging	CustomLoggingModule; installed by feature selection
Request Monitor	RequestMonitorModule; installed by feature selection
SECURITY FEATURES	
Anonymous Authentication	AnonymousAuthenticationModule; installed automatically as part of the core installation
Basic Authentication	BasicAuthenticationModule; installed by feature selection
Client Certificate Mapping Authentication	CertificateMappingAuthenticationModule; installed by feature selection
Digest Authentication	DigestAuthenticationModule; installed by feature selection
IIS Client Certificate Mapping Authentication	IISCertificateMappingAuthenticationModule; installed by feature selection
IP and Domain Restrictions	IpRestrictionModule; installed by feature selection
Request Filtering	RequestFilteringModule; installed by feature selection
URL Authorization	UrlAuthorizationModule; installed by feature selection
Windows Authentication	WindowsAuthenticationModule; installed by feature selection
PERFORMANCE FEATURES	
Dynamic Content Compression	DynamicCompressionModule; installed by feature selection
Static Content Compression	StaticCompressionModule; installed by feature selection
File Cache	FileCacheModule; must be manually installed after setup
.NET Integration	ManagedEngine; must be manually installed after setup
Token Cache	TokenCacheModule; must be manually installed after setup
URI Cache	UriCacheModule; must be manually installed after setup

Introducing the Managed Modules

A managed module is a .NET Framework Class Library contained within an assembly. Because managed modules are installed automatically as part of the .NET Framework, they do not need to be installed. However, managed modules do need to be activated for use. Managed modules also require the installation and activation of the ManagedEngine module, which provides the necessary integration functionality between IIS and the .NET Framework.

The IIS installation ships with 11 managed modules. As Table A-2 shows, these modules provide the core functionality ASP and ASP.NET applications need for authorization and authentication in addition to utility functions for caching, session management, and URL mapping.

TABLE A-2 Managed Modules Shipped with IIS

SECURITY FUNCTIONS	
Anonymous Identification	System.Web.Security.DefaultAuthenticationModule
File Authorization	System.Web.Security.FileAuthorizationModule
Forms Authentication	System.Web.Security.Forms.AuthenticationModule
Profile Management	System.Web.Profile.ProfileModule
Role Management	System.Web.Security.RoleManagerModule
URL Authorization	System.Web.Security.UrlAuthorizationModule.
Windows Authentication	System.Web.Security.WindowsAuthenticationModule
UTILITY FUNCTIONS	
Output Cache	System.Web.Caching.OutputCacheModule
Session Management	System.Web.SessionState.SessionStateModule
URL Mapping	System.Web.UrlMappingsModule

IIS Native Module Reference

In the following section, you'll find a reference for the native modules that ship with IIS. Native modules are used by both administrators and developers.

AnonymousAuthenticationModule

Implements Anonymous authentication

Description   Anonymous authentication is one of several authentication mechanisms available in IIS. If Anonymous authentication is enabled, any user can access content without being required to provide credentials. The actual component within IIS that implements Anonymous authentication is the AnonymousAuthenticationModule. This module allows Anonymous authentication by creating the necessary *HttpUser* object. The *HttpUser* object is an IIS data structure. The IIS core installation checks to ensure that this object is populated after the authentication phase. See Chapter 4, "Managing Web Server Security," for more information on Anonymous authentication.

> **Note**   At least one authentication module must be configured. Because of this, if you disable Anonymous authentication, you must ensure that another authentication mechanism is enabled. If the *HttpUser* object is not populated as would be the case when there are no configured authentication mechanisms, the IIS server core generates a 401.2 error.

Executable   *%Windir%*\System32\Inetsrv\Authanon.dll

Dependencies   None

Configuration Element
system.webServer/security/authentication/*anonymousAuthentication*

ApplicationHost.config Usage Examples

```
<anonymousAuthentication enabled="true" userName="IUSR" />

<anonymousAuthentication enabled="true" userName="IUSR" password="[enc:
AesProvider:jAAAAAECAAADZgAAAKQAAJbG5Vze9+qBIwzs3YYUfw4w1FhMxydEPXSIQN3
WjxTI9s7y8a6VsU9h+bMHUsPibqPGbT0ZwEovDXWzVG0Fg3A/bi7uJAOphgDDP4/xPl8XDw
```

S0rm+22Yyn44lLPbG6d4BGBy7G+b/O2ywozBFbsdckm7bKyNp1NinWKY9dSzKfa9l2SmYVq
vHEQEQjUMXSvg==:enc]" />

Element Attributes   Anonymous authentication is controlled through the system.webServer/security/authentication/*anonymousAuthentication* element. Table A-3 summarizes the standard attributes of the *anonymousAuthentication* element.

TABLE A-3 Standard Attributes of the *anonymousAuthentication* Element

defaultLogonDomain	Sets the optional name of the default domain against which the anonymous users are authenticated. The default logon domain is an empty string.
enabled	Controls whether Anonymous authentication is enabled or disabled. The default is true.
logonMethod	Sets the optional logon method for the anonymous user account as Interactive, Batch, Network, or ClearText. The default is ClearText.
password	Sets the optional password of the account used for anonymous access. This is an optional attribute that must be used only if the account used for anonymous access is assigned a user-managed password. The password is expected to be passed as an encrypted string.
userName	Sets the name of the account used for anonymous access to IIS. You can set this to a specific user or use an empty attribute value (*userName=""*) to use the application pool identity. By default, this value is set to IUSR, the name prefix of the Internet Guest Account created when you installed IIS. The actual account is named in the form: *Prefix_ComputerName*. For example, if the prefix is set as IUSR and the computer name is WebServer81, the account is named IUSR_WebServer81.

BasicAuthenticationModule

Implements Basic authentication

Description   Basic authentication requires a user to provide a valid user name and password to access content. Although all browsers support this authentication mechanism, browsers transmit the password without encryption, making it possible for a password to be compromised. If you want to require basic authentication, you should disable Anonymous authentication. The actual component within IIS that implements Basic authentication is the BasicAuthenticationModule. This module implements HTTP Basic authentication described in RFC 2617.

The BasicAuthenticationModule creates the *HttpUser* object used by and validated by IIS after the authentication phase. If the *HttpUser* object is not populated as would be the case when there are no configured authentication mechanisms, the IIS core installation generates a 401.2 error. See Chapter 4 for more information on Basic authentication.

Executable   *%Windir%\System32\Inetsrv\Authbas.dll*

Dependencies   None

Configuration Element
system.webServer/security/authentication/*basicAuthentication*

ApplicationHost.config Usage Example

```
<basicAuthentication enabled="false" realm="magic1"
defaultLogonDomain="imagined1" />
```

Element Attributes   Basic authentication is controlled through the system.webServer/security/authentication/*basicAuthentication* element. Table A-4 summarizes the standard attributes of the *basicAuthentication* element.

TABLE A-4 Standard Attributes of the *basicAuthentication* Element

defaultLogonDomain	Sets the name of the default domain against which users are authenticated by default. Any users who do not provide a domain name when they log on are authenticated against this domain. No default logon domain is set.
enabled	Controls whether Basic authentication is enabled or disabled. The default is false.
logonMethod	Sets the optional logon method for the anonymous user account as Interactive, Batch, Network, or ClearText. The default is ClearText.

realm	Sets the optional name of the Domain Name System (DNS) domain or Web address that will use the credentials that have been authenticated against the default domain. No default realm is set.

CertificateMappingAuthenticationModule

Maps client certificates to Active Directory accounts for authentication

Description Active Directory Client Certificate authentication maps client certificates to Active Directory accounts. When the CertificateMappingAuthenticationModule is enabled, the module performs the necessary Active Directory Certificate mapping for authentication of authorized clients. As with Anonymous and Basic authentication, the CertificateMappingAuthenticationModule also creates the *HttpUser* object used by and validated by IIS after the authentication phase. If the *HttpUser* object is not populated as would be the case when there are no configured authentication mechanisms, the IIS core installation generates a 401.2 error. See Chapter 4 for more information on Active Directory Client Certificate authentication.

Executable *%Windir%*\System32\Inetsrv\Authcert.dll

Dependencies For this module to work, the Web server must be a member of an Active Directory domain and be configured to use SSL.

Configuration Element
system.webServer/security/authentication/*clientCertificateMappingAuthenticatio n*

ApplicationHost.config Usage Examples

```
<clientCertificateMappingAuthentication enabled="false" />

<clientCertificateMappingAuthentication enabled="true" />
```

Element Attributes Certificate mapping is controlled through the system.webServer/security/authentication/*clientCertificateMappingAuthenticatio*

n element. The enabled attribute of the *clientCertificateMappingAuthentication* element controls whether certificate mapping is enabled or disabled.

CgiModule

Implements the Common Gateway Interface (CGI) specification for use with IIS

Description   In IIS, the Common Gateway Interface (CGI) specification is implemented through the CgiModule. CGI describes how programs specified in Web addresses, also known as *gateway scripts*, pass information to Web servers. Gateway scripts pass information to servers through environment variables that capture user input in forms in addition to information about users submitting information.

The CgiModule has a managed handler that specifies that all files with the .exe extension be handled as CGI programs. The way CGI programs are handled is determined by the *cgi* element defined in the Application.Host.config or Web.config file. If this module is removed, CGI programs stop working.

The *isapiCgiRestriction* element contains the extension restriction list configuration to control which functionality is enabled or disabled on the server. You use the *add* element to specify the full file path to the .exe for the CGI program or the .dll for the ISAPI extension and to specify the allowed status of the application. Optionally, you can also provide a group name for easier management of similar applications and a description of the application.

If you remove this module, IIS will not be able to run CGI programs. See Chapter 1, "Running IIS Applications," for more information on CGI and ISAPI.

Executable   *%Windir%*\System32\Inetsrv\Cgi.dll

Dependencies   None

Configuration Elements   system.webServer/*cgi*

system.webServer/*isapiCgiRestriction*

ApplicationHost.config Usage Examples

```
<cgi createCGIWithNewConsole="false" createProcessAsUser="true"
timeout="00:15:00" />

<isapiCgiRestriction notListedIsapisAllowed="false"
notListedCgisAllowed="false">
  <clear />
  <add path="c:\Windows\system32\inetsrv\asp.dll" allowed="true"
groupId="ASP" description="Active Server Pages" />
  <add path="c:\Windows\Microsoft.NET\Framework\v2.0.50727\
aspnet_isapi.dll" allowed="true" groupId="ASP.NET v2.0.50727"
description="ASP.NET v2.0.50727" />
  <add path="c:\Windows\system32\msw3prt.dll" allowed="true"
groupId="W3PRT" description="Internet Printing" />
</isapiCgiRestriction>
```

Element Attributes   CGI is controlled through the system.webServer/*cgi* element. Table A-5 summarizes the standard attributes of the *cgi* element. The *isapiCgiRestriction* element contains *add* sub-elements that control which functionality is enabled or disabled on the server. These *add* elements can use the attributes summarized in Table A-6.

TABLE A-5 Standard Attributes of the *cgi* Element

createCGIWithNewConsole	Indicates whether the gateway script runs in its own console. The default is false. If set to false, gateway scripts run without a console. If set to true, each gateway application creates a new console when it is started.
createProcessAsUser	Specifies whether a CGI process is created in the system context or in the context of the requesting user. The default is true. If set to false, CGI processes run in the system context. If set to true, CGI processes run in the context of the requesting user.
Timeout	Sets the timeout for gateway scripts. The default is 15 minutes.

TABLE A-6 Standard Attributes of the *isapiCgiRestriction\add* Element

path	Sets the full file path to the .exe for the CGI program or the .dll for the ISAPI extension. No default path is set.

allowed	Indicates whether the application is allowed to run. If set to true, the application can run. If set to false, the application cannot run. The default is false.
groupId	Sets an optional group name for adding the restriction to a group for easier management. No default *groupID* is set.
description	Sets an optional description of the application being added. No default description is set.
notListedIsapiAllowed	Controls whether an ISAPI extension is listed as allowed in IIS Manager. If set to false, the ISAPI extension is not listed as allowed. If set to true, the ISAPI extension is listed as allowed. The default is false.
notListedCGIAllowed	Controls whether a CGI program is listed as allowed in IIS Manager. If set to false, the CGI program is not listed as allowed. If set to true, the CGI program is listed as allowed. The default is false.

ConfigurationValidationModule

Implements configuration validation and related error reporting

Description

When the ConfigurationValidationModule is enabled, IIS validates the configuration of the server and its applications by default. If a server or application is improperly configured, IIS generates errors that can help detect and diagnose the problem. If this module is removed, IIS will not validate the configuration and also will not report configuration errors.

Executable   *%Windir%*\System32\Inetsrv\Validcfg.dll

Dependencies   None

Configuration Element   system.webServer/*Validation*

ApplicationHost.config Usage Examples

```
<validation validateIntegratedModeConfiguration="false" />

<validation validateIntegratedModeConfiguration="true" />
```

Element Attributes   Configuration validation is controlled through the system.webServer/*Validation* element. By default, the *Validation* element has no content, and its attribute values are taken from the schema. In the schema, the *Validation* element has a single attribute: *validateIntegratedModeConfiguration*. This attribute, set to true by default, controls whether IIS validates the server and application configuration. If you don't want IIS to validate the configuration, set the *validateIntegratedModeConfiguration* attribute to false.

CustomErrorModule

Implements custom error and detailed error notification

Description   The CustomErrorModule implements custom error and detailed error notification. When this module is enabled and the server encounters an error, the server can return a customer error page to all clients regardless of location, a detailed error message to all clients regardless of location, or a detailed error for local clients and a custom error page for remote clients. The custom error page displayed is based on the type of HTTP error that occurred. If you remove this module, IIS will return minimal error information when HTTP errors occur. See Chapter 8 in *Web Server Administration: The Personal Trainer*.

Executable   *%Windir%*\System32\Inetsrv\Custerr.dll

Dependencies   None

Configuration Element   system.webServer/*httpErrors*

ApplicationHost.config Usage Examples

```
<httpErrors errorMode="DetailedLocalOnly" defaultPath=""
defaultResponseMode="File">
 <error statusCode="401" prefixLanguageFilePath="%SystemDrive%
\inetpub\custerr" path="401.htm" />
 <error statusCode="404" prefixLanguageFilePath="%SystemDrive%
\inetpub\custerr" path="404.htm" />
 <error statusCode="500" prefixLanguageFilePath="%SystemDrive%
\inetpub\custerr" path="500.htm" />
</httpErrors>
```

Element Attributes Custom errors are controlled through the system.webServer/*httpErrors* element. Table A-7 summarizes the standard attributes of the *httpErrors* element. Table A-8 summarizes the standard attributes of the *error* element.

TABLE A-7 Standard Attributes of the *httpErrors* Element

allowAbsolutePathsWhenDelegated	Controls how paths are used. When true, absolute paths are allowed for custom error pages. When false, only paths that are relative to the site root are allowed. (IIS 7.5 only)
defaultPath	Sets the default path when the execute URL or redirect mode is used.
defaultResponseMode	Sets the response mode as File, ExecuteURL, or Redirect. Use the default response mode, File, when you want IIS to serve the client browser a Web document. Use the Redirect mode when you want to redirect users to a local or remote Web address. Use the ExecuteURL mode when you want IIS to execute a specific, relative URL. The resource specified in the URL must be on the current server. The URL itself cannot contain the following characters: ? : @ & = . > < .
detailedMoreInformationLink	Sets the URL used for the More Information link. The default value is *http://go.microsoft.com/fwlink/?LinkID=62293*.
errorMode	Sets the type of error reporting desired. If this attribute is not assigned a value or set to DetailedLocalOnly, local clients see detailed errors and remote clients see custom error pages. Set *errorMode*="Detailed" for detailed error reports only. Set *errorMode*="Custom" for custom error reports only.
existingResponse	Determines how an existing response is handled. The default, Auto, specifies that existing responses are handled automatically with either Replace or Passthrough as appropriate. Use Replace to force IIS to replace the existing response. Use Passthrough to force IIS to pass the existing response through to the client.

TABLE A-8 Standard Attributes of the *Error* Element

path	Sets the file name of the custom error page within a language-specific subdirectory. No default is set. The path cannot be set to an empty string.
prefixLanguageFilePath	Sets the full path to the base directory for custom error pages. For each language pack installed, IIS looks in a language-specific subdirectory based on the default language of the client browser, such as en-US. No default path is set.
responseMode	Sets the response mode as File, ExecuteURL, or Redirect. Use the default response mode, File, when you want IIS to serve the client browser a Web document for the specific status and substatus code. Use the Redirect mode when you want to redirect users to a local or remote Web address. Use the ExecuteURL mode when you want IIS to execute a specific, relative URL.
statusCode	Indicates the HTTP status code the custom error page should handle. No default value is set for this required field. Valid values are from 400 to 999. For example, if this attribute is set to 404, the custom error page is for HTTP 404 errors.
subStatusCod	Sets the related substatus code. With the default value, −1, IIS does not display or handle the substatus code. Valid values are from −1 to 999.

CustomLoggingModule

Implements custom logging using the Component Object Model (COM)

Description   The CustomLoggingModule implements the ILogPlugin interface. This COM interface is a deprecated feature that allows you to extend IIS logging. Rather than using this module, Microsoft recommends that you create a managed module and subscribe to the RQ_LOG_REQUEST notification.

Executable   *%Windir%*\System32\Inetsrv\Logcust.dll

Dependencies   None

Configuration Element

system.applicationHost/*sites*

ApplicationHost.config Usage Examples

```
<sites>
 <site name="Default Web Site" id="1">
  <application path="/">
   <virtualDirectory path="/"
physicalPath="%SystemDrive%\inetpub\wwwroot" />
  </application>
  . . .
 </site>
 <siteDefaults>
  <logFile logFormat="custom" customLogPluginClsid ="{3a2a4e84-4c21-
4981-ae10-3fda0d9b0f83}" />
  . . .
</sites>
```

Element Attributes   Custom logging is controlled through the system.applicationHost/sites/site/*logFile* element. This element has two attributes that determine whether and how custom logging is used: *logFormat* and *customLogPluginClsid*. To turn on custom logging, you must set *logFormat*="Custom" and then use the *customLogPluginClsid* attribute to set the CLSID of the COM object being used for logging.

Although included as a feature of IIS 7.5, this module is provided as a separate download for IIS 7.0.

DefaultDocumentModule

Allows IIS to serve default documents when directory-level URLs are requested

Description   When a user enters a request with a trailing /, such as *http://www.imaginedlands.com/*, IIS can redirect the request to the default document for the Web server or directory. The DefaultDocumentModule determines whether and how default documents are used. When working with default documents, keep the following in mind:

- When a default document is assigned and available, IIS returns the default document whose file name matches one of those listed as acceptable.

- When there are multiple default documents in a directory, IIS returns the default document with the highest precedence.

- When a default document does not exist and directory browsing is enabled, IIS generates a listing of the contents of the specified directory.

If neither the DefaultDocumentModule nor the DirectoryListing Module handle a request for a directory-level URL, an empty response will be returned.

For optimal performance, you should list the default document you use the most first and then reduce the overall list of default documents to only those that are absolutely necessary. See Chapter 8 in *Web Server Administration: The Personal Trainer* for more information on default documents.

Executable *%Windir%*\System32\Inetsrv\Defdoc.dll

Dependencies None

Configuration Element system.webServer/*defaultDocument*

ApplicationHost.config Usage Examples

```
<defaultDocument enabled="true">
<files>
<add value="Default.htm" />
<add value="Default.asp" />
<add value="index.htm" />
<add value="index.html" />
<add value="iisstart.htm" />
<add value="default.aspx" />
</files>
</defaultDocument>
```

Element Attributes You can use the *defaultDocument* element to control whether default documents are used. To configure IIS to stop using default documents, set the *enabled* attribute of the *defaultDocument* element to false. To have IIS use default documents, set the *enabled* attribute of the *defaultDocument* element to true.

You can use the files and *add* elements to control how default documents are used. The *files* element contains *add* elements that define the acceptable default documents. Each acceptable default document must be defined using a separate *add* element. The *value* attribute of the *add* element sets the name of the default document, such as Default.htm. The order of the *add* elements sets the relative priority of the related default documents.

DigestAuthenticationModule

Implements digest authentication as described in RFC 2617

Description   Digest authentication uses a Microsoft Windows domain controller to authenticate user requests for content. Digest authentication can be used through firewalls and proxies. As with other types of authentication, the DigestAuthenticationModule also creates the *HttpUser* object used by and validated by IIS after the authentication phase. If the *HttpUser* object is not populated as would be the case when there are no configured authentication mechanisms, the IIS server core generates a 401.2 error. See Chapter 4 for more information on Digest authentication.

If you want to require Digest authentication, you should disable Anonymous authentication.

Executable   *%Windir%\System32\Inetsrv\Authmd5.dll*

Dependencies   IIS must part of an Active Directory domain. The client browser must support HTTP 1.1.

Configuration Element
system.webServer/security/authentication/*digestAuthentication*

ApplicationHost.config Usage Examples

```
<digestAuthentication enabled="false" />

<digestAuthentication enabled="true" realm="MagicL" />
```

Element Attributes   Digest authentication is controlled through the system.webServer/security/authentication/*digestAuthentication* element. Table A-9 summarizes the standard attributes of the *digestAuthentication* element.

TABLE A-9 Standard Attributes of the *digestAuthentication* Element

enabled	Controls whether digest authentication is enabled or disabled.
realm	Sets the name of the DNS domain or Web address against which the credentials will be authenticated. If this attribute is not set, credentials are authenticated against the user's default (logon) domain.

DirectoryListingModule

Implements directory browsing functionality

Description   When a user enters a request with a trailing /, such as *http://www.imaginedlands.com/*, IIS can display a listing of the directory. The DirectoryListingModule in conjunction with the DefaultDocumentModule determines whether and how directory listings are used. When default documents are enabled but there is no current default document, IIS can use this module to generate a listing of the contents of the specified directory. If neither the DefaultDocumentModule nor the DirectoryListing Module handle a request for a directory-level URL, an empty response will be returned. See Chapter 7 in *Web Server Administration: The Personal Trainer* for more information on directory browsing.

Executable   *%Windir%*\System32\Inetsrv\Dirlist.dll

Dependencies   None

Configuration Element   system.webServer/*directoryBrowse*

ApplicationHost.config Usage Examples

```
<directoryBrowse enabled="false" />

<directoryBrowse enabled="true" showFlags="LongDate, Extension, Size, T
ime, Date" />
```

Element Attributes Directory browsing is controlled through the system.webServer/*directoryBrowse* element. Table A-10 summarizes the standard attributes of this element.

TABLE A-10 Standard Attributes of the *directoryBrowse* Element

enabled	Controls whether directory browsing is enabled or disabled.
showFlags	Controls the listing details by specifying the desired details in a comma-separated list of values. In addition to file names, IIS can return details about the date, time, long date, file size, and file extension by using the *Date*, *Time*, *LongDate*, *Size*, and *Extension* flags respectively. The default flags are: *Date*, *Time*, *Size*, and *Extension*.
virtualDirectoryTimeout	Sets the amount of time in seconds the service will use to retrieve the timestamp information for virtual directories. The default is 5.

DynamicCompressionModule

Implements in-memory compression of dynamic content

Description

Compression squeezes the extra space out of files, resulting in small files and greatly reducing the amount of bandwidth needed to transmit content over a network in most cases. Because compressed files generally are smaller than uncompressed files, users perceive a performance improvement.

IIS supports static compression through the StaticCompressionModule and dynamic compression through the DynamicCompressionModule. With static compression, IIS performs an in-memory compression of static content upon first request and then saves the compressed results to disk for subsequent use. With dynamic content, IIS performs in-memory compression every time dynamic content is requested. IIS must compress dynamic content every time it is requested because dynamic content changes.

Executable *%Windir%*\System32\Inetsrv\Compdyn.dll

Dependencies None

Configuration Elements   system.webServer/*httpCompression*

system.webServer/*urlCompression*

ApplicationHost.config Usage Examples

```
<httpCompression directory="%SystemDrive%\inetpub\temp\IIS Temporary Co
mpressed Files">
 <scheme name="gzip" dll="%Windir%\system32\inetsrv\gzip.dll" />
 <dynamicTypes>
  <add mimeType="text/*" enabled="true" />
  <add mimeType="message/*" enabled="true" />
  <add mimeType="application/x-javascript" enabled="true" />
  <add mimeType="*/*" enabled="false" />
 </dynamicTypes>
 <staticTypes>
  <add mimeType="text/*" enabled="true" />
  <add mimeType="message/*" enabled="true" />
  <add mimeType="application/x-javascript" enabled="true" />
  <add mimeType="*/*" enabled="false" />
 </staticTypes>
</httpCompression>

<urlCompression doDynamicCompression="true" />
```

Element Attributes   Compression is controlled through the
system.webServer/*httpCompression* and system.webServer/*urlCompression*
elements. The system.webServer/*httpCompression* element controls how IIS uses
HTTP compression. The system.webServer/*urlCompression* element controls per-
URL compression. Whereas HTTP compression has many standard configuration
settings, URL Compression has no values set by default, which means that the
values are taken from the schema.

In a standard configuration, IIS compresses content in the following folder:
%SystemDrive%\Inetpub\Temp\IIS Temporary Compressed Files. By using the
directory attribute of the *httpCompression* element, you can specify an
alternative directory.

The type of compression IIS uses is set through the *scheme* element. By default,
IIS uses GZip compression. The *name* and *dll* attributes of the *scheme* element
set the descriptive name of the compression type and the full file path to the
DLL that performs the compression.

The *staticTypes* and *dynamicTypes* elements are used to specify how compression can be used. The related *add* elements have *mimeTYPE* attributes that set the Multipurpose Internet Mail Extensions (MIME) type being referenced and enabled attributes that specify the compression status for the identified MIME type. When compression is enabled in a standard configuration, all text- and message-related MIME types for static content are compressed automatically as are scripts written in JavaScript. When dynamic compression is enabled in a standard configuration, the same is true for dynamic content.

When the *doDynamicCompression* attribute of the *urlCompression* element is set to true, compression of dynamic content is enabled. Otherwise, dynamic compression is disabled.

The standard attributes of the *httpCompression* element and the *urlCompression* element are summaried in Table A-11 and Table A-12 respectively.

TABLE A-11 Standard Attributes of the *httpCompression Element*

cacheControlHeader	Sets the maximum time a header can be cached. The default value, max–age=86400, sets the header to expire after 86,400 seconds (24 hours).
Dll	Sets the DLL of the compression utility to use. This value cannot be set to an empty string.
doDiskSpaceLimiting	Controls whether IIS limits the amount of disk space used for caching compressed files. The default value, true, enables disk space limiting.
doDynamicCompression	Controls whether dynamic compression is used by IIS. The default is true, which means that IIS will try to use dynamic compression if no other restrictions apply.
doStaticCompression	Controls whether static compression is used by IIS. The default is true, which means that IIS will try to use static compression if no other restrictions apply.
dynamicCompressionBufferLimit	Sets the maximum amount of dynamically compressed data that IIS will buffer before flushing the buffer to the client. The default is 65536 bytes. (IIS 7.5 only)

dynamicCompressionDisableCpuUsage	Controls whether dynamic compression is disabled when the CPU percent utilization reaches or exceeds a specific level. By default, dynamic compression is disabled when the CPU utilization is 90 percent or higher. The valid range is from 0 to 100.
dynamicCompressionEnableCpuUsage	Controls whether dynamic compression is enabled but throttled when the CPU percent utilization reaches or exceeds a specific level. By default, dynamic compression is enabled when the CPU utilization is 50 percent or higher. The valid range is from 0 to 100.
dynamicCompressionLevel	Sets the level of compression used with dynamic content. The default compression level is 0. Compression level can be set from 0 (minimal) to 7 (maximum).
expiresHeaders	Sets the default expiration header. The default value, Wed, 01 Jan 1997 12:00:00 GMT, forces expiration by setting a date earlier than the current date.
maxDiskSpaceUsage	Sets the maximum disk space that can be used for caching compressed files (when disk space limiting is enabled). The default value is 100 MB.
minFileSizeForComp	Sets the minimum file size for compression. Files smaller than the minimum file size are not compressed. For IIS 7.0, the default is 256 bytes. For IIS 7.5, the default is 2700 bytes.
noCompressionForHttp10	Controls whether compression is used with HTTP 1.0. The default is true, which means that compression is not used with HTTP 1.0.
noCompressionForProxies	Controls whether compression is used when transmitting through a proxy. The default is true, which means that compression is not used with proxies.
noCompressionForRange	Controls whether compression is used for clients on the local network. The default is true, which means that compression is not used with local clients.
sendCacheHeaders	Controls whether IIS sends the cached header to the client. The default value is false.

staticCompressionDisableCpuUsage	Controls whether static compression is disabled when the CPU percent utilization reaches or exceeds a specific level. By default, static compression is disabled when the CPU utilization reaches 100 percent. The valid range is from 0 to 100.
staticCompressionEnableCpuUsage	Controls whether static compression is enabled but throttled when the CPU percent utilization reaches or exceeds a specific level. By default, static compression is enabled when the CPU utilization is 50 percent or higher. The valid range is from 0 to 100.
staticCompressionLevel	Sets the level of compression used with static content. The default compression level is 7. Compression level can be set from 0 (minimal) to 7 (maximum).

TABLE A-12 Standard Attributes for the *urlCompression* Element

doDynamicCompression	Controls whether dynamic compression is used for per-URL compression. The default is true, which means that IIS will try to use dynamic compression if no other restrictions apply.
doStaticCompression	Controls whether static compression is used for per-URL compression. The default is true, which means that IIS will try to use static compression if no other restrictions apply.
dynamicCompressionBeforeCache	Controls whether IIS performs per-URL compression before caching the file. The default is false, which means that IIS caches a file (as appropriate per the current configuration) and then performs compression.

FailedRequestsTracingModule

Implements tracing of failed requests

Description   Failed request tracing is designed to help administrators and developers more easily identify and track failed requests. In previous versions of IIS, you could check for certain HTTP error codes in the IIS logs to identify failed requests but could not easily get detailed trace information that would help resolve related issues. Request traces can be logged automatically when an error code is generated or when the time taken for a request exceeds a specified duration. For general tracing for debugging or other purposes, you can also configure general tracing on a per-URL basis.

You control the way tracing works using Failed Request Tracing Rules. With each rule, you specify:

- The type of content to trace as either all content (*), ASP.NET (*.aspx), ASP (*.asp), or custom.

- The conditions under which a request should be traced, including event severity (Error, Critical Error, or Warning), HTTP status code, and time taken. For general tracing, you can also trace information and other non-error events.

- The provider through which to track the request, including ASP, ASPNET, ISAPI Extension, and WWW Server.

Executable   *%Windir%*\System32\Inetsrv\Iisfreb.dll

Dependencies   None

Configuration Elements   system.webServer/*httpTracing*

system.webServer/*tracing*

ApplicationHost.config Usage Examples

```
<httpTracing>
 <traceUrls>
  <add value="\test.aspx"
 </traceUrls>
</httpTracing>

<tracing>
 <traceFailedRequests>
  <add path="*.aspx">
   <traceAreas>
    <add provider="ASP" verbosity="Verbose" />
    <add provider="ISAPI Extension" verbosity="Verbose" />
    <add provider="WWW Server" areas="Authentication,Security,Filter,St
aticFile,CGI,Compression,Cache,RequestNotifications"
```

```
verbosity="Verbose" />
   </traceAreas>
   <failureDefinitions timeTaken="00:00:30" statusCodes="500"
verbosity="Error" />
  </add>
 </traceFailedRequests>

 <traceProviderDefinitions>
  <add name="WWW Server" guid="{3a2a4e84-4c21-4981-ae10-3fda0d9b0f83}">
   <areas>
    <clear />
    <add name="Authentication" value="2" />
    <add name="Security" value="4" />
    <add name="Filter" value="8" />
    <add name="StaticFile" value="16" />
    <add name="CGI" value="32" />
    <add name="Compression" value="64" />
    <add name="Cache" value="128" />
    <add name="RequestNotifications" value="256" />
   </areas>
  </add>
  <add name="ASP" guid="{06b94d9a-b15e-456e-a4ef-37c984a2cb4b}">
   <areas>
    <clear />
   </areas>
  </add>
  <add name="ISAPI Extension" guid="{a1c2040e-8840-4c31-ba11-
9871031a19ea}">
   <areas>
    <clear />
   </areas>
  </add>
 </traceProviderDefinitions>
</tracing>
```

Element Attributes   The system.webServer/*httpTracing* element configures request tracing for whenever a specific URL is accessed. Each URL that you want to trace is specified with the value attribute of an *add* element nested within an *httpTracing\traceUrls* element. The way tracing is handled for a particular file is based on the trace rules you've defined.

In the following example, two URLs are configured for tracing whenever they are accessed:

```
<httpTracing>
 <traceUrls>
  <add value="\test1.aspx">
  <add value="\test2.asp">
</traceUrls>
</httpTracing>
```

Because you can configure separate tracing rules for .asp and .aspx files, IIS may handle tracing for these files in different ways. Keep in mind that if you've configured tracing rules to track only errors, you won't see the general or information events that may be needed for more general tracing of requests.

The system.webServer/*tracing* element allows you to define tracing rules. Within the system.webServer/*tracing* element, request tracing is implemented through two subelements:

- **traceProviderDefinitions** Defines the available trace providers

- **traceFailedRequests** Allows you to define tracing rules

Because you'll rarely, if ever, want to modify the provider definitions, you'll work mostly with the *traceFailedRequests* element. Within this element, you define a type of document to trace using the *path* attribute of the *add* element and then define the related rule within the context of the *add* element. The following snippet of code defines a rule for .aspx files:

```
<add path="*.aspx">
 <traceAreas>
  <add provider="ASP" verbosity="Verbose" />
  <add provider="ISAPI Extension" verbosity="Verbose" />
  <add provider="WWW Server" areas="Authentication,Security,
Filter,StaticFile,CGI,Compression,Cache,RequestNotifications"
verbosity="Verbose" />
 </traceAreas>
 <failureDefinitions timeTaken="00:00:30" statusCodes="500" verbosity="
Error" />
</add>
```

As shown in this example, the *add* element denotes the start and end of the rule:

```
<add path="*.aspx">
...
</add>
```

In this case, the rule applies to all ASP.NET files. ASP.NET files have the .aspx file extension. You could apply a Failed Trace Request Rule to all content by using:

```
<add path="*">
...
</add>
```

You could apply a Failed Trace Request Rule to all ASP files by using:

```
<add path="*.asp">
...
</add>
```

Or you could apply a Failed Trace Request Rule to a custom file type or name by using wildcards as appropriate, such as:

```
<add path="curr*.asp">
...
</add>
```

The *traceAreas* element defines the providers to which the rule applies in addition to how the rule applies to each provider. Failed requests can be traced through one or more of the following providers:

- **ASP**   Traces the failed request through Active Server Pages (%*Windir%*\System32\Inetsrv\Asp.dll)

- **ISAPI Extension**   Traces the failed request through ISAPI extension for ASP.NET (%*Windir%*\Microsoft.NET\Framework\V2.0.50727\Aspnet_isapi.dll)

- **WWW Server**   Traces the failed request through the IIS server core

You specify a provider to use with the *provider* attribute of the *add* element. You then use the *verbosity* attribute to specify the types of information to trace as follows:

- **General**   Trace general information about a request

- **CriticalError**   Trace critical errors related to a request

- **Error**   Trace standard errors related to a request

- **Warning**   Trace warnings related to a request

- **Information**   Trace information events related to a request

- **Verbose**   Trace all available information and errors related to a request

In the following example, tracing for the ASP provider is set to track critical errors:

```
<add provider="ASP" verbosity="CriticalError" />
```

When using WWW Server as the provider, you can specify the area within the IIS server core to trace as any combination of the following:

- **Authentication**   Traces the failed request through authentication-related modules

- **Security**   Traces the failed request through authentication-related modules

- **Filter**   Traces the failed request through the IsapiFilterModule, the RequestFilteringModule, or both

- **StaticFile**   Traces the failed request through the StaticFile module

- **CGI**   Traces the failed request through the CgiModule

- **Compression**   Traces the failed request through the StaticCompressionModule or the DynamicCompressionModule

- **Cache**   Traces the failed request through cache-related modules

- **RequestNotifications**   Traces the failed request through the RequestMonitorModule

The following examples enables tracing of all areas for the WWW Server:

```
<add provider="WWW Server" areas="Authentication,Security,Filter,
StaticFile,CGI,Compression,Cache,RequestNotifications"
verbosity="Verbose" />
```

After you define the trace areas, you must define the type of related failure or events to trace using the attributes of the *failureDefinitions* element. Tracing can be initiated based on two types of events: the time taken to respond as specified with the *timeTaken* attribute and specific status codes as specified with the *statusCodes* attribute. You use the *verbosity* attribute of the *failureDefinitions* element to specify the event severity to track. To see how this works, consider the following example:

```
<failureDefinitions timeTaken="00:00:30" statusCodes="500"
verbosity="Error"/>
```

Here, IIS traces the previously specified file type when the time taken to handle a response is more than 30 seconds or when an HTTP 500 error is generated and tracks events with an Error severity level. The *verbosity* attribute of the *failureDefinitions* element can use the following flags: *Ignore*, *CriticalError*, *Error*, and *Warning*. The default value is *Ignore*.

FastCgiModule

Implements the multithreaded Common Gateway Interface (CGI) specification for use with IIS

Description   See CgiModule.

Executable   %Windir%\System32\Inetsrv\Iisfcgi.dll

Dependencies   None

Configuration Elements   system.webServer/fastCgi

system.webServer/*isapiCgiRestriction*

ApplicationHost.config Usage Examples

```
<fastCgi>
 <application fullpath="c:\php\cgi-php.exe"
   maxInstances="10" idleTimeout="120">
</fastCgi>
```

Element Attributes   FastCGI is controlled through the
system.webServer/fastCgi/application element. Table A-13 summarizes the
standard attributes of the fastCgi/application element.

TABLE A-13 Standard Attributes of the *fastCgi/application* Element

activityTimeout	Sets the activity timeout in seconds. If an active request has been working with longer than this value, it is stopped. The default value is 30 seconds. The maximum activity time is 3,600 seconds (1 hour).
arguments	Sets command-line arguments to pass to the application. This value is a string and must be enclosed in quotation marks.
flushNamedPipe	Controls whether named pipes are flushed. The default value is false. If set to true, named pipes are flushed when requests are terminated.
fullPath	Sets the full file path to the executable for the application to be processed through FastCGI. This value is required and cannot be set to an empty string.
idleTimeout	Sets the idle timeout for FastCgi applications in seconds. If the application has not been used and this time elapses, the application instance is deleted. The default value is 300 seconds (5 minutes). The maximum idle time is 604,800 seconds (7 days).
instanceMaxRequests	Sets the maximum number of requests that each application instance can service. The default is 200 requests. The maximum is 10,000,000.
maxInstances	Sets the maximum number of concurrent instances of the application that can run for multithreading. The default value is 4 instances. The maximum number is 10,000.
monitorChangesTo	Allows you to pseicfy a file to monitor that might change the behavior of a FastCGI application, such as PHP.INI. (IIS 7.5 only)
protocol	Sets the communication protocol for the application. The default value is NamedPipe. Applications can also use TCP IP by setting a value of Tcp.

queueLength	Sets the size of the request queue. If this number of requests are waiting to be processed, additional requests are ignored. The default is 1,000, meaning up to 1,000 requests can be waiting to be processed. The maximum queue size is 100,000,000.
requestTimeout	Sets the request timeout in seconds. If the server has not responded to a request before this time elapses, the request is terminated. The default request timeout is 90 seconds. The maximum request time is 604,800 seconds (7 days).
signalBeforeTerminateSeconds	Specifies the time to wait after IIS signals a FastCGI application that it needs to shut down, allowing the application to clean up any settings before IIS terminates. (IIS 7.5 only)
stderrMode	Controls how IIS handles errors returned from a FastCGI application through the STDERR stream. (IIS 7.5 only)

FileCacheModule

Caches file handles (*not installed by default*)

Description   The FileCacheModule caches file handles for files opened by the server engine and related server modules. If file handles are not cached, the files have to be opened for every request, which can result in performance loss. In a standard configuration, this module is not added even if you select all available features during installation of IIS.

Executable   *%Windir%\System32\Inetsrv\Cachfile.dll*

Dependencies   None

Configuration Elements   None

HttpCacheModule

Implements output caching and kernel-mode caching

Description   HTTP.sys is the server process that listens for requests made on a Web site. HTTP.sys also performs caching and logging operations on the server. Caching improves performance by returning a processed copy of a requested

Web page from cache, resulting in reduced overhead on the server and faster response times. IIS supports several levels of caching including output caching in user mode and output caching in kernel mode. When kernel-mode caching is enabled, cached responses are served from the kernel rather than from IIS user mode, giving IIS an extra boost in performance and increasing the number of requests IIS can process.

Executable   *%Windir%\System32\Inetsrv\Cachhttp.dll*

Dependencies   None

Configuration Elements   System.webServer/*asp*

System.webServer/asp/*cache*

System.webServer/*caching*

ApplicationHost.config Usage Examples

```
<asp>
 <cache diskTemplateCacheDirectory="%SystemDrive%\inetpub\temp\ASP
Compiled Templates" />
</asp>

<caching enabled="true" enableKernelCache="true" maxCacheSize="200"
maxResponseSize="262144">
 <profiles>
  <add extension=".axd" policy="CacheForTimePeriod"
duration="00:00:30" />
  <add extension=".aspx" policy="CacheUntilChange"
varyByHeaders="HTTP_ACCEPT" varyByQueryString="Locale" />
 </profiles>
</caching>
```

Element Attributes   Caching is controlled through the System.webServer/asp/*cache* and System.webServer/*caching* elements. As summarized in Table A-14, general caching settings for dynamic files are configured through the attributes of the System.webServer/asp/*cache* element. Table A-15 summarizes the attributes of the System.webServer/*caching* element.

TABLE A-14 Standard Attributes of the System.webServer/asp/*cache Element*

diskTemplateCacheDirectory	Sets the name of the directory that ASP uses to store compiled ASP templates to disk after overflow of the in-memory cache. This attribute cannot be set to an empty string. The default value is *%SystemDrive%*\Inetpub\Temp\ASP Compiled Templates.
maxDiskTemplateCacheFiles	Sets the maximum number of compiled ASP templates that can be stored on disk. The default value is 2,000. The valid range is from 0 to 2,147,483,647 files.
scriptFileCacheSize	Sets the maximum number of precompiled script files to cache in memory. The default value is 500 files. The valid range is from 0 to 2,147,483,647 files.
scriptEngineCacheMax	Sets the maximum number of scripting engines that IIS will keep cached in memory. The default value is 250 cached scripting engines. The valid range is from 0 to 2,147,483,647 files.
enableTypelibCache	Determines whether Type Library caching is enabled. The default value, true, enables Type Library caching.

TABLE A-15 Standard Attributes of the System.webServer/*caching* Element

enabled	Controls whether caching is enabled or disabled.
enableKernelModeCache	Controls whether output caching in kernel mode is enabled. If set to true, kernel mode caching is enabled. Otherwise, kernel-mode caching is disabled.
maxCacheSize	Sets the maximum size, in megabytes, of the in-memory cache used by IIS. If this attribute is not set or is set to zero, IIS controls the maximum size of the cache.
maxResponseSize	Sets the maximum size, in bytes, of responses that can be stored in the output cache. The default value is 262144 bytes (256 KB). If the response size is large than this value, the response is not stored in the output cache.

The *caching* element can contain a *profiles* element. Within the *profiles* element, you can use *add* elements to define output caching rules. Each rule specifies how specific types of files should be handled. You can cache files until they change or until a specified time interval has elapsed. You also can have multiple cached versions of files based on query string variables or HTTP headers. For example, you may want to allow multiple cached versions of files based on locale. This would allow IIS to store different language versions of a file in cache. The following example ensures that ASP.NET files are cached until they change:

```
<profiles>
  <add extension=".aspx" policy="CacheUntilChange" />
</profiles>
```

To allow multiple language versions of files to be cached, you can use the Locale query string variable as shown in the following example:

```
<profiles>
  <add extension=".aspx" varyByQueryString="Locale" />
</profiles>
```

To allow multiple versions of files to be cached based on HTTP headers, you can specify the type of HTTP header to track. The following example tracks the HTTP_USERAGENT header:

```
<profiles>
  <add extension=".aspx" varyByHeaders="HTTP_USERAGENT" />
</profiles>
```

Table A-16 lists and describes the attributes of the *add* elements used within the *profiles* element.

TABLE A-16 Standard Attributes of the *profiles/add* Element

enabled	Controls whether caching is enabled or disabled.
policy	Sets the overall monitoring policy for cached files. Use *DontCache* to turn off caching. Use *CacheUntilChange* to cache files until they change. Use *CacheForTimePeriod* to cache files for a specified time period.
kernelCachePolicy	Sets the monitoring policy for cached files when in kernel mode. Use *DontCache* to turn off kernel-mode caching. Use *CacheUntilChange* to cache files in kernel mode until they change. Use *CacheForTimePeriod* to cache files in kernel mode for a specified time period.

duration	Sets the time period for caching files; must be used with *CacheForTimePeriod*. The default value is 00:00:30.
location	Specifies the locations for which caching should be used. The default value is Any. You can also use Client, Server, ServerAndClient, Downstream, and None.
varyByQueryString	Allows multiple cached file versions that vary by query string variable, such as Locale.
varyByHeaders	Allows multiple cached file versions that vary by HTTP header, such as HTTP_ACCEPT.

HttpLoggingModule

Implements standard IIS logging

Description IIS can be configured to use one log file per server or one log file per site. Use per server logging when you want all Web sites running on a server to write log data to a single file. With per server logging, you can use one of two logging formats: centralized binary logging or World Wide Web Consortium (W3C) extended log file format. With centralized binary logging, the log files contain both fixed-length records and index records that are written in a raw binary format called the Internet Binary Log (IBL) format, giving the log file an .ibl extension. Professional software applications or tools in the IIS Software Development Kit can read this format.

Use per site logging when you want to track access separately for each site on a server. With per site logging, you can configure access logs in several formats. The standard formats are:

- National Center for Supercomputer Applications (NCSA) Common Log File Format Use the NCSA Common Log File Format when your reporting and tracking needs are basic. With this format, log entries are small, which reduces the amount of storage space required for logging.

- Microsoft Internet Information Services (IIS) Log File Format Use the IIS Log File Format when you need a bit more information from the logs but don't need to tailor the entries to get detailed information. With this format, log entries are compact, which reduces the amount of storage space required for logging.

- World Wide Web Consortium (W3C) Extended Log File Format   Use the W3C Extended Log File Format when you need to customize the tracked information and obtain detailed information. With this format, log entries can become large, which greatly increases the amount of storage space required. Recording lengthy entries can also affect the performance of a busy server.

> **Note**   With per site logging, you can also configure custom logging or ODBC logging. Custom logging uses the CustomLoggingModule, which implements the ILogPlugin interface. ODBC logging is a type of custom logging that writes access information directly to an ODBC-compliant database. These advanced logging configurations can be managed only through the ApplicationHost.config file.

With all the standard log file formats, you can specify the log file encoding format as ANSI for standard ASCII text encoding or UTF8 for UTF-8 encoding. You can also specify whether and when log files roll over. For example, you can configure IIS to create new log files every day by configuring daily log file rollover. See Chapter 9 in *Web Server Administration: The Personal Trainer* for more information on logging.

Executable   *%Windir%\System32\Inetsrv\Loghttp.dll*

Dependencies   None

Configuration Elements   system.webServer/*httpLogging*

system.webServer/*odbcLogging*

system.applicationHost/*log*

ApplicationHost.config Usage Examples

```
<httpLogging dontLog="false" />
```

```
<odbcLogging />
```

```
<log logInUTF8="false" centralLogFileMode="CentralW3C">
 <centralBinaryLogFile enabled="true"
 directory="%SystemDrive%\inetpub\logs\LogFiles" period="Weekly"
 localTimeRollover="true" />
 <centralW3CLogFile enabled="true"
 directory="%SystemDrive%\inetpub\logs\LogFiles" period="Hourly"
 localTimeRollover="false" logExtFileFlags="HttpSubStatus, Host,
 ProtocolVersion, Referer, Cookie, UserAgent, ServerPort, TimeTaken,
 BytesRecv, BytesSent, Win32Status, HttpStatus, UriQuery, UriStem,
Method,
 ServerIP, ComputerName, SiteName, UserName, ClientIP, Time, Date" />
 </log>

<sites>
 <site name="Default Web Site" id="1">
  <application path="/">
   <virtualDirectory path="/"
physicalPath="%SystemDrive%\inetpub\wwwroot" />
  </application>
  . . .
 </site>
 <siteDefaults>
  <logFile logFormat="W3C" directory="%SystemDrive%\inetpub\logs\
LogFiles" />
  . . .
</sites>
```

Element Attributes   Logging is controlled through three configuration
elements: system.webServer/*httpLogging*, system.webServer/*odbcLogging*, and
system.applicationHost/*log*. The *dontLog* attribute of the *httpLogging* element
controls whether HTTP logging is enabled for the IIS server. With
dontLog="false", HTTP logging is enabled. With *dontLog*="true", HTTP logging is
disabled.

With the *httpLogging* element, you can configure selective logging using the
following flags for the *selectiveLogging* attribute:

- **LogAll**   Logs both successful and failed access requests. This is the default.

- **LogSuccessful**   Logs only successful access requests.

- **LogError**   Logs only access request failures.

The *odbcLogging* element controls ODBC logging when HTTP logging is disabled. By default it has no content and attribute values are taken from the schema. The default schema values are:

```
<sectionSchema name="system.webServer/odbcLogging">
 <attribute name="dataSource" type="string" defaultValue="InternetDb" />
 <attribute name="tableName" type="string" defaultValue="InternetLog" />
 <attribute name="userName" type="string" defaultValue="InternetAdmin" />
 <attribute name="password" type="string" encrypted="true" />
</sectionSchema>
```

As summarized in Table A-17, the attributes of the *odbcLogging* element control the way ODBC logging is performed.

TABLE A-17 Standard Attributes of the *odbcLogging* Element

dataSource	Sets the Data Source Name (DSN) that IIS can use to connect to the database. Typically, you'll want to use a system DSN.
tableName	Sets the name of the table used to which logging data should be stored within the logging database.
username	Sets the user name of the account you want to use to log on to the database.
password	Sets the password of the account you want to use to log on to the database. The password is expected to be passed as an encrypted string.

Setting the attribute values in ApplicationHost.config overrides the schema default values as shown in the following example:

```
<httpLogging dontLog="true" />
<odbcLogging dataSource="LoggingDB" tableName="WebServer85Log" username=
"IISAdmin" password="[enc:AesProvider:jAAAAAECAAADZgAAAKQAAJbG5Vze9+qBI
wzs3YYUfw4w1FhMxydGFXXSIQN3WjxTI9s7y8a6VsU9h+bMHUsPibqPGbT0ZwEovDXWzVG0
Fg3A
/bi7uJAOphgDDP4/xP18XDwS0rm+22Yyn441LPbG6d4BGBy7G+b/O2ywozBFbsdckm7bKyN
p1NinWKY9dSzKfa9l2SmYVqvHEQEQjUMXSvg==:enc]" />
```

HttpRedirectionModule

Implements HTTP redirect functionality

Description You can use HTTP redirection to redirect users from an old site to a new site. In the default configuration for redirection, all requests for files in the old location are mapped automatically to files in the new location you specify. You can change this behavior in several ways. You can:

- Redirect requests to the destination URL without adding any other portions of the original URL. You can use this option to redirect an entire site or directory to one location. For example, you could redirect all requests for any page or resource at *http://www.imaginedlands.com* to *http://www.reagentpress.com/wemoved.htm*.

- Redirect requests for a parent directory to a child directory. For example, you could redirect your home directory (designated by /) to a subdirectory named /Current.

Using status codes, you can indicate to the client browser whether a redirection is a standard redirection (HTTP status code 302), a temporary redirection (HTTP status code 307), or a permanent redirection (HTTP status code 301). Use redirect wildcard characters to redirect particular types of files to a specific file at the destination. For example, you can use redirect wildcard characters to redirect all .htm files to Default.htm and all .asp files to Default.asp. The syntax for wildcard character redirection is:

```
*;*.EXT;FILENAME.EXT[;*.EXT;FILENAME.EXT...]
```

where *.EXT* is the file extension you want to redirect and *FILENAME.EXT* is the name of the file to use at the destination. As shown, begin the destination URL with an asterisk and a semicolon and separate pairs of wildcard characters and destination URLs with a semicolon. Be sure to account for all document types that users might request directly, such as .htm, .html, .asp, and .aspx documents.

Executable *%Windir%*\System32\Inetsrv\Redirect.dll

Dependencies None

Configuration Element   system.webServer/*httpRedirect*

ApplicationHost.config Usage Examples

```
<!-- Redirect requests relative to destination (the default) -->
<httpRedirect enabled="true" destination="
http://www.imaginedlands.com/" />

<!-- Redirect all request to the exact destination -->
<httpRedirect enabled="true" destination="http://www.reagentpress.com/
wemoved.htm" exactDestination="true" />

<!-
- Redirect requests to content in this directory (not subdirectories) -
->
<httpRedirect enabled="true" destination="/Current" childOnly="true" />

<!-- Set a status code for redirection -->
<httpRedirect enabled="true" destination="
http://www.imaginedlands.com/"  httpResponseStatus="Permanent" />
```

Element Attributes   The system.webServer/*httpRedirect* element controls
HTTP redirection. Table A-18 summarizes the attributes of this element.

TABLE A-18   Standard Attributes of the *profiles/add* Element

enabled	Controls whether redirection is enabled or disabled. If set to true, redirection is enabled and you must provide a destination for redirection. The default is false.
destination	Sets the location to which clients are redirected. This attribute cannot be set to an empty string.
exactDestination	Controls whether clients are redirected to a relative or absolute location. If set to false, all requests for files in the old location are mapped automatically to files in the new location you specify. If set to true, all requests for any page or resource are redirected to the exact location specified in the destination. The default is false.
childOnly	Controls whether requests for a parent directory are redirected to a child directory. If set to true, requests for a parent directory are redirected to a child directory. If set to false, requests for a parent directory are not redirected to a child directory. The default is false.

httpResponseStatus	Sets the HTTP status code for the redirection. Use Found to indicate a standard redirection (HTTP status code 302). Use Temporary to indicate a temporary redirection (HTTP status code 307). Use Permanent to indicate a permanent redirection (HTTP status code 301).

IISCertificateMappingAuthenticationModule

Implements SSL client certificate mapping

Description   The IISCertificateMappingAuthenticationModule maps SSL client certificates to a Windows account. With this method of authentication, user credentials and mapping rules are stored within the IIS configuration store. At least one authentication module must be configured. When this authentication method is enabled, client certificates can be mapped to Windows accounts in two ways:

- On a one-to-one basis, in which each client must have its own SSL client certificate

- On a many-to-one basis, in which multiple clients can use the same SSL client certificate

This module allows SSL client certificate mapping by creating the necessary *HttpUser* object. The *HttpUser* object is an IIS data structure. The IIS server core checks to ensure that this object is populated after the authentication phase. See Chapter 4 for more information on authentication.

Executable   *%Windir%*\System32\Inetsrv\Authmap.dll

Dependencies   The server must be configured to use SSL and to receive client certificates.

Configuration Element   system.webServer/security/authentication */iisClientCertificateMappingAuthentication*

ApplicationHost.config Usage Examples

```
<iisClientCertificateMappingAuthentication enabled="false">
</iisClientCertificateMappingAuthentication>
```

Element Attributes   SSL client certificate authentication is handled through the *iisClientCertificateMappingAuthentication* element. Table A-19 summarizes the standard attributes of this element.

TABLE A-19 Standard Attributes of the *iisClientCertificateMappingAuthentication* Element

defaultLogonDomain	Sets the optional name of the default domain against which the client certificates are authenticated. The default logon domain is an empty string.
enabled	Controls whether client certificate authentication is enabled or disabled. The default is false.
logonMethod	Sets the optional logon method for the related user account as Interactive, Batch, Network, or ClearText. The default is ClearText.
oneToOneCertificateMappingsEnabled	Controls whether one-to-one certificate mapping is enabled. When client certificate authentication is enabled, the default is true.
manyToOneCertificateMappingsEnabled	Controls whether many-to-one certificate mapping is enabled. When client certificate authentication is enabled, the default is true.

When SSL client certificate authentication is enabled, certificate mapping relationships, rules, or both must also be defined. With many-to-one certificate mapping, each mapping has a relationship entry and one or more rule definitions in addition to an enabled value that indicates whether the mapping is enabled or disabled. The basic syntax for a many-to-one mapping is as follows:

```
<iisClientCertificateMappingAuthentication enabled="true">
 <manyToOneCertificateMappings>
  <add name="AllClients" description="The default mapping for clients"
enabled="true" permissionMode="Allow" username="authUser"
password="[enc:AesProvider:...:enc]">
```

```
  <rules>
    <add certificateField="Subject" certificateSubField=""
matchCriteria="" compareCaseSensitive="">
    <add certificateField="Issuer" certificateSubField=""
matchCriteria="" compareCaseSensitive="">
  </rules>
 </manyToOneCertificateMappings>
</iisClientCertificateMappingAuthentication>
```

With one-to-one certificate mapping, each mapping has only a relationship entry. The entry specifies the Windows user, the user's encrypted password, and the related certificate as an enabled value that indicates whether the mapping is enabled or disabled. The basic syntax for a one-to-one mapping is as follows:

```
<iisClientCertificateMappingAuthentication enabled="true">
 <oneToOneCertificateMappings>
   <add enabled="true" userName="wrstanek" password="[enc:AesProvider:..
.:enc]" certificate="">
</oneToOneCertificateMappings>
</iisClientCertificateMappingAuthentication>
```

IpRestrictionModule

Implements Internet Protocol (IP) address and domain name restrictions

Description   By default, IIS resources are accessible to all IP addresses, computers, and domains, which presents a security risk that might allow your server to be misused. To control use of resources, you might want to grant or deny access by IP address, network ID, or domain.

Granting access allows a computer to make requests for resources but doesn't necessarily allow users to work with resources. If you require authentication, users still need to authenticate themselves.

Denying access to resources prevents a computer from accessing those resources. Therefore, users of the computer can't access the resources—even if they could have authenticated themselves with a user name and password.

The settings you specify when defining a restriction controls how the restriction is used. For a single computer, provide the exact IP address for the computer, such as 192.168.5.50. For groups of computers, provide the subnet address, such as 192.168.0.0, and the subnet mask, such as 255.255.0.0. For a domain name, provide the fully qualified domain name (FQDN), such as *eng.microsoft.com*.

Executable   *%Windir%*\System32\Inetsrv\Iprestr.dll

Dependencies   Transmission Control Protocol/Internet Protocol (TCP/IP)v4 must be installed on the server.

Configuration Element   system.webServer/security/*ipSecurity*

ApplicationHost.config Usage Example

```
<ipSecurity allowUnlisted="true" />
```

Element Attributes   The system.webServer/security/*ipSecurity* element controls IP address and domain name restrictions. Table A-20 summarizes the standard attributes of the *ipSecurity* element. The *ipSecurity* element can contain *add* elements, which define the restrictions you want to use. The attributes of the *ipSecurity*/*add* element are summarized in Table A-21.

TABLE A-20 Standard Attributes of the *ipSecurity* Element

enableReverseDNS	Controls whether IIS can perform reverse DNS lookups. This is useful when you are restricting by domain and the computer has only an IP address set. The default is false, which means that reverse lookups are not used.
allowUnlisted	Determines whether IP addresses not specifically listed as allowed are granted access to server resources. The default value is true, which means that all IP addresses are granted access.

TABLE A-21 Standard Attributes of the *ipSecurity*/*add* Element

ipAddress	Sets the IP address of the computer or network for which you want to grant or deny access.
subnetMask	Sets the subnet mask of the computer or network for which you want to grant or deny access. The default value is 255.255.255.255.

domainNam	Sets the domain name for which you want to grant or deny access.
allowed	Controls whether a computer, network, or domain is granted or denied access. If set to true, IIS grants access. If set to false, IIS denies access. The default is false.

Examples of configuring grant and deny restrictions follow:

Allow unrestricted access

```
<ipSecurity allowUnlisted="true" />
```

Restrict access to a specific grant list

```
<ipSecurity allowUnlisted="false">
 <add ipAddress="192.168.5.53 allowed="true">
 <add ipAddress="192.168.5.62 allowed="true">
</ipSecurity>
```

Allow open access except for specific computers

```
<ipSecurity allowUnlisted="true">
 <add ipAddress="192.168.5.53 allowed="false">
 <add ipAddress="192.168.5.62 allowed="false">
</ipSecurity>
```

Allow open access except for specific networks

```
<ipSecurity allowUnlisted="true">
 <add ipAddress="192.168.10.0 subnetMask="255.255.0.0" allowed="false">
 <add ipAddress="192.168.11.0 subnetMask="255.255.0.0" allowed="false">
</ipSecurity>
```

Allow open access except for specific domains

```
<ipSecurity allowUnlisted="true">
 <add domain="eng.microsoft.com" allowed="false">
</ipSecurity>
```

IsapiFilterModule

Implements ISAPI filter functionality

Description   IIS uses ISAPI filters to provide additional functionality. If you selected ASP.NET during initial configuration, an ASP.NET filter is configured to provide this functionality. Each version of ASP.NET installed on the Web server must have a filter definition that identifies the version and path to the related filter. After you install new versions of ASP.NET, you can add definitions for the related filter. If you remove this module, IIS will not be able to load ISAPI filters, and applications might stop working, which could expose sensitive content.

Executable   *%Windir%*\System32\Inetsrv\Filter.dll

Dependencies   None

Configuration Element   system.webServer/*isapiFilters*

ApplicationHost.config Usage Examples

```
<isapiFilters>
 <filter name="ASP.Net_2.0.50727.0"
path="%windir%\Microsoft.NET\Framework\
v2.0.50727\aspnet_filter.dll" enableCache="true"
preCondition="bitness32" />
</isapiFilters>
```

Element Attributes   The system.webServer/*isapiFilters* element determines which filters are available. Each filter you want to use must have a corresponding *filter* element. Table A-22 summarizes the standard attributes of the filter element.

TABLE A-22 Standard Attributes of the *isapiFilters* Element

name	Sets the unique name of the filter.
path	Sets the full file path to the DLL for the filter.
enabled	Controls the availability of the filter. If set to true, the filter is available. If set to false, the filter is not available. The default is true.
enableCache	Determines whether the filter can use the caching features of IIS. If set to true, the filter can use caching. If set to false, the filter cannot use caching. The default is false.
precondition	Sets any necessary prerequisites for the filter.

IsapiModule

Implements ISAPI Extension functionality

Description   The IsapiModule makes it possible to use ISAPI Extension functionality. In the IIS core installation, several components rely on handlers that are based on ISAPI extensions, including ASP and ASP.NET. The IsapiModule has a managed handler that specifies that all files with the .dll extension are handled as ISAPI extensions. If you remove this module, ISAPI Extensions mapped in the <handlers> section or explicitly called as ISAPI Extensions will no longer work.

This module is used with the system.webServer/*isapiCgiRestriction* element. See the "CgiModule" section of this appendix for more information.

Executable   *%Windir%*\System32\Inetsrv\Isapi.dll

Dependencies   None

Configuration Elements   system.webServer/*isapiCgiRestriction*

system.webServer/*handlers*

ApplicationHost.config Usage Examples

```
<!-- related handler definitions -->
<add name="ASPClassic" path="*.asp" verb="GET,HEAD,POST"
modules="IsapiModule" scriptProcessor="%windir%\system32\inetsrv
\asp.dll" resourceType="File" />
<add name="SecurityCertificate" path="*.cer" verb="GET,HEAD,POST"
modules="IsapiModule" scriptProcessor="%windir%\system32\inetsrv
\asp.dll" resourceType="File" />
<add name="AXD-ISAPI-2.0" path="*.axd" verb="GET,HEAD,POST,DEBUG"
modules="IsapiModule" scriptProcessor="%windir%\Microsoft.NET
\Framework\v2.0.50727\aspnet_isapi.dll" preCondition="classicMode,
runtimeVersionv2.0,bitness32" responseBufferLimit="0" />
<add name="PageHandlerFactory-ISAPI-2.0" path="*.aspx"
verb="GET,HEAD,POST,DEBUG" modules="IsapiModule"
scriptProcessor="%windir%\Microsoft.NET\Framework\v2.0.50727\aspnet_
isapi.dll" preCondition="classicMode,runtimeVersionv2.0,bitness32"
responseBufferLimit="0" />
<add name="SimpleHandlerFactory-ISAPI-2.0" path="*.ashx" verb="GET,
```

```
HEAD,POST,DEBUG" modules="IsapiModule" scriptProcessor="%windir%
\Microsoft.NET\Framework\v2.0.50727\aspnet_isapi.dll" preCondition="
classicMode,runtimeVersionv2.0,bitness32" responseBufferLimit="0" />
<add name="WebServiceHandlerFactory-ISAPI-2.0" path="*.asmx"
verb="GET,HEAD,POST,DEBUG" modules="IsapiModule"
scriptProcessor="%windir%\Microsoft.NET\Framework\v2.0.50727\aspnet_
isapi.dll" preCondition="classicMode,runtimeVersionv2.0,bitness32"
responseBufferLimit="0" />
<add name="HttpRemotingHandlerFactory-rem-ISAPI-2.0" path="*.rem"
verb="GET,HEAD,POST,DEBUG" modules="IsapiModule"
scriptProcessor="%windir%\Microsoft.NET\Framework\v2.0.50727
\aspnet_isapi.dll" preCondition="classicMode,runtimeVersionv2.0,
bitness32" responseBufferLimit="0" />
<add name="HttpRemotingHandlerFactory-soap-ISAPI-2.0" path="*.soap"
verb="GET,HEAD,POST,DEBUG" modules="IsapiModule"
scriptProcessor="%windir%\Microsoft.NET\Framework\v2.0.50727
\aspnet_isapi.dll" preCondition="classicMode,runtimeVersionv2.0,
bitness32" responseBufferLimit="0" />
<add name="ISAPI-dll" path="*.dll" verb="*" modules="IsapiModule"
resourceType="File" requireAccess="Execute" allowPathInfo="true" />
```

Element Attributes   See the "CgiModule" section of this appendix for details.

ManagedEngine

Implements ASP.NET integration (*not installed by default*)

Description   ManagedEngine provides the necessary functionality for IIS integration with the ASP.NET runtime engine. If you remove this module, ASP.NET integration will be disabled. As a result, none of the managed modules declared in the <modules> section or ASP.NET handlers declared in the <handlers> section will be called when the application pool runs in Integrated mode. In a standard configuration, this module is not added even if you select all available features during installation of IIS.

Executable   *%Windir%*\Microsoft.NET\Framework*Version*\Webengine.dll

Dependencies   None

Configuration Elements   None

ApplicationHost.config Usage Examples

```
<!-- globalModules installation definition -->
<add name="ManagedEngine" image="%windir%\Microsoft.NET\Framework
\v2.0.50727\webengine.dll" preCondition="integratedMode,runtime
Versionv2.0,bitness32" />

<!-- modules activation definition -->
<add name="ManagedEngine" preCondition="integratedMode,
runtimeVersionv2.0,bitness32" />
```

ProtocolSupportModule

Implements keep-alive support, custom headers, and redirect headers

Description   The ProtocolSupportModule makes it possible for IIS to use the TRACE and OPTIONS verbs in HTTP headers. These features are used with HTTP keep-alive, custom headers, and redirect headers. If you remove this module, IIS will return a "405 Method not allowed" error message any time you attempt to use these features.

Executable   *%Windir%*\System32\Inetsrv\Protsup.dll

Dependencies   None

Configuration Element   system.webServer/*httpProtocol*

ApplicationHost.config Usage Examples

```
<httpProtocol>
 <customHeaders>
  <clear />
   <add name="X-Powered-By" value="ASP.NET" />
 </customHeaders>
 <redirectHeaders>
  <clear />
 </redirectHeaders>
</httpProtocol>
```

Element Attributes   The *httpProtocol* element controls the use of keep-alive support, custom headers, and redirect headers. The basic syntax for working with these features follows:

```
<httpProtocol>
 <customHeaders>
 .  .  .
</customHeaders>
 <redirectHeaders>
 .  .  .
</redirectHeaders>
</httpProtocol>
```

Generally, you set either a custom header or a redirect header, but not both. Before using these features, you should clear out the current values by using an empty clear element, such as:

```
<redirectHeaders>
 <clear />
</redirectHeaders>
```

Using the *add* element, you can then define the necessary custom header or redirect header. The *add* element has two basic attributes: *name* and *value*. As shown in the following example, the *name* attribute sets the type of header, and the *value* attribute sets the contents of the header:

```
<customHeaders>
 <clear />
 <add name="X-Powered-By" value="ASP.NET" />
</customHeaders>
```

RequestFilteringModule

Implements request filtering

Description The RequestFilteringModule is designed to reject suspicious requests by scanning URLs sent to the server and filtering out unwanted requests. You can filter requests in several ways. You can:

- Specify that only requests with specified file extensions be allowed

- Specify that all requests except specified file extensions be allowed

- Specify that certain code segments are hidden so that they cannot be accessed in clients

By default, IIS is configured to block requests for file extensions that could be misused and also blocks browsing of critical code segments. If you uninstall or disable the RequestFilteringModule, you will reduce the overall security of the server and may open the server to attack.

Executable   *%Windir%*\System32\Inetsrv\Modrqflt.dll

Dependencies   None

Configuration Element   system.webServer/security/*requestFiltering*

Related elements include alwaysAllowedUrls, alwaysAllowedQueryStrings, denyQueryStringSequences, and filteringRules.

ApplicationHost.config Usage Examples

```
<requestFiltering>
 <fileExtensions allowUnlisted="true" applyToWebDAV="true">
  <add fileExtension=".asax" allowed="false" />
  <add fileExtension=".ascx" allowed="false" />
  …
 </fileExtensions>
 <verbs allowUnlisted="true" applyToWebDAV="true"/>
 <hiddenSegments applyToWebDAV="true">
  <add segment="web.config" />
  <add segment="bin" />
  <add segment="App_code" />
  <add segment="App_GlobalResources" />
  <add segment="App_LocalResources" />
  <add segment="App_WebReferences" />
  <add segment="App_Data" />
  <add segment="App_Browsers" />
 </hiddenSegments>
</requestFiltering>
```

Element Attributes   Within the *requestFiltering* element, you can use the *fileExtensions* element to define file extensions that are either allowed or blocked and the *hiddenSegments* element to define segments that should be hidden from clients.

To allow all requests except specified file extensions, you use the following basic syntax:

```
<fileExtensions allowUnlisted="true" applyToWebDAV="true">
  <add fileExtension=".asax" allowed="false" />
  . . .
</fileExtensions>
```

Here the *allowUnlisted* attribute of the *fileExtensions* element is set to true to allow all file requests by default. The *add* element is then used to define exceptions to this rule. The *fileExtension* attribute of the *add* element sets the file extension for the exception. The *allowed* attribute specifies whether requests for files with the extension are allowed or blocked. If allowed="true", requests for files with the extension are allowed. If allowed= "false", requests for files with the extension are blocked.

To specify that only requests with specified file extensions be allowed, you use the following basic syntax:

```
<fileExtensions allowUnlisted="true" applyToWebDAV="true">
  <add fileExtension=".asax" allowed="true" />
  . . .
</fileExtensions>
```

Here the *allowUnlisted* attribute of the *fileExtensions* element is set to false to block all file requests by default. The *add* element is then used to define exceptions to this rule as discussed previously.

To specify that certain segments are hidden so that they cannot be accessed in clients, you use the following basic syntax:

```
<hiddenSegments applyToWebDAV="true">
  <add segment="bin" />
  . . .
</hiddenSegments>
```

Here, the *segment* attribute of the *add* element is used to specify a code segment that is hidden.

RequestMonitorModule

Implements a run-time interface for making queries

Description   The RequestMonitorModule implements the IIS Run-Time State and Control Interface (RSCA). RSCA makes it possible for applications and clients to query for run-time information, such as details on currently executing requests, the run state of a Web site, or the currently executing application domains. If you remove this module, applications and clients won't be able to query the run-time environment.

Executable   *%Windir%*\System32\Inetsrv\Iisreqs.dll

Dependencies   None

Configuration Elements   None

ApplicationHost.config Usage Examples

```
<!-- globalModules installation definition -->
<add name="RequestMonitorModule" image="%windir%\System32\inetsrv
\iisreqs.dll" />

<!-- modules activation definition -->
<add name="RequestMonitorModule" />
```

ServerSideIncludeModule

Implements Server-Side Includes (SSI)

Description   When you install and activate the ServerSideIncludeModule, IIS can use Server-Side Includes (SSI). This module has managed handlers that specify that it is executed only for files with the .stm, .shtm, and .shtml extensions. If you remove this module, .stm, .shtm and .shtml files will be handled by the static file module.

> **Note**   In the Application.Host.config file you define MIME types the server can handle using *mimeMap* elements. The Application.Host.config file does not have *mimeMap* definitions for the extensions used for Server-Side Includes (SSI). This is as designed, and you should not change this. If you create *mimeMap* definitions for the .stm, .shtm, and .shtml extensions, files with these extensions will be served as text (rather than

content that needs to be executed to process the Server-Side Includes (SSI).

Executable   *%Windir%*\System32\Inetsrv\Iis_ssi.dll

Dependencies   None

Configuration Element   system.webServer/*serverSideInclude*

ApplicationHost.config Usage Examples

```
<!-- related handler definitions -->
<add name="SSINC-stm" path="*.stm" verb="GET,POST"
modules="ServerSideIncludeModule" resourceType="File" />
<add name="SSINC-shtm" path="*.shtm" verb="GET,POST"
modules="ServerSideIncludeModule" resourceType="File" />
<add name="SSINC-shtml" path="*.shtml" verb="GET,POST"
modules="ServerSideIncludeModule" resourceType="File" />

<!-- element usage examples -->
<serverSideInclude ssiExecDisable="false" />
```

Element Attributes   The *ssiExecDisable* attribute of the *serverSideInclude* element can be used to enable or disable Server-Side Includes (SSI) without having to uninstall or remove the ServerSideIncludeModule. To disable Server-Side Includes (SSI) globally by default, you can set this attribute as shown in this example:

```
<serverSideInclude ssiExecDisable="true" />
```

To enable Server-Side Includes (SSI) globally by default, you can set this attribute as shown in this example:

```
<serverSideInclude ssiExecDisable="false" />
```

You can edit an application's Web.config file to override the default setting.

StaticCompressionModule

Implements compression of static content

Description   You can use the StaticCompressionModule to enable compression of static content. This module uses both in-memory as well as persistent in-the-file-system compression to reduce the size of files sent to client browsers, decreasing transmission time and improving performance. If you remove this module, compression of static content is disabled and uncompressed content is sent to client browsers.

See the "DynamicCompressionModule" section of this appendix for specific details on how compression can be configured.

Executable   *%Windir%*\System32\Inetsrv\Compstat.dll

Dependencies   None

Configuration Elements   system.webServer/*httpCompression*

system.webServer/*urlCompression*

ApplicationHost.config Usage Examples

```
<!-- globalModules installation definition -->
<add name="StaticCompressionModule"
image="%windir%\System32\inetsrv\compstat.dll" />

<!-- modules activation definition -->
<add name="StaticCompressionModule" />
```

StaticFileModule

Implements static file handling

Description   Sends out static files with the file extension .html, .jpg, and many others. The list of file extensions is determined by the *staticContent/mimeMap* configuration collection. Potential issues when removing this module include static files no longer being served and requests for files return a "200 - OK" message with an empty entity body.

Executable   *%Windir%*\System32\Inetsrv\Static.dll

Dependencies   None

Configuration Element   system.webServer/*staticContent*

ApplicationHost.config Usage Examples

```
<staticContent lockAttributes="isDocFooterFileName">
<mimeMap fileExtension=".323" mimeType="text/h323" />
. . .
<mimeMap fileExtension=".zip" mimeType="application
/x-zip-compressed" />
</staticContent>
```

TokenCacheModule

Implements security token caching for password-based authentication schemes (*not installed by default*)

Description   The TokenCacheModule caches Windows security tokens for password-based authentication schemes, including Anonymous authentication, Basic authentication, and Digest authentication. Once IIS has cached a user's security token, the cached security token can be used for subsequent requests by that user. If you disable or remove this module, a user must be logged on for every request, which can result in multiple logon user calls, which could substantially reduce overall performance.

Executable   *%Windir%*\System32\Inetsrv\Cachtokn.dll

Dependencies

None

Configuration Elements   None

ApplicationHost.config Usage Examples

```
<!-- globalModules installation definition -->
<add name="TokenCacheModule"
image="%windir%\System32\inetsrv\cachtokn.dll"

<!-- modules activation definition -->
<add name="TokenCacheModule" />
```

TracingModule

Implements event tracing and trace warning (*not installed by default*)

Description   The TracingModule implements event tracing and trace warning. If you remove or disable this module, event tracing and warning won't work. For details on how tracing can be configured, see the "FailedRequestsTracingModule" section in this appendix.

Executable   *%Windir%*\System32\Inetsrv\Iisetw.dll

Dependencies   None

Configuration Element   system.webServer/*httpTracing*

ApplicationHost.config Usage Examples

```
<!-- globalModules installation definition -->
<add name="TracingModule"
image="%windir%\System32\inetsrv\iisetw.dll" />

<!-- modules activation definition -->
<add name="TracingModule" />
```

UriCacheModule

Implements a generic cache for URL-specific server state (*not installed by default*)

Description   The UriCacheModule implements a generic cache for URL-specific server state, such as configuration details. With this module, the server will read configuration information only for the first request for a particular URL. For subsequent requests, the server will use the cached information as long as the configuration does not change. If you remove or disable this module, the server must retrieve the state information for every request, which could reduce the overall performance of the server.

Executable   *%Windir%*\System32\Inetsrv\Cachuri.dll

Dependencies   None

Configuration Elements   None

ApplicationHost.config Usage Examples

```
<!-- globalModules installation definition -->
<add name="UriCacheModule"
image="%windir%\System32\inetsrv\cachuri.dll" />


<!-- modules activation definition -->
<add name="UriCacheModule" />
```

UrlAuthorizationModule

Implements authorization based on configuration rules

Description   The UrlAuthorizationModule implements authorization based on configuration rules. When you enable and configure the features of this module, you can require logon and allow or deny access to specific URLs based on user names, .NET roles, and HTTP request method. If you remove or disable this module, managed URLs will no longer be protected.

Executable   *%Windir%*\System32\Inetsrv\Urlauthz.dll

Dependencies   None

Configuration Element   system.webServer/security/*authorization*

ApplicationHost.config Usage Examples

```
<authorization>
  <add accessType="Allow" users="*" />
</authorization>
```

Element Attributes   The system.webServer/security/*authorization* element is used to allow or deny access to managed URLs. The attributes of the related *add* element are summarized in Table A-23.

TABLE A-23 Standard Attributes of the *authorization/add* Element

accessType	Sets the access type for the specified user, role, or HTTP request. If set to Allow, the specified user, role, or HTTP request is granted access. If set to Deny, the specified user, role, or HTTP request is denied access.
passLoginPages	Controls whether a user can bypass the logon page. If set to true, IIS can use the user's current credentials for logon and will allow the user to bypass any logon page. If set to false, IIS will require the user to log on through an applicable logon page.
roles	Sets the name of the .NET role or roles to which the authorization rule applies. If set to *, the rule applies to all .NET roles.
users	Sets the name of the user or users to which the authorization rule applies. If set to *, the rule applies to all users.
verbs	Sets the name of the HTTP request method to which the authorization rule applies, such as GET, HEAD, or POST. If set to *, the rule applies to all HTTP request methods.

WindowsAuthenticationModule

Implements Windows authentication using NTLM, Kerberos, or both

Description   The WindowsAuthenticationModule implements Windows authentication by using NTLM, Kerberos, or both. At least one authentication module has to be configured. As necessary, the WindowsAuthenticationModule creates the *HttpUser* object used by and validated by IIS after the authentication phase. If the *HttpUser* object is not populated as would be the case when there are no configured authentication mechanisms, the IIS server core generates a 401.2 error.

With IIS 7.5, you can use advanced settings to either accept or require extended protection. With extended protection, channel-binding data is encoded using a Channel Binding Token and service-binding data is encoded using a Service Principal Name. See Chapter 4 for more information on Windows authentication.

Executable   *%Windir%*\System32\Inetsrv\Authsspi.dll

Dependencies   None

Configuration Element

system.webServer/security/authentication/*windowsAuthentication*

../windowsAuthentication/extendedProtection

ApplicationHost.config Usage Examples

```
<windowsAuthentication enabled="true">
 <providers>
  <add value="Negotiate" />
  <add value="NTLM" />
 </providers>
</windowsAuthentication>
```

Element Attributes   The *enabled* attribute of the *windowsAuthentication* element can be used to enable or disable Windows authentication without having to uninstall or remove the WindowsAuthenticationModule. To disable Windows authentication globally by default, you can set this attribute as shown in this example:

```
<windowsAuthentication enabled="false">
```

To enable Windows authentication globally by default, you can set this attribute as shown in this example:

```
<windowsAuthentication enabled="true">
```

Within the *providers* element, the attributes of the related *add* element control the permitted authentication mechanisms. You can permit NTLM, Negotiate (Kerberos), or both, as shown in the following example:

```
<providers>
 <add value="Negotiate" />
 <add value="NTLM" />
</providers>
```

Because Negotiate (Kerberos) is more secure, it is the mechanism you want to try first. So always list it first when you allow both NTLM and Kerberos.

IIS Managed Module Reference

In the following section, you'll find a reference for the managed modules that ship with IIS. Managed modules are used primarily by application developers.

AnonymousIdentificationModule

Manages anonymous identifiers for ASP.NET applications

.NET Framework Class Library
System.Web.Security.AnonymousIdentificationModule

ApplicationHost.config Usage Examples

```
<!-- modules activation definition -->
<add name="AnonymousIdentification" type="System.Web.Security
.AnonymousIdentificationModule" preCondition="managedHandler" />
```

Microsoft Visual Basic Usage

```
Public NotInheritable Class AnonymousIdentificationModule
    Implements IHttpModule
Dim instance As AnonymousIdentificationModule
```

C# Usage

```
public sealed class AnonymousIdentificationModule : IHttpModule
```

Dependencies   The ManagedEngine module must be installed.

Configuration Elements   None

DefaultAuthenticationModule

Ensures that an authentication object is provided in the current context

.NET Framework Class Library
System.Web.Security.DefaultAuthenticationModule

ApplicationHost.config Usage Examples

```
<!-- modules activation definition -->
<add name="DefaultAuthentication" type="System.Web.Security.Default
AuthenticationModule" preCondition="managedHandler" />
```

Visual Basic Usage

```
Public NotInheritable Class DefaultAuthenticationModule
    Implements IHttpModule
Dim instance As DefaultAuthenticationModule
```

C# Usage

```
public sealed class DefaultAuthenticationModule : IHttpModule
```

Dependencies   The ManagedEngine module must be installed.

Configuration Element   system.web/*authentication*

FileAuthorizationModule

Verifies that a user has permission to access the requested file

.NET Framework Class Library   System.Web.Security.FileAuthorizationModule

ApplicationHost.config Usage Examples

```
<!-- modules activation definition -->
<add name="FileAuthorization" type="System.Web.Security.File
AuthorizationModule" preCondition="managedHandler" />
```

Visual Basic Usage

```
Public NotInheritable Class FileAuthorizationModule
    Implements IHttpModule
Dim instance As FileAuthorizationModule
```

C# Usage

```
public sealed class FileAuthorizationModule : IHttpModule
```

Dependencies   The ManagedEngine module must be installed.

Configuration Elements   None

FormsAuthenticationModule

Allows you to manage client registration and authentication at the application level instead of relying on the authentication mechanisms in IIS

.NET Framework Class Library
System.Web.Security.Forms.AuthenticationModule

ApplicationHost.config Usage Examples

```
<!-- modules activation definition -->
<add name="FormsAuthentication" type="System.Web.Security.
FormsAuthenticationModule" preCondition="managedHandler" />
```

Visual Basic Usage

```
Public NotInheritable Class FormsAuthenticationModule
    Implements IHttpModule
Dim instance As FormsAuthenticationModule
```

C# Usage

```
public sealed class FormsAuthenticationModule : IHttpModule
```

Dependencies   The ManagedEngine module must be installed.

Configuration Element   system.web/*authentication*

Library Settings   Table A-24 summarizes the standard settings used with forms-based authentication.

TABLE A-24 Settings Used with Forms Authentication

Authentication cookie time-out	Sets the time interval, in minutes, after which the cookie expires. The default value is 30 minutes. If sliding expiration is allowed, the *time-out* attribute is a sliding value, expiring at the specified number of minutes after the time the last request was received. Persistent cookies do not time out.

Extend cookie expiration on every request	Specifies whether sliding expiration is enabled. If sliding expiration is allowed, the time-out attribute is a sliding value, expiring at the specified number of minutes after the time the last request was received. By default, this is enabled.
Login URL	Sets the URL to which the request is redirected for logon if no valid authentication cookie is found. The default value is login.aspx.
Mode	Specifies where to store the Forms authentication ticket. The options are: **Don't use cookies** Cookies are not used. **Use cookies** Cookies are always used, regardless of device. **Auto-detect** Cookies are used if the device profile supports cookies. Otherwise, no cookies are used. ASP.NET checks to determine whether cookies are enabled. **Use device profile** Cookies are used if the device profile supports cookies. Otherwise, no cookies are used. ASP.NET does not check to determine if cookies are enabled. This is the default setting.
Name	Sets the name of the Forms authentication cookie. The default name is .ASPXAUTH.
Protection Mode	Specifies the type of protection, if any, to use for cookies. The options are: **Encryption and validation** Specifies that both data validation and encryption are used to help protect the cookie. This is the default and recommended value. **None** Specifies that both encryption and validation are disabled. **Encryption** Specifies that the cookie is encrypted using Triple-DES or DES, but data validation is not performed on the cookie. **Validation** Specifies that a validation scheme verifies that the contents of a cookie have not been changed in transit.
Requires SSL	Specifies whether an SSL connection is required in order to transmit the authentication cookie. By default, this setting is disabled.

OutputCacheModule

Implements output Caching functionality in managed code for a scalable and fast native alternative

.NET Framework Class Library   System.Web.Caching.OutputCacheModule

ApplicationHost.config Usage Examples

```
<!-- modules activation definition -->
<add name="OutputCache" type="System.Web.Caching.OutputCacheModule"
preCondition="managedHandler" />
```

Dependencies   The ManagedEngine module must be installed. Potential issues when removing this module include managed content no longer being able to store content in the managed output cache.

Configuration Element   system.web/caching/*outputCache*

ProfileModule

Manages the creation of user profiles and profile events

.NET Framework Class Library   System.Web.Profile.ProfileModule

ApplicationHost.config Usage Examples

```
<!-- modules activation definition -->
<add name="Profile" type="System.Web.Profile.ProfileModule"
preCondition="managedHandler" />
```

Visual Basic Usage

```
Public NotInheritable Class ProfileModule
    Implements IHttpModule
Dim instance As ProfileModule
```

C# Usage

```
public sealed class ProfileModule : IHttpModule
```

Dependencies   The ManagedEngine module must be installed.

Configuration Elements   None

RoleManagerModule

Manages the .NET role–based security information for the current HTTP request, including role membership

.NET Framework Class Library   System.Web.Security.RoleManagerModule

ApplicationHost.config Usage Examples

```
<!-- modules activation definition -->
<add name="RoleManager" type="System.Web.Security.RoleManagerModule" pr
eCondition="managedHandler" />
```

Visual Basic Usage

```
Public NotInheritable Class RoleManagerModule
    Implements IHttpModule
Dim instance As RoleManagerModule
```

C# Usage

```
public sealed class RoleManagerModule : IHttpModule
```

Dependencies   The ManagedEngine module must be installed.

Configuration Elements   None

SessionStateModule

Manages session state services for ASP.NET applications

.NET Framework Class Library   System.Web.SessionState.SessionStateModule

ApplicationHost.config Usage Examples

```
<!-- modules activation definition -->
<add name="Session" type="System.Web.SessionState.SessionStateModule" p
reCondition="managedHandler" />
```

Visual Basic Usage

```
Public NotInheritable Class SessionStateModule
    Implements IHttpModule
Dim instance As SessionStateModule
```

C# Usage

```
public sealed class SessionStateModule : IHttpModule
```

Dependencies   The ManagedEngine module must be installed.

Configuration Element   system.web/*sessionState*

UrlAuthorizationModule

Verifies that a user has permission to access the requested URL. This implementation in managed code provides a scalable and fast native alternative to the like-named native module.

.NET Framework Class Library   System.Web.Security.UrlAuthorizationModule

ApplicationHost.config Usage Examples

```
<!-- modules activation definition -->
<add name="UrlAuthorization" type="System.Web.Security.Url
AuthorizationModule" preCondition="managedHandler" />
```

Visual Basic Usage

```
Public NotInheritable Class UrlAuthorizationModule
    Implements IHttpModule
Dim instance As UrlAuthorizationModule
```

C# Usage

```
public sealed class UrlAuthorizationModule : IHttpModule
```

Dependencies   The ManagedEngine module must be installed.

Configuration Elements   system.web/*authorization*

UrlMappingsModule

Implements a URL mapping functionality for ASP.NET applications

.NET Framework Class Library   System.Web.UrlMappingsModule

ApplicationHost.config Usage Examples

```
<!-- modules activation definition -->
<add name="UrlMappingsModule" type="System.Web.UrlMappingsModule"
preCondition="managedHandler" />
```

Dependencies   The ManagedEngine module must be installed.

Configuration Elements   None

WindowsAuthenticationModule

Allows Windows authentication to be used to set the identity of a user for an
ASP.NET application. With Windows authentication, you can use the existing
Windows domain security to authenticate client conne1ctions. Windows
authentication works only in intranet environments. Because of this, clients must
access the internal network to use this authentication mechanism.

.NET Framework Class Library
System.Web.Security.WindowsAuthenticationModule

ApplicationHost.config Usage Examples

```
<!-- modules activation definition -->
<add name="WindowsAuthentication" type="System.Web.Security.Windows
AuthenticationModule" preCondition="managedHandler" />
```

Visual Basic Usage

```
Public NotInheritable Class WindowsAuthenticationModule
    Implements IHttpModule
Dim instance As WindowsAuthenticationModule
```

C# Usage

```
public sealed class WindowsAuthenticationModule : IHttpModule
```

Dependencies   The ManagedEngine module must be installed. Both the client and server must be in an internal domain.

Configuration Element   system.web/*authentication*

About the Author

William Stanek (http://www.williamstanek.com/) has more than 20 years of hands-on experience with advanced programming and development. He is a leading technology expert, an award-winning author, and a pretty-darn-good instructional trainer. Over the years, his practical advice has helped millions of programmers, developers, and network engineers all over the world. His current and books include *Windows 8.1 Administration Pocket Consultants, Windows Server 2012 R2 Pocket Consultants* and *Windows Server 2012 R2 Inside Outs.*

William has been involved in the commercial Internet community since 1991. His core business and technology experience comes from more than 11 years of military service. He has substantial experience in developing server technology, encryption, and Internet solutions. He has written many technical white papers and training courses on a wide variety of topics. He frequently serves as a subject matter expert and consultant.

William has an MS with distinction in information systems and a BS in computer science, magna cum laude. He is proud to have served in the Persian Gulf War as a combat crewmember on an electronic warfare aircraft. He flew on numerous combat missions into Iraq and was awarded nine medals for his wartime service, including one of the United States of America's highest flying honors, the Air Force Distinguished Flying Cross. Currently, he resides in the Pacific Northwest with his wife and children.

William recently rediscovered his love of the great outdoors. When he's not writing, he can be found hiking, biking, backpacking, traveling, or trekking in search of adventure with his family!

Find William on Twitter at www.twitter.com/WilliamStanek and on Facebook at www.facebook.com/William.Stanek.Author.

www.ingramcontent.com/pod-product-compliance
Lightning Source LLC
LaVergne TN
LVHW081515050326
832903LV00025B/1504